Dancing on the
FRONTIER

Dancing on the
FRONTIER

Travels by Land through China and Tibet

NICO HOBHOUSE

To order additional copies of this book, contact:
Xlibris Corporation
0-800-644-6988
www.xlibrispublishing.co.uk
Orders@xlibrispublishing.co.uk
304760

CONTENTS

Chapter 1   New Life; New Job...9
Chapter 2   The Leaves Start to Fall.....................................30
Chapter 3   Colder, Darker, Murkier.....................................46
Chapter 4   Who's in Charge? 57
Chapter 5   Capital Apathy..71
Chapter 6   Poverty, Tradition and Respect 80
Chapter 7   The Booming Yangtze Delta...............................89
Chapter 8   Back to the Sun..120
Chapter 9   Towards the Ethnic Minorities..........................144
Chapter 10 Yunnan 154
Chapter 11 Shattered Illusions in Kham.............................173
Chapter 12 The Way to the Holy Mountain.........................210
Chapter 13 When the Battle is Won....................................223
Chapter 14 One Province; Two Worlds...............................232
Chapter 15 Down the Silk Road...261
Chapter 16 Cities of the Future...269
Chapter 17 On the Mighty Yangtze.....................................284
Chapter 18 The End of all my Exploring.............................294

About the Author...312

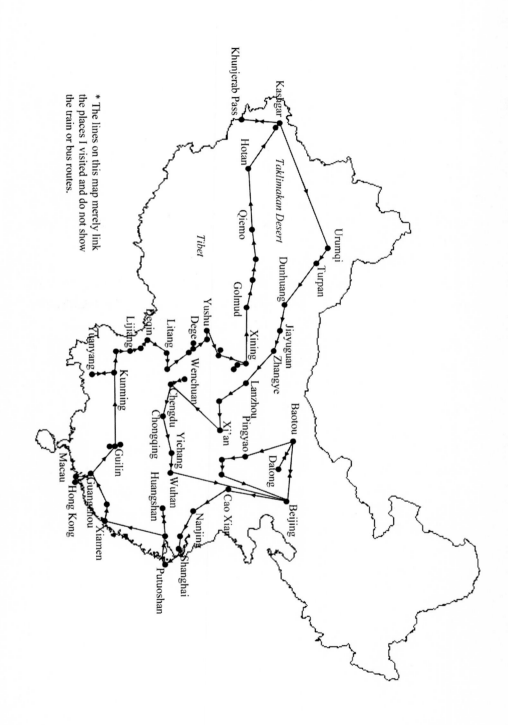

Khunjerab Pass

Kashgar

Taklimakan Desert

Hotan

Qiemo

Tibet

Golmud

Urumqi

Turpan

Dunhuang

Jiayuguan

Zhangye

Xining

Lanzhou

Yushu

Dege

Litang

Wenchuan

Pingyao

Baotou

Deqin

Lijiang

Chengdu

Chongqing

Yichang

Xi'an

Dalong

Tuanyang

Kunming

Huangshan

Wuhan

Beijing

Guilin

Nanjing

Cao Xian

Macau

Guangzhou

Xiamen

Putuoshan

Shanghai

Hong Kong

NOTES

At the time of travelling, from August 2010 to July 2011, 1RMB exchanged for approximately £0.10

I have used the Chinese names for towns (as written in pinyin), with the exceptions of places more familiar to the West by other names. For example, I have used 'Urumqi' instead of 'Wulumuqi.'

CHAPTER 1

New Life; New Job

I stepped out of the metro station and strode towards the only landmark in sight. The massive Bird's Nest dominated the darkness but only in a discreet way; the red glow warm and reassuring. Separating it and its little sister, the bulbous Water Cube, was a promenade that dwarfed them both. It must have been one of the largest open spaces in Beijing, that thoroughfare. Everywhere else in the capital, empty space was being plundered, traditional blocks razed and apartment towers thrust towards the sky. Apart from a few tourists and the odd person selling plastic children's toys, the place felt empty and a heavy silence reigned. This was the China the whole world looked at when the Olympics came to town in 2008. This was the China the Chinese wanted the world to see.

*

A couple of days later I was on the overnight train to Baotou. It was the largest city in Inner Mongolia and sat near the mighty Yellow River at the tip of its northern bend. I had been forewarned that, despite the connotations of boundless steppe that the name 'Mongolia' inspired, horse riding had long been out and heavy industry was most certainly in. Awaking after a cramped night's sleep on the top bunk of my hard sleeper compartment and staring out of the window, I saw large piles of coal beside the tracks and lines of trucks chugging slowly down the motorway beyond. Except for the stretch of hills to the north—hills beyond which lay the Gobi desert—the landscape was flat, arid and dusty.

I went to Baotou because an agency had arranged a teaching placement for me there. On arrival, I discovered that it was a sprawling city. It embraced a population of almost 2.5 million and covered three major districts, of which I went to live in the westernmost Kundulun district. There the tree-lined roads were laid out in a grid pattern and the street names were written in three languages: Chinese, Mongolian and pinyin—the Romanised Chinese script. Visible even from the city centre were the parched brown ranges to the north.

My school was private and occupied the ground floor of a residential block. Five classrooms lay along one side of a corridor while on the other side, separated by a glass screen, were some dormitories and two bedrooms. I was given one room and Kris, a teaching colleague who was also new to Baotou, was given another.

The big disadvantage of living in the school itself became apparent on my very first morning. I was awoken before eight o'clock by students coming for classes and by their teacher, who for reasons unknown used a microphone to project her voice across the tiny classroom.

The school's name was O'Sullivans and its raison d'etre was explained to me by my new boss, Yaming: "The quality of English teaching is awful in Baotou and in China as a whole. Everyone goes to state-run schools and class sizes are huge, up to seventy students. The teachers just say, 'come in, sit down, shut up,' and then set written exercises."

I learnt that many Baotou children took extra classes in the evenings and at weekends at so called 'training schools.' My new job was at one of these. They were everywhere; two in my street alone. Although in theory children went to these schools to get ahead, they were so popular that getting extra tuition was more about not falling behind.

*

Over the first week, I spent my daytimes exploring Baotou. It was the end of August and large numbers of people were out on the streets. Often they would mutter to each other excitedly as I passed or bark out, "laowai"-"foreigner" to alert every Chinese person in the vicinity to my presence. At first I found this annoying but I quickly learnt to ignore it. There were only a handful of foreigners in Baotou so it was unsurprising that I was viewed with curiosity.

In the evenings, Kris and I were kept busy with invitations to dinner from people linked to O'Sullivans. Mountains of food were showered upon us by our new 'friends' and we were never allowed to share the bill. Exotic delicacies were heaped into our helpless bowls when we were already full to bursting: silkworm, lamb stomach, pig trotter, chicken feet and the succulent skewers of Inner Mongolian barbecued lamb.

Friendly offers came thick and fast. I was promised guided tours around Baotou, introductory courses in Buddhism, Chinese lessons and even Kung Fu master-classes. After it all settled down nothing much came of these words. Everybody became 'too busy' and so no one guided me in Baotou, I was not initiated into Buddhism, I was left to teach myself Chinese and I never mastered Kung Fu.

One of my new colleagues, Cathy Wang, was particularly welcoming in those early days. Her primary job was at a public school but she taught a couple of evening classes at O'Sullivans to boost her earnings. One evening as I ate dinner at her house, I asked Cathy why she had become an English teacher.

"I didn't want to become an English teacher!" She replied. "My dream was to do foreign trade in the south of China."

"Why didn't you?"

"I did do it for two years but then my family said I had to come back to Baotou to get married."

Her husband was eating beside me but could not understand English. Occasionally he would laugh in a high-pitched voice at something that Cathy had translated. Like her, he was roughly thirty years old.

"And what does your husband do?" I asked, feeling self-conscious that I was speaking about a man sat right next to me.

"He is an architect," she said with a hint of pride. But then her tone darkened and she added, "He is leaving Baotou next week to go and work in Ordos, another city in Inner Mongolia."

"How long will he be gone for?"

"Maybe two months. He has only been home for three weeks."

"That is difficult! It must be sad for you when he is away," I remarked in an effort to be sympathetic.

"Yes it is. But this is a normal situation for a good job."

Cathy had a one-year-old daughter who was looked after during the daytimes by her mother-in-law. Every aspect of Cathy's life seemed to involve challenging compromise but, when I voiced my thoughts, she looked at me with a hardened glint in her eye. "It sounds stressful to an Englishman like you," she said, "But that is normal here. That is China."

The fruit of her and her husband's hard work was a small two bedroom apartment with a large flat screen TV and plush furniture. After dinner, Cathy showed me her wedding pictures from two years earlier. To my eye they looked naff and Cathy herself was unrecognisable after all the photo shopping. Attired in showroom suits and dresses, she and her husband looked very unnatural against the computerised backgrounds. In most of the snaps she was in a Western bridal dress.

In answer to my question about this she explained, "I did not get married in those clothes. The Chinese tradition is to wear a red dress. I just wore a white dress for the photos."

As I subsequently discovered, Chinese couples were prepared to fling vast amounts of money at their weddings. Interestingly, more was often spent on peripheral things such as the photos than on the ceremony itself. This reflected a societal obsession with status. What mattered was not what the wedding was like to be part of but what it looked like to outsiders.

*

Biyu was the elder sister of a student at my school. She was twenty one years old, had studied for two years at a good university in Shanghai, spoke excellent English and, to top it all off, was good looking. Life should have been going swimmingly but strangely she was not going back to Shanghai for the next academic year.

When I enquired why, as I sat with her in the entrance to the school one morning, she replied cryptically that I would not understand because, "This is China and you are English."

I probed further until she confided that her mother lay behind the decision. Money was not an issue in her case but Shanghai lay far from the safety net of family and friends and it was thought that Biyu, despite being an adult, ought to return to the fold. She herself was unequivocal about where she wanted to be, exclaiming, "I love Shanghai!"

Biyu's mother no doubt vetoed her university career for reasonable and loving reasons. Nonetheless I could not help but reflect that the lot of women in China was a difficult one.

Biyu repeated, "You cannot understand. You are English and it is different for you. I want to be free but I must listen to my mother and father."

*

Eager to understand more about the place I found myself in, I went to Baotou's Buddhist monastery. It stood on the outskirts of the city, in the shadow of a power station. At that time much of it was in a state of disrepair. The surrounding neighbourhood was poor and dirty. It was explained to me that Buddhism had gone underground during the early years of Communist rule and had still not fully recovered, despite the relaxation of religious restrictions.

It was sad to see the degradation but there was slight cause for optimism. A monastic community of about 30 men was in residence. All of them were old, which indicated that the recruitment of novices from younger generations was proving difficult. Nonetheless it was a positive step that monks were allowed to be there at all. Furthermore, the main hall was being repaired and was under scaffolding. Most uplifting was the number of worshippers, who all packed into the monastery's dining hall for a free vegetarian lunch. After the meal a few ladies volunteered to wash the dishes to improve their karma.

In the home, I discovered that Buddhism was also far from dead. Many families in Baotou had small shrines to Buddhist deities at which they offered food, incense and small money. Particularly popular was the deity Caishen, god of wealth and good fortune. Of course the main thing people prayed for was to become rich.

*

After the rounds of welcomes and introductions were over, I had to start doing my job. I had never taught before but had completed a TEFL qualification before coming to China. The theory behind TEFL is that a teacher can be effective without speaking the native language of their students. Before I even started it seemed an overly optimistic methodology. Many of my first classes passed in a blur of mutual misunderstanding. As I talked I received encouraging smiles from my flock but, whenever I stopped talking and asked a question, the smiles were replaced by blank looks. Fortunately, being a teacher guaranteed me automatic respect and so my students did not hold my failings against me.

I saw this respect manifested at the birthday party of one pupil, John Paul. The party was held in the main ballroom of the Baotou's smartest hotel and was a glamorous affair.

"How old is John Paul?" I asked Yaming as we walked in. I had never met the boy and had received an invitation only by proxy.

"Twelve. It is an important birthday in Inner Mongolia because it is when a boy comes of age," she replied.

This seemed a bit of an understatement. I counted no fewer than twenty tables placed around the central stage, though only two seemed to be for children. The rest were occupied by adults in suits and formal gowns. It was evidently more a party for the parents than for the birthday boy. Yaming had dressed up for the event, clearly well used to this sort of affair. Kris and I had not been warned what to expect and were in jeans and T-shirts.

The three of us were seated at a kids' table, clearly with the intention that the children would learn something useful over the course of the evening. At all the other tables, guests were drinking alcohol and were receiving a wide range of dishes. Our table was bedecked with fizzy pops, hot dogs, crisps and cake.

Events were overseen by a team of professional hosts. A camera crew hovered around, zooming into the faces of the eating guests and projecting their gormless expressions onto a big screen.

"The parents must be pretty wealthy to throw a twelfth birthday party like this," I commented to Yaming as I chewed a mini hamburger.

"There are plenty of rich people in Baotou. A lot of the wealth has come because farmers have sold their land to the government for mining."

Beneath the ground to the south of Baotou was the world's most abundant source of rare earth, an extremely valuable collection of minerals. In the years before I came to Baotou, the government bought out most of the farmers on the land. Going by the well reported standards of the rest of the country, the displaced residents probably had little choice in the matter, though they apparently were amply compensated.

Yaming told me a joke about the new wealth in China: "The son of a wealthy businessman is given a BMW by his father. Every day he drives it to University but one day he stops doing so. His father asks why. 'All the other students take metros to the University,' the son replies, 'and so I feel out of place in a BMW.' The father scratches his head and says, 'Oh dear! Even a BMW isn't enough. Well then, here's 20 million RMB to go and buy a metro train!'"

The evening dragged by slowly. Endless acts were performed. Dancers, singers, a saxophonist, a violinist, a cocktail juggler and a magician followed one another in an endless procession across the stage. Some were lousy and some were quite good. None made much of an impression on the several hundred people in the hall. Nobody applauded. Nobody seemed to be having a good time. It was a very stilted party; more a status parade than anything else.

At the climax John Paul himself appeared, emerging from a plastic orb in a burst of light, noise and dry ice. Standing barely four and a half feet off the ground and looking awkward in a white suit, he reeled off a couple of rehearsed lines before being joined by his smiling parents on stage. His mother was looking elegant; her sparkle enhanced by the diamond necklace around her neck. The father—clearly the money—was lean and older. Interestingly, both had crooked and yellowing teeth. Dentistry did not come free in China and dairy products were scarcely eaten. Many otherwise faultless visages were marred by imperfect smiles.

John Paul presented his Mum and Dad with flowers, bowed to them and thanked them for being his parents. Suddenly everyone in the room turned to look at Yaming, Kris and me. I could not understand what was going on but my face had appeared on the big screen. I hastily dropped my sausage roll and, before I knew it, the three of us were on stage.

Attendants conveniently on hand passed John Paul more flowers and he submissively bowed before each of us in turn, murmuring, "Thank you for being my teacher."

Then Yaming had the microphone, presumably saying some sycophantic words in praise of the boy. After finishing, she shoved it over to me.

I seized the moment: "On behalf of me, Kris and the whole of Britain, Happy Birthday John Paul!" Yaming translated to appreciative applause.

On descending from the stage, Kris and I were suddenly the toast of the party. Shots of alcohol were pressed into our hands, we were collared for photographs and had our hands shaken by senior relatives. Nobody seemed concerned that between us we had barely taught a lesson in our lives. Nor was it a problem that we had never met John Paul before. We were white, spoke English and were 'foreign teachers'. Petty details did not matter.

Kris succinctly remarked to me afterwards, "We were just face whores."

Just as the party was taking a turn for the better, Yaming said we were going home. She was a Buddhist and teetotal.

*

I had dived into teaching at the deep end and after two weeks I felt more confident in the classroom, albeit still with frequent misunderstandings. I gradually got to know my students. The One Child Policy meant virtually every one of them was an only child, though a small handful of them did have a sibling. The result of this was that their parents had to pay a fine to the family planning authorities.

China was a competitive place for students, with future prospects almost completed related to exam success. The parents of my pupils pushed their children hard. They crowded in the street to the side of the school, peering through windows and keeping a close eye on how their kids were performing. More gathered in the corridors and occasionally nudged the doors open to see what was going on. They tried to catch their children's eyes and exhort them to volunteer answers. Some parents even wanted to sit in the classroom and were surprised if I said they could not.

Part of the reason for this pushiness seemed to be normal parental ambition. But it was also because each parent knew their own old age security was linked to the success of their child. Chinese retirees received little pension or no pension at all. Personal savings and the family were all that could be relied on.

And so the parents pressurised their children but I also saw them try other means. Giving gifts to teachers was standard practice, as was inviting them out to dinner and crooning over them on the occasion of a chance encounter in the street. Seeing as class sizes in Baotou's public schools could exceed seventy, a lot of pupils got lost in the crowd. Guaranteeing a bit of favourable treatment and attention for one's child made sense.

The majority of the students who came to my school ranged between the ages of eight and fourteen. It quickly became clear that many recited texts very well—something they did a lot of in their day schools—but came apart when asked to invent any fresh sentences of their own. Although there were a lot of intelligent and conscientious students in my classes, almost all of them were held back by fear of making mistakes.

The strict discipline of the Chinese public school system encouraged this attitude. The huge class sizes meant that order was best kept by a dictatorial silence. Chirpy or combative students were cut little slack and often found themselves in trouble. Part of the challenge of my job was extricating intelligent children from the mire of self-doubt and robotic performance that this style of teaching impressed on them.

A particularly noticeable and saddening trait was an inability to understand criticism as constructive. After a wrong answer some students retreated into their shells, perceiving a loss of 'mianzi'-'face.' I was not a fan of the concept of 'face' because I felt it inhibited honesty. I tried to create a classroom atmosphere where getting things wrong was not a problem. There was only so much I could do because the 'face' principle permeated all Chinese society. Adults went out of their way to avoid speaking home truths in public. When they did, fireworks went off. One evening the school's cleaner got into an argument with Yaming's mum. This fight went on for at least an hour and both women were hoarse and in tears by the time it was broken up. Too much 'face' had been lost for the cleaner to feel she could continue in her job so the next day there was a new person sweeping the floors.

My primary responsibility as a foreign teacher was to improve the speaking fluency of my students. I did, however, have some smaller tasks. One was to give an 'English name' to new pupils. Seeing as most people kept these for life, I took it seriously and stuck with convention: James, Sophie, Edward . . .

Usually naming took all of a minute and then the matter was over, but complications were possible. In a beginners' class of mine was a boy who had been given an English name by a previous teacher. Unfortunately he could neither remember how to spell it nor how to pronounce it. From the 'guntir' he wrote on the name sheet and from the strange grunt he uttered in answer to the question, "What is your name?" I surmised that he was called Gunther. Kris also taught him and from the same stimuli registered him as Quentin. We only found out that he was one and the same boy several months down the line.

*

The Chinese calendar was littered with festivals; some of them traditional lunar events and some more recent additions. Teacher's Day arrived in mid-September. Yaming invited all the staff linked to my school for dinner at a restaurant. Thin strips of meat and vegetables were dropped into a sizzling broth and then wolfed down in deliciously juicy mouthfuls. I was informed that this 'hot pot' was an Inner Mongolian speciality.

Around the table were roughly ten people and at the head of it sat Professor Li. I was never sure whether Professor Li was actually a professor but that was what everyone called him. Now about seventy, he had made his name teaching Chinese language privately to students preparing for their public exams. It seemed that everyone who was anyone in Baotou had been taught by Professor Li. His classes on Monday evenings were packed. Over fifty students crammed themselves into the school's largest classroom to hang on his every word. Even the parents of the children stood around the edges of the classroom so as to cultivate themselves. As far as I could establish, Professor Li never raised his voice in class. He never had to.

One evening Yaming confided that she did not charge Professor Li for using the classrooms in her school. "I couldn't charge him!" She exclaimed in horror at the thought, "He used to be my teacher. I respect him too much."

At the restaurant on that Teachers' Day, Professor Li barely said a word. He had a pot belly and slit like eyes. Looking at him called to mind Milefo, the corpulent Laughing Buddha. On one occasion I thought I saw his veneer crack and his eyes twinkle with delight at how well life had turned out, but maybe I just imagined it.

The first and best morsels of meat were put on his plate and he accepted them without thanks. The women at the table were fussing over him so diligently that they barely had a chance to eat themselves. From the day of this spectacle onwards I always referred to Professor Li as 'The Great Professor Li.'

*

Despite being only a twelve hour train ride from Beijing, Baotou felt a long way away. The eyes of China were trained on the east coast and towards the big economic cities of the south. No one was looking over their shoulder to the dusty industrial backwaters of the northern plains.

I received warning from a colleague, an Irishman called Tony, about the actuality of Baotou life. He had lived in the city for many years. "You've just arrived so you haven't seen any of this yet, but Baotou is run by a load of thugs," he told me after class one evening. "Most directives from Beijing are ignored here."

"For example?" I asked, curious.

"Ok, a couple of years back the government said that middle school students—thirteen to fifteen year olds—should only be given one hour of homework per night. There was an article about it in China Daily, which I showed to one of my classes. They all laughed and told me that they were still getting three or four hours of homework per night."

I expressed my disgust but Tony had more: "There are worse things than that. I'll tell you this one. A few years back I had serious problems getting a work visa because a senior policeman was friends with the owner of a rival school. They tried to have me kicked out of the country. Here it's about knowing the right people and giving money to the right people."

I saw for myself evidence of this incompetent provincial rule shortly afterwards. Over the summer a large refurbishment project had taken place in Baotou's public schools. Classrooms had been redone, equipment replaced and facilities added. Come the beginning of September and the nationally fixed start of term, the work had not yet finished. By the time the public schools did finally open in the third week of the month, a huge amount of lesson time had been lost. Concerned that middle and high school students would not have enough time to complete their courses, the Baotou authorities decided they should all have classes on Saturdays as well.

Everyone tried to make the best of a bad job but nobody seemed to be complaining publically about whoever had caused the mess. The political apathy was even apparent in people who were being severely messed about by it all, not least Yaming. She was forced to cram a large number of classes that would otherwise have taken place on Saturdays into Sunday slots. I went to challenge her about what was going on, asking why nobody was complaining.

For my trouble I received a patronising look and the words, "It doesn't work like that here. Complaining doesn't do any good."

"Maybe it would do some good if you actually tried it!" I proclaimed, idealistically. "It would force the people who've caused the problems to be responsible for them."

"It would make no difference. It's just a way to get into trouble."

Yaming seemed a little disinterested but I pressed on, "Don't you think that's a bad thing?"

"No I think it is fine here."

"But there's no accountability," I stressed, exasperated. "Do you even know who your local leaders are?"

"There's one called Wang and then . . . erm . . . Anyway you might be interested in politics but I bet most people in England don't know who their leaders are! You're very naïve."

I tried persisting with no success. Any implication that it was better in England just pushed her onto the defensive. It was frustrating to me that a question about the merits of a political system descended into a nationalist slugfest. My experience of Chinese newspapers suggested that was the way the state media liked to present the discussion too.

*

Once the students had returned to their public schools, I was left with a steady weekly timetable. Tuesdays and Wednesdays were my 'weekend'. After more than three weeks in Baotou, I wanted to make an excursion out of the city and so I went with Kris to the Mausoleum of Genghis Khan.

This lay at Ejin Horo, a few hours to the south of Baotou. We had to change buses several times to get there and quickly learnt that politeness while queuing was a recipe for a long wait. The little old ladies with the crooked backs were the worst, using their iron coated elbows to carve their way through the scrums. After we had missed a couple of buses Kris and I decided to lay our Englishness aside and got stuck in.

All the way to the Mausoleum I optimistically hoped the scarred, dusty and polluted landscape would give way to sweeping grasslands. It never did. The only feature of interest during an otherwise thoroughly bland drive lay about 20km north of the city of Dongsheng. Visible from the road was a town that appeared to have been dropped there by accident. Some buildings were still under construction but the majority were finished. There was absolutely no sign of life. All the apartments stood empty. There were no cars. No people anywhere. Nor was there anything in the vicinity that suggested why all the new homes had been built.

As I later learnt, this 'Dongsheng Ghost Town' was quite iconic. It was built with the capacity to hold three hundred thousand people, who it was hoped would pour in to capitalise on the increasing economic success of the region. Almost nobody had come. Ninety per cent of the available housing remained unused.

Baotou had a similarly contradictory landmark: a football stadium built on a stretch of land near the motorway. Baotou had no football team. These were the unsustainable paradoxes of China's economic growth.

Money was being poured into massive construction projects but some of the ideas were so poorly thought through and so hastily executed that massive wastage was the only consequence.

We eventually reached Genghis Khan's Mausoleum, which was situated in the middle of nowhere. A large white building with three domed roofs perched at the top of a flight of steps. This was built in the 1950s and the title 'Mausoleum' was misleading because the Genghis was never been buried there. I found some items, which had purportedly belonged to the Great Khan, displayed inside traditional Mongolian gers. I had been warned before I visited that these were fakes and that any remaining genuine relics were destroyed in the Cultural Revolution. On the drive down to the Mausoleum I had seen that the surrounding grasslands had been heavily exploited for mining purposes. Taken as a whole, there seemed to me to be little Mongolian heritage left in Inner Mongolia.

*

In late September came the Mid-Autumn Festival. Kris and I celebrated by eating lunch with the relatives of a friend. It was a lively meal. 'Baijiu'—'rice liquor,' which was misleadingly referred to as 'wine', was poured into our glasses. Every couple of minutes one of the men around the table would say, "Lai, ganbei!"-"Come on. Drink!" After two large glasses of the fifty per cent spirit, I felt pleasantly merry.

After lunch we went back to their home in a residential apartment compound, the like of which most Baotou residents occupied. Over a few more drinks, I was taught how to play mah-jong. It was one of the most popular games in China but came with a stigma attached. The Chinese were big on gambling; both men and women. In my experience, younger people played cards when they wanted to put their money on the line; older people played mah-jong. I learnt that a few licensed places existed in Baotou where people could play, but that it was the illegal dens in private houses that were especially notorious. There the real money could change hands. Directly above my bedroom was one such place. Every couple of weeks I spent a sleepless night listening to the loud click of mah-jong tiles until dawn.

In a nod to tradition on that Mid-Autumn Festival, after our game, when the sun had set, fruit was offered up to the full moon. It seemed that, in China, superstition was less at war with modernity and more a partner to it.

It was a very enjoyable day but the aftermath was far from enjoyable. Because the day-off had left the public school students even further behind, the authorities decided to arrange catch-up classes in the evenings. The decision makers were clearly improvising as they went along and students often only found out when they had to attend these compulsory classes at a few hours' notice.

For a school like O'Sullivans, which had a schedule based around the availability of its students, the public school confusion meant chaos. Arranging future class times was unsurprisingly difficult when the students themselves did not know whether they would be forced to attend unscheduled classes at a moment's notice. The cause was not helped by a complete absence of communication between O'Sullivans' Chinese staff and its foreign staff. The Chinese teachers tended to arrange their class times independently and then not tell anyone. Inevitably, large numbers of students turned up for classes when nobody was expecting them and it repeatedly fell to me or Kris to pick up the pieces. Having to teach ninety minutes off the cuff to large and dispirit groups started to wear me down but my objections met with little sympathy. Yaming was of the opinion that I had no right to complain about working conditions as long as I was getting paid, and I never got an apology even when the blame for the balls-up lay entirely with her poor communication. Her approach to management was that she was always right and that I was just there to do what she told me. She felt that this made her a good businesswoman.

Despite the lack of order being very clear, none of the Chinese teachers seemed to mind and were perfectly happy to teach classes spontaneously. The students, too, seemed unperturbed by having three different teachers for three successive lessons. As for the parents, far from being critical of the organisational troubles, many took advantage of the situation to dump their kids at O'Sullivans every day of the week, hiding behind the excuse that they did not know when their child's next class was and hoping to pick up some free tuition. Clearly everyone was well used to dealing with this sort of thing and, moreover, was opportunistic about it.

*

Baotou was normally a very dry city, lying as it did near desert and otherwise arid land. Nothing, therefore, was designed to cope with large quantities of water. One day at the end of September it rained hard. The drains in the streets overflowed and brought traffic to a standstill. Inside the school, the roof leaked. Low-quality construction was the norm across China and I frequently experienced this in Baotou. The school occupied a rented space in a prematurely ageing block. Yaming told me that, many years before, after the school had already been set up, the landlord had given her a tenancy contract to sign. She had wanted to take it to a lawyer and check the wording but the landlord had told her she could sign it immediately or get out. The school had nowhere else to go and so she had signed. The landlord had deviously removed himself of any obligation to mend the leak and so we just had to put down buckets and wait for the drip to stop.

The same problems applied to the school's toilet, which was a more persistent nuisance. Sometimes the pipes carrying the sewage from upstairs leaked. Combined with the inevitable mess made by negligent aim of the pupils, the toilets smelt like a water treatment facility by the end of most days.

Outside, the poor quality control and safety regulations were similarly problematic. One day I received a nasty electric shock from a wire hanging down from a traffic light. Fortunately I was wearing rubber soled shoes. I glanced up to see the green man had stopped flashing. When I passed the spot again a couple of weeks later, the light had still not been repaired.

*

In the first week of October came the National Holiday to commemorate the 1949 declaration of the People's Republic. Kris and I said we wanted to go to neighbouring Shanxi province. Yaming told us not to worry because she would arrange everything. She did arrange everything, but only on the night before we left. Forward planning was not in the vocabulary.

We hired a driver and went to Wutai Shan, the earthly home of Wenshu, Bodhisattva of Wisdom. Much of the drive there was ugly. Even after we had crossed into Shanxi Province via a restored Great Wall fort and left the motorway behind, the narrow roads were still dominated by belching trucks. Scattered homesteads, many of them radiating poverty and neglect, were dotted around. But then the road started to wind and climb into forest covered mountains. Prayer flags shivered in the breeze as we crested the top of the climb. From there the road wound down into the sacred valley.

Scattered along it were over fifty monasteries. The valley was ringed by five snow-flecked peaks, the highest rising above 3000m. Pilgrims and interested tourists fill the area, climbing steep steps up to the most famous temples and prostrating themselves before the golden Buddhas. I joined in where possible, feeling a long way from Baotou. The green bulks of the enclosing mountains shut out the outside world.

In the evening Kris and I went for a stroll. Everywhere was stillness and silence. The Milky Way stretched above us and a meteor shower sent shooting stars whistling across the sky. A taxi drove past and stopped outside the gates of a monastery in the gloom ahead of us. The silhouettes of robed monks climbed out and quietly slipped through a side door. They looked for all the world like truant students returning from a late night on the lash.

On the way back to Baotou, we stopped off at the Yungang Grottoes, a sacred hillside dotted with Buddhist caves. The site owed its existence to the imperial patronage of the Northern Wei dynasty in the 5th Century AD; a time when Buddhism was first on the rise in China. It was therefore a part testament to the dynamic relationship between state and religion, which had brought in equal measure flourishing and destruction over the long course of Chinese history. Needless to say, recent Chinese history had exemplified the latter rather more than the former.

Huge Buddhist statues, carved from the solid rock, sat passively inside enormous caves. Several of the colossi were over 15m tall. Age and vandalism had taken their toll but the sense of power was undimmed. But outside the caves the broad sweep of millennia distilled back to the realities of the present. The city of Datong, situated nearby, had been a dynastic capital at the time of the caves' construction but was now a polluted metropolis. Time did not stand still. I went back to work.

CHAPTER 2

The Leaves Start to Fall

When I returned from Shanxi I discovered that Miss Gao, a colleague at O'Sullivans, had left. Miss Gao was from Hohhot, the capital city of Inner Mongolia, which lay two hours' drive to the east of Baotou. She worked at a factory in Hohhot from Monday to Friday and caught a train on Saturday mornings to teach her classes at the school. On Sunday evenings she returned home. Miss Gao was 29 years old, pretty and single. Or at least she had been.

The evening I got back, Yaming came to see me. "You're going to have to take a couple of extra classes, Nico," she said. "I've just got a call from Miss Gao. She's getting married and not coming back to teach."

Apparently Miss Gao's parents, exasperated by their daughter's inability to find a spouse, had taken matters into their own hands. They had contacted some acquaintances with an unmarried son and arranged a match. Miss Gao had agreed. The incident reminded me of others I had heard about, albeit that Miss Gao's were quite peculiar circumstances. Arranged marriages were very rare but women in China were put under a lot of pressure to find a husband before they turned thirty.

After the adjustments made to accommodate the absence of Miss Gao, from the second week of October I was able to settle into a routine that continued until the end of the term. One notable thing was the complete absence of ethnic Mongolian children. I taught in the region of one hundred and fifty students; every single one of them Han Chinese. But by that point I had understood that Baotou contained almost no Mongolian inhabitants anyway. Although Inner Mongolia was technically an 'Autonomous Region' for the Mongolian people, its population was eighty per cent Han Chinese. Moreover the Han wre clustered into the economic and political centres in the south of the region, meaning Baotou's total population was barely three per cent ethnic Mongolian. The spiky Mongolian script on street signs—a feature of the Government's nominally friendly policy towards ethnic minorities—was the only visible indication that Baotou was in Inner Mongolia at all.

*

I first learned on the BBC website that Liu Xiaobo had won the Nobel Peace Prize. It did not receive coverage in the Chinese press. I asked several people whether they knew who Liu Xiaobo was and invariably met with blank looks. I tried explaining to Yaming that Liu Xiaobo was an imprisoned dissident imprisoned.

"If he's in prison then he's a criminal," She pointed out, simply.

"No, he's broken no real laws. He's been locked up because he wants democracy."

"Well he shouldn't have criticised the government should he? The government knows what it's doing. The leaders are very clever men."

"Yes they probably are clever but the system's bad. Don't you see? If you can't criticise them then how can you stop them doing bad things?"

"They're not doing bad things. I'm happy with the government."

"Maybe, but if you weren't happy you wouldn't be able to do anything about it either."

"But I am happy! Anyway you should stop being so high minded. In England your government is just controlled by people with money. You think you can criticise them but in fact you can't make a difference! All governments are the same!" She retorted.

"Maybe they are, but at least our government in England is democratically elected. Everybody in my country at least has the right to vote. Everybody is politically equal. Everybody can criticise if they want to."

Yaming rolled her eyes and then said, "You know Animal Farm by George Orwell? What he says is what I feel. All animals are equal but some animals are more equal than others. I think that! Some people are definitely more equal than others!"

I was frustrated by how completely she had missed the point Orwell was trying to make. For years Orwell's works had been banned in China but now even Yaming had a copy of *1984*. And yet, infuriatingly to me, though she was able to read Orwell's books she did not even understand them! Undaunted, I tried a different approach to prove my point and showed her the leading article from a copy of *China Daily*, the English language newspaper, which was little more than a mouthpiece for the Communist Party line. I chose an old paper at random from a pile, knowing that any would suit my purpose. The copy I grabbed featured a dispute over Sino-Japanese contested waters as its title story. One sentence read, "The new and inexperienced Japanese administration has found . . . (a Chinese government) refusing to compromise on China's territorial integrity." The rest of the article continued in a similar vein and uttered not a single word of dissent against the government's actions.

"So?" asked Yaming. "I want them to write articles like that. That article is what I think. I hate the Japanese. Everyone hates the Japanese!"

I gave up. After all it was stupid to make her angry while trying to criticise something that I was suggesting should itself be making her angry. My comments only served to entrench her in support of a system with which she might otherwise have had qualms. It was a lesson to a man soaked in Western values like me that discussion required a different approach in China. In that and many subsequent experiences, I found that direct criticism of China only threw people onto the defensive.

The collective Chinese animosity against the Japanese that I frequently saw in Baotou had its origin in the latter's invasion and occupation of China, which began in Manchuria in 1931 and continued until the end of the Second World War in 1945. That terrible period of Chinese history still aroused much emotion in the population and the Government was seemingly prepared to whip up nationalist feeling when it suited its purpose. For the country's leaders, turning anger outwards served to draw criticism away from themselves.

*

The weather in October was perfect. I took advantage of the blue skies and mild temperature to go out for strolls. Baotou's main shopping street was a five minute walk from my school. Every shop along it had speakers pumping out different dance music, so that passers-by found themselves dragged into a vortex of beats that changed with every twenty paces. Emerging at the other end of the street, I invariably felt invigorated and well exercised.

Near the pedestrian street was Baotou's largest department store. Inside, a huge shot of Julia Roberts gazed down on shoppers. Even the Chinese models on the posters were subtly westernised: their eyes rounded, their breasts filled out. On the various floors of the store, designer outlets sold clothes at western prices, which were disproportionately high compared to average Chinese salaries. For those with money, buying western brands was a way of flaunting that wealth. The economic inequalities in Baotou were revealed to me when Jiang Wei, a friend who worked in one such designer outlet, had to pay for an item of clothing that had gone missing whilst she and another girl were on shift. Its value, 4000RMB, was the equivalent of four months of her wage.

But top-range shops made up only a tiny section of the Baotou market and elsewhere it was a free-for-all. Whole streets were occupied by shops selling identical hardware. There was a street for DIY equipment, a street for bicycles, a street for bathroom items and a street for locks . . . Every shop owner no doubt dreamt of expanding and becoming dominant but it was hard to see how that would happen. Everyone bought their goods from the same depot and everyone sold them from the same place. It was a risky business trying to set up a shop in a different area from one's competitors because every buyer knew which street to go to if they wanted a particular item.

A large number of low and mid-range clothes malls existed in the city centre. The small outlets were leased out and most were snapped up by young women. While I was walking around an almost deserted mall one day, a girl dressed in a long T-shirt and baggy jeans came over. She introduced herself by the 'English name' of Yuki and said that she wanted to practise her English. I asked her what she did.

"I have a shop but there is nobody there so I feel bored. I only set up here two months ago. I am a business student in Hohhot, the capital city of Inner Mongolia, but this year I have to do work experience," she replied, looking unenthusiastic.

I went to look at her shop, a small outlet in the back corner of the third floor. A cardboard sign over the door had the name 'Crazy Girl' printed in Chinese characters. The clothes were all Indie-type pieces for girls.

"Is business good?" I enquired.

"No it is very bad. I shouldn't have rented in this building. It's only old women who come here. They do not like my style of clothes. Only about five people come into my shop every day. Most of the time I watch movies on my laptop. It's so boring."

"Where do you buy your clothes from?"

"From a big warehouse in Beijing."

"And do you sell any at all?"

"Last week I sold three things. All the customers bargain and want a low price. I am losing money!"

I looked around the rest of the mall. There was considerably more on sale than was ever going to be bought. Many of the clothes were almost identical from shop to shop. It was little wonder that customers bargained hard because if they did not like a price they could always go next door and buy the same thing.

On the whole, the people of Baotou were quite careful with their cash. The rise of the middle class was a major demographic change in China but, in Baotou at least, I found that normal people were still not spending massively on non-essential items. As a result of this the same economic pressures that applied to shops also applied to businesses such as restaurants and hairdressers. Because there were too few consumers and too many prospective entrepreneurs for the market, small businesses went to great lengths to grab attention. In mid-October a new hairdresser opened opposite the school in a tidal wave of noise. Lines of bangers were exploded continually for about twenty minutes. Chinese bangers were uncomfortably loud for anyone unfortunate enough to be caught outside. They also set off the alarms of every car in the vicinity. I peered into the new shop a few days later and saw the hairdressers sitting around looking bored. There were no customers.

*

In the opposite direction from the city centre was a large park. It was a pleasant place in late autumn. Grass could not grow in the dry climate but there were plenty of trees, winding paths and artificial lakes. There was also a deer enclosure. Baotou's Mongolian name meant 'Deer City.' Around the enclosure were always a few couples having their wedding pictures taken. Funky photographers with striking haircuts contorted themselves while the husband-and-wife-to-be posed dreamily. Usually the bride was in jeans and trainers beneath the billowing meringue of her white dress but that did not matter because everything was going to be photo-shopped anyway. I had seen examples of the end product.

A day with a photographer could cost several thousand RMB, an extortionate amount. But just as buying western brands was a way for the nouveau riche to flaunt wealth, posing in western bridal gear was good for social status. Many young couples considered the cost worthwhile, particularly as it was only a once-in—a-lifetime expense. More to the point, they considered it worthwhile because everybody else did it. Seeing as the lifestyles of people in Baotou were still quite standardised, everyone looked over each other's shoulders to monitor the little differences. As I understood it the relative lifestyle conformity across China had its origins in the not-so-distant era of genuine communism.

Part of the reason it lingered was that most people still lacked sufficient money to lead a radically different life. Many also lacked the imagination and single-mindedness. The system did not promote individuality.

Apart from the brides, the deer and the occasional woodpecker, most of the people in the park were retirees. The older generation formed a very visible part of the population. Retirement age was not fixed across China but I was told that in Baotou it was 60 for men and 55 for women. However, a number of exceptions existed. Women doing manual work, for example, retired at 50. Chinese retirees rarely received a pension, relying instead on money put away and eventually on their children for financial support. China's 'ageing population' was a buzz topic and I just had to step outside in Baotou to see it.

These 'oldies'—as I affectionately referred to them—kept themselves busy and came outside en masse when the weather was fine. Pairs of old men played Chinese chess for hours on the pavement. Aged passers-by often stopped to watch and then stayed indefinitely. It was very normal to see ten or fifteen people clustered around a board but there was never any gossiping or laughter; everyone's attention was focussed intently on the moves.

But it was in the parks especially that the elder generation dominated. I often saw practitioners of Tai chi balanced flamingo-like on one leg; power-walkers clapping their hands together rhythmically to improve circulation; geriatrics bumping against tree trunks to loosen their backs; ladies swinging on the yellow and blue painted exercise machines with all the abandon of children on climbing frames. Then there were groups of musical friends rehearsing Beijing Opera in secluded spots and dancers with CD players hopping the afternoons away. They all looked so healthy! They were so healthy! Not one was overweight or arthritic. Not one was dying any time soon and, for the Chinese authorities, the longevity of people like them was proving a headache.

I enjoyed strolling around and watching them whiling away the hours. I was fascinated by what they must have experienced in their lives. Born in Mao's China, they had to live through the carnage that accompanied much of his rule. Then, when Deng Xiaoping emerged as leader after Mao's death in 1976 and brought in the reforms that gradually opened China's doors to the world, they saw the country they had known transformed. By the time the possibilities of wealth were revealed to them, their human habits were too engrained to change. Most still dress plainly: the men in shirts, trousers and black shoes; the women usually in trousers too. There were no designer brands and no flashy wrist watches. They were the generation that was young when China started to modernise; they were now old and would never be modern. In a country trying to forget recent history and training its eye on the future, they were a little lost; not that it appeared to bother them. I found them very reassuring.

Many retained an unsavoury idiosyncrasy from old China: spitting. Most young people I spoke to found spitting disgusting, but not the old. 'Better out than in,' seemed to be their mantra. With a rasping noise they would draw the phlegm and mucus into their mouths, roll it all into shape with their tongues and then eject a small and neat sphere onto the ground.

Yaming's mother, 'Auntie', hailed from that generation. She was a teenager when the Cultural Revolution started. At that time, people in elevated positions throughout society were brought crashing down in a tide of red fervour. Auntie's father was an important official in Baotou and the family therefore had a difficult time. On two occasions their home was broken into and vandalised. All the while Auntie was memorising the quotations of Chairman Mao and attending feverish rallies with her Little Red Book. I could not help thinking that she and those like her must bear huge psychological scars. If so, they buried them deep.

Forty years on from the Cultural Revolution, Auntie was a divorcee, kept a number of small dogs and exhibited her youthful agility on the table tennis table whenever given a chance. She had retired from her job as a construction worker some five years earlier and now spent her days helping out at the school. In China, family members were always ready to support each other. Events had a tendency to overtake normal people and few expected to rely on the state. The family was the core stabilising influence in Chinese life.

*

The public schools took a break from midday until two o'clock and O'Sullivans provided a day-care service for some students who could not go home. Every day about twenty students from the nearby Number 35 Middle School came for lunch. They all wore the blue and white tracksuit that was their school uniform. Tracksuits and khaki were the two most common uniforms in Baotou.

I liked to go and sit with the day-care students and practise my Chinese. From when I had first arrived in Baotou, I had spent a lot of time trying to learn the language. I had decided to ignore Chinese characters so as to focus all my energies on spoken Mandarin. I had also been deterred from writing by the testament of my pupils. Virtually all of those over the age of twelve wore reading glasses and blamed the study of the tiny characters in textbooks for their premature loss of sight. In light of this, it seemed sensible to stick to speaking.

By mid-October I was able to string simple sentences together; something that made teaching to my youngest students much easier. It was worthwhile practising speaking with the day-care students because they spoke standard Mandarin. Nationwide this was the gold standard but in daily life people tended to communicate in their regional dialect. In Baotou the strong Inner Mongolian twang was very difficult for me to understand.

After eating lunch, the day-care students retired to the dormitories next to mine and Kris' rooms. By one o'clock, all were invariably asleep and not a stir was ever heard until they were woken by Auntie just before two. One day Auntie fell asleep herself. It was only at half past two that she woke up and hurriedly roused the unconscious students, every single one of whom had been sleeping like a log. They were attending public schools six days a week and were receiving excessive amounts of homework on top of that. They were exhausted in a way that no young teenagers should have been.

*

Teaching younger students was formulaic and structured around text books. I did, however, have one class of older students. With them I was free to do as I chose. Some of the class were excellent at English. All could read and write well. As for speaking, the pattern was very clear: those who had studied at my school with a foreign teacher for many years were quite fluent; those who had just joined struggled.

The main obstacle to getting what I wanted from my lessons was not the English ability of the students. The problem—exacerbated by years of public schooling so that it was a much greater problem with elder students than with younger—was that most were afraid to push boundaries. The best students stuck to simple sentences and the average students often gave one word answers. Getting it right and nothing more was deemed better than going for broke and slipping up.

I was interested in their life ambitions and discovered that all had a plan. One wanted to be a doctor, a second a teacher, a third a businessman in the south of China . . . All were highly focused but unimaginative. The possibility of living an unconventional sort of life had either not occurred to any of them or else had been discarded as impossible. A combination of societal and family pressures had discouraged them from pursuing success in anything other than a structured manner. Their dreams had been reduced to a few targets, which with hard work and exam success might be achievable.

When I enquired why each wanted to be whatever it was he or she wanted to be, I received a unanimous response. All hoped to become rich; not necessarily exorbitantly rich but, in the words of one, "To have enough money that I don't need to work so hard."

The bane of their lives, which gave each of them limited time to do anything else, was homework. They griped about it constantly and bemoaned their absence of free time. Even when one boy, Lawrence, remarked, "I want to visit America because the life there is relaxed and everyone sits on the beach," I suspected that his Hollywood-inspired Californian idyll said more about his desire for a break than a genuine interest in American culture.

I felt they needed some fun in their lives and tried to keep my classes relatively informal. Some responded well to the atmosphere I tried to create. Others were so used to disciplining themselves in the classroom that, when they realised they could let themselves go slightly, they went too far. More than anything, this revealed their lopsided personal development. Because they had so little free time to relax in the company of other people their own age, their impressive work ethic and dedication was complimented by a marked social immaturity. Some of the students in my eldest class were eighteen years old but I occasionally had to bring class discussions to a halt because one of the boys had excitedly sworn or said something sexually explicit. The girls remained more careful but not always. It transpired that one of the boys, Woody, was in a relationship. Some of the girls, clearly envious, took every opportunity to poke fun at him.

"Woody won't be here next week because he'll be with his *girlfriend*," they would jibe. "What did you see at the cinema that time Woody? You know, that time with your *girlfriend* . . ."

I laughed along but wondered whether they ought to have already grown out of that sort of thing.

*

Baotou University occupied a campus in the south of the city near the railway station. When I first visited, large amounts of construction were going on all around it. About ten concrete tower blocks were being built and a fancy new library had recently been completed nearby.

In late October I became friends with some of the students. They came from all parts of China but had one thing in common: they had all performed badly on the final high school exam. The results in this, the feared 'gaokao', were the only determining factor for university entrance in China. Baotou University was low-rated and was located in an unpopular region of the country. My new friends' 'gaokao' results had left them no choice.

University students across China slept in dormitories. That was the only way to pack them all in. The only variable was how many people lived in each. At Baotou University the standard seemed to be six per dorm. Unsurprisingly, all dorms were single sex. The dormitory buildings were supervised—no one could get in without a swipe card—and curfew was eleven o'clock.

For my friends in relationships, the living arrangements made their sex lives complicated. Most were forced to go to hotels but because they were students and tended not to have much disposable cash, they preferred places where hourly rooms were available. I was told that many of Baotou's hotels catered for this.

In the middle of the Baotou University campus were the huge buildings housing classrooms and lecture theatres. When I was shown around, every single classroom was occupied by people. On the lower floors the occupants were mostly doing work. As we climbed higher the number of people diminished and the odd couple skulked about, trying in vain to find a quiet corner. In other parts of the campus were tennis courts, badminton courts, basketball courts and a large football pitch. All were well used, particularly the basketball courts. It was perhaps counterintuitive that basketball had become the most popular sport in China. After all, a notable thing that most Chinese men lacked was height. But basketball it was and the superstars of the American NBA dominated the sports advertising on Chinese television.

Considering that every one of them had only achieved the bottom bracket of high school grades, most Baotou University students came across as pretty intelligent. Their common failing seemed to be laziness, not shortage of brains. In an education system based entirely on jumping through hoops, work ethic mattered much more than grey matter. David was an excellent example of this. When I first met him, I was surprised by his powerful physique. He stood well above six feet tall. His English was excellent. He could speak British English, American English and Australian English, and flaunted each accent with the arrogance of an actor. His build and facial features were different from what I was used to. It emerged that he was of the Muslim Hui ethnic minority, a group whose population was represented all over China but was particularly concentrated in the provinces to the west of Inner Mongolia.

"Do you believe strongly in Islam?" I asked.

"No, not really," David replied. "My father has strong faith but he does not force me to be strict. I observe important festivals but I very rarely go to worship."

David was determined not to miss the opportunity to have a serious conversation. I was a little taken aback by the tide of questions that come my way once we had moved beyond small talk. Most disconcerting was the Oxford drawl with which they rolled off his tongue. "Which factors do you feel were primarily to blame for the world financial crisis? . . . Tell me, are you a supporter of the British monarchy or do you feel it is a dated institution? . . . Surely you agree that American culture is immature and lacks depth?"

I blustered through. After what seemed a very long time, he eased up and started teaching me Chinese swear words. As we parted he shook my hand warmly and said, "Be careful around Baotou. The Mongolians like fighting. It can be very dangerous here. Fortunately for myself I am a big man and can fight them off. You should stay out of harm's way."

I tried not to be offended by this reminder that I was an outsider. Besides, David's warning seemed unnecessary: I was not sure whether I had even seen a Mongolian in Baotou, let alone had the opportunity to start fighting one. The fact that David, a man of non-Han ethnicity, made the derogatory remark about the Mongolians also gave me food for thought. I knew there were fifty six ethnic minorities in China and it was easy to think of them in terms of 'the Han versus the rest.' I realised that was a foolish simplification.

*

At the end of October, I took my bike and cycled to the west of the city, to the Baogang Iron and Steel Factory. This had been built in the 1954 and was still the largest single employer in Baotou. The factory's assets were worth more than 50 billion RMB and, among other things, included schools and real estate dotted around the city.

On this day the factory looked solid and peaceful. A sonorous rumbling was emanating from within and plumes of smoke were billowing from towers. As the evening wore on the sky behind glowed with unnatural colour. Oranges, pinks and deep reds silhouetted the concrete chimneys and made them seem almost beautiful. Baotou's air was not visibly smoggy but the pollution that dogged all of China's industrial cities was revealed in that moment.

As I returned home, the winds picked up and the air filled with sand. I had been warned that sandstorms sweeping off the nearby desert routinely struck the city in late autumn. Everything turned a murky yellow and I cycled with care.

CHAPTER 3

Colder, Darker, Murkier

The day of the sandstorm was one of the final times I took my bike out. November arrived and with it the temperature started to plummet. In the park, the fish were taken out of the lakes and the water was drained away to prevent it freezing. Everyone put on thick thermal layers and got on with life. Many hardy locals even continued working on the streets: fruit sellers and phone card hawkers kept plying their trade, as did the lady with no legs who begged down by the central post office. Pedestrians hurried a little faster from A to B; bicyclists and electric scooter riders accelerated more quickly away from traffic lights, and most women wore face masks to protect their lips from chaffing in the cold, dry air. Otherwise Baotou continued pretty much as it had done before.

I found it less easy than the locals to adjust to the cold and came down with a throat inflammation. Yaming boiled up some herbs and told me to drink the tar flavoured broth. In this manner I croaked my way through teaching.

My throat was not helped by kindergarten classes. While all other teaching had become much easier as time went on, Thursday mornings with the toddlers had by November become the hardest part of my week.

Yaming had first set up links to the kindergarten in September, with the intention of attracting new students to our school. She had made the arrangements with the help of an acquaintance, Joseph. I came across plenty of middle-men like Joseph in Baotou. Like informal agents, they claimed financial rewards in return for bringing people and businesses together. Social networks were essential in China and all people were interlinked by webs of obligation. These networks were so entrenched that the polite response to an apology in Chinese, "mei you guanxi," implied, "You don't owe me one." I routinely heard the cultivation of social networks hailed as more important than talent. The idea that, 'It's not what you know but who you know,' did not seem to inspire cynicism but rather was treated positively: being a good networker was considered an art form.

Joseph took half the money that Kris and I earned from the kindergarten. It was a source of annoyance to me that he profited from my hard work. He had a slippery character, which seemed all the more untrustworthy because of his effeminate mannerisms, and he used every opportunity he had to try and prise me away from O'Sullivans. He enquired about my salary, told me he could arrange for me to make much more elsewhere and bought me a pair of gloves as a goodwill gesture. He even told me about several foreigners for whom he had arranged good jobs, including one who, he explained with a slight snigger, was, "How to say? . . . Gay . . . But he is a very good teacher."

That sort of remark did not exactly endear me to Joseph, and his persistent efforts to get me to switch jobs did not please Yaming either. The two of them were, in a manner of speaking, old friends. But as she told me, "(In business) there's no such thing as a true friend in China."

That teaching at kindergarten had become the hardest part of my week was a problem of my own making. For the trial lesson I had driven the kids into frenzy and from then on frenzy was all they wanted. Their regular teachers always took the opportunity of my presence to take a breather and in the circumstances the only way for me to prevent leaderless chaos in the classroom was to lead the chaos.

The tots had an insatiable appetite for movement and were more than happy to do anything that involved running around. Their teachers led them in outdoor dance routines whatever the weather. One catchy song, which routinely bellowed from the megaphones, had lyrics along the lines of: *'Sing, sing, sing/ We play football in the playground/ We have fun and lots of laughter/ Sing, sing, sing.'*

Fun and lots of laughter were not exactly words I would have used to describe my experiences of kindergarten teaching. Week after week I limped home in exhaustion, having jumped, skipped, hopped, danced and sang my charges into ecstasy.

*

With the temperatures making it less enjoyable to be outside, I looked around for indoor activities and decided to try out my first bathhouse. These were very common in Baotou and some were less legitimate than others.

Once, when I was sitting on the steps outside the school, a tall and muscular figure walked past. Wearing a short dress, high heels and lots of eye make-up, he was laughing in an exaggeratedly high pitched voice at something his similarly dressed but slightly shorter companion had said. He caught sight of me and beckoned. I did not budge. He shrugged his broad shoulders and went into the bathhouse further down the street.

I decided to check out the rather more luxurious spa in the Haide Hotel, which catered to men, women and children alike. Even so, a friend warned me not to accept any invitations from staff to go into 'private rooms' lest I end up with a larger bill than I could afford to pay. On the day I went along and handed over 200RMB, which was very expensive for Baotou. I was given a pair of bath slippers and went into the bathing area. Heated pools, steam rooms, saunas and showers greeted me. Everyone was naked. I stripped down and hurried straight for one of the hot tubs. The Chinese men had no such qualms. They stalked around with their crotches thrust out. As a general rule they had little to flaunt. In one corner were benches. Pairs of friends were taking it in turns to rub each other down. On reaching the groin, whoever was doing the scrubbing took his friend's ball sack and flipped it over so as to clean underneath. I decided to miss out the rub down and went to collect a pair of pyjamas before heading upstairs to the communal area. There were computers, a pool table, a table tennis table, reclining couches with TVs attached, a gym . . . Best of all was the free food served from a buffet. It was spotlessly clean, there was plenty of space and attendants were on hand at every turn.

I knew that the majority of people in Baotou could not afford the luxurious experience offered at the Haide but cheaper equivalents were scattered around the city. One thing almost all had in common was that they offered massages. When I ordered a massage at the Haide, the masseuse arrived wearing a miniskirt and a tight corset. Although there were old ladies and toddlers around, her clothes betrayed who the most important clients were. The shyness with which she avoided catching my eye made me feel sorry for her. That her boss made her dress like a prostitute for work was presumably quite humiliating, particularly as she was properly trained in health massage. Any lingering doubts I had about her credentials disappeared when she pulverised by helpless foot and made it hurt in ways I had never conceived possible.

*

Driving in Baotou was anarchic. Cars came from every direction of the compass. It was perfectly acceptable for a driver to overtake into oncoming traffic as long as he used the horn first. What with the horn being more of an indicator than anything else, at rush hour the main roads became pretty noisy places. Crashing red lights, speeding, making illegal turns in the road: everything went. The law of the jungle ruled and buses were the big beasts. Coming up to a left turn on a three lane main road it was normal for bus drivers to slip into the right hand lane and then cut across the two lanes on their side and the three lanes on the other, bringing all other vehicles to furious but impotent halts.

I thought it was dangerous at the best of times, and it became increasingly lethal as the days got shorter and the evenings darker. One November evening there was commotion outside the school. A pupil, Billy, had been hit by a scooter as he tried to cross the road and had broken his arm. Billy had been crossing the road while taking a break between two successive classes at the school. That placed Yaming in a sticky position and she was worried about getting sued.

Fortunately the Billy's mother decided not to blame the school and instead tried for financial compensation from the rider of the scooter. She did this informally because, to the best of my knowledge, there was no formal procedure for dealing with the aftermath of accidents. I saw several low speed crashes take place; they seemed to happen on a daily basis as an inevitable consequence of the lax traffic laws. After a bump, both drivers would usually begin an argument about who was to blame. Bystanders and witnesses often joined in. Eventually a traffic policeman would appear to see what was going on. This official would mediate and some sort of financial agreement would be made. Then everyone would disperse. The behaviour of people in these situations was often dramatic. Usually the drivers would leave their vehicles parked in the middle of the road so as to begin their shouting match, oblivious to the traffic jams they were causing.

That everything was so anarchic said a lot about the negligence of Baotou's traffic police. I had my own experience of this a few days after Billy's accident. I was driven home by a traffic policeman who I had eaten dinner with at the house of a friend. He was very enthusiastic to meet me and kept offering to help me out if I ever got into trouble. That was questionable enough behaviour given his position but more remarkable was the way he drove. He spent most of the time looking at his mobile and texting. His eyes were rarely on the road and he frequently drifted. At one horrifying moment a female bicyclist appeared in the headlights and he swerved violently to avoid mowing her down. He had drifted so far that he had been travelling down the wrong side of the road.

Baotou's traffic police only stopped being negligent when the end of the month came round. At that time, their funds running low, they would set up blockades in the road and breathalyse the driver of every car that passed. Anyone who had touched a drop before heading out was given an on the spot cash fine.

*

The cold caused me to spend more time drinking. Or at least I spent more time drinking when it was cold, perhaps only deluding myself that there was a causal relationship. Bars had yet to really catch on in Baotou. There were only a handful of places available when I was there and most had number names. There were 7 Bar, 9 Bar, 88 Bar and 89 Bar. The Chinese word for 'bar' was a homophone for 'ninety eight,' which perhaps explained the naming system. There were not even enough customers to support the tiny number of establishments and these therefore sprung up and closed down at sporadic intervals. 9 Bar, which was opened with great fanfare by a wealthy businessman, received such a small clientele that it closed only a couple of months later.

Rather than going out to bars and clubs, people in Baotou preferred drinking in restaurants or at home. Even amongst the under-thirties I knew, the favourite entertainment was reserving a private room in a karaoke bar. They thought drinking behind closed doors was safer and more comfortable. Many bars had bad reputations.

The most popular spot in Baotou was 88. It had a small dance floor but, even when the place was pumping, most people just danced around their tables. Performers sang covers of popular songs, and then mingled with the guests. The guests rarely mingled with each other. Going to 88 was viewed as a fun way to spend time with friends, not a means to meet people. It was very rare to see anybody kissing inside. The women tended to drink little and danced with each other because their men were usually shy of dancing. The way the men impressed their girlfriends was by spending money and playing drinking games. They liked to invite foreigners over and challenge us. On most nights-out I was gestured over to a table, offered a cigarette and given a glass of alcohol. With a cry of, "ganbei!"—"dry the cup!" my host would drain his glass and I would follow suit. Then my glass would be refilled. Chinese men loved drinking like this. They were usually lightweight so this knocking back of drinks quickly got them drunk.

Some of my hosts were genuinely friendly. Others just monopolised my company to show off to the girls with them. Being 'friends' with a foreigner was good for status, especially in less developed areas of China like Baotou; a strange state of affairs given that foreigners were also held up as hairy, sweaty and smelly. But I could not have cared less about hidden motives. Often I went a whole night without having to buy myself a drink.

Over time, I discovered that the bad reputation of the bar scene did not come undeserved. One freezing November night I was at 88 when a tall young man in an expensive suit came over. He had broad shoulders and the whiff of alcohol was potent on his breath. He ignored me and without any warning whatsoever took my friend, Ryan, by the throat. "Fucking Japanese!" He snarled in English, "Fucking Jap."

Ryan was actually Filipino, but the drunkard was having none of it. After a backward and forward tussle, Ryan managed to disentangle himself and we made a run for it. Outside were a line of taxis. We leapt into the first one and I told the taxi driver to hurry up and start the car. The young man appeared outside and shouted something. Our driver refused to set off. We clambered out and climbed into the taxi behind, only to meet with the same reaction. I distracted the assailant, who did not have anything against me, while Ryan tried every single taxi in the rank. All of the drivers refused to take him.

The man worked his way into a state; opened the door of his Porsche, which was parked at the front of the bar; turned the headlights on full beam and pranced about yelling, "Fucking Japanese. I'll kill you fucking Japanese."

All the security guards of the club were standing around hesitantly. They seemed intimidated by him. With no help forthcoming, Ryan and I sprinted off on foot.

Afterwards, I wondered why the taxi drivers and the security guards had been so unhelpful. Ryan's tormentor had clearly been wealthy, which might have been a factor, but I suspected that there was more to it than that. My mind turned to the Li Gang incident, a scandal that had disgusted China a couple of months previously. A young man had run over two female students outside a university. One girl been killed and the other seriously injured. When the police had come to arrest him, he had dared them to try and sue him, proclaiming, "My father's Li Gang." On investigation it had emerged that Li Gang was the Deputy Commissioner of the local Public Security Bureau. I knew that corruption of that sort was widespread and speculated whether Ryan's attacker could have been somebody's relation.

*

Teaching proceeded according to the established routine. The only change came when Yaming asked me to write plays for the younger students to rehearse and perform at Christmas. I dutifully knocked together as fine a creation as I could using only the sentences: "What is your name?", "Where are you from?", "How old are you?" and "What do you do?"

In an early rehearsal I met with a problem. I had written "I am a gentleman" into the dialogue in answer to the question, "What do you do?" It was perhaps disingenuous of me to give children the idea that being a gentleman counts as a job, but first I had to overcome the difficulty that none of the students knew what the word 'gentleman' meant. Explaining subtle meanings using only context and my then mediocre Chinese was something I regularly had to do in class. On this occasion I tried for an explanation by association. "Englishmen are gentlemen," I said to the assembled group. "Do you understand?"

Nobody's eyes lit up. With hindsight I suppose it was a fairly pathetic line of reasoning. Nonetheless I ploughed on with my attempt. "Englishmen are gentlemen because we are nice," I said.

"No you're not," Annabelle, a bright ten year old, retorted defiantly. "In one . . . eight . . . four . . . zero . . . fight . . . . Err . . ."

I realised that she was referring to the 1840 Opium War. The short war and the 'Unequal Treaties' that followed it were often cited as examples of the Western Imperial Powers humiliating China at a time when she was weak. Although still at primary school, Annabelle had already studied this period. The horrors of the twentieth-century Japanese occupation also figured prominently in childhood education. The result was that young children came away with an instinctive suspicion of foreign motives. By contrast, the more recent turbulent years of communism were not covered in detail on the history syllabus.

*

By late November I had established quite a large group of friends within Baotou. I was invited out to dinner on a regular basis. Usually we went to barbecue restaurants. Barbecue food was a Baotou speciality and was cheap, delicious and filling. It did not matter what was ordered because the heavily-salted skewers of meat all ended up tasting the same anyway.

One night I and some Chinese friends went for a late meal. Piles of food were ordered. I ate my way through lamb chunks, barbecued dumplings and chicken wings until I was full to bursting. Another lump of meat was placed on my plate. I asked what it was but did not understand the response. I wolfed it down anyway. It was juicy, fatty and had roughly the same flavour as everything else, albeit with a slightly stronger aftertaste. A second was placed before me.

"I am completely stuffed. I can't eat anymore," I said, shoving it away.

My host pushed it back with his chopsticks. "You must eat a second one," he said.

"Why?"

He smiled wryly and gestured to his midriff, "Because we have two"

They were not kidneys.

*

Towards the end of the month, Kris and I went to visit Wudang Zhao, a Tibetan Buddhist monastery in the mountains to the north of Baotou. Just as we had seen on the drive to Wutai Shan, a short way outside the city any sense of modernity was extinguished. The bus passed through small villages where poverty was very apparent. Low crumbling brick houses stood by the roadside.

The monastery was large and sat in a valley of brown hills, which in that season were flecked with snow. Simple square huts sprawled up these hillsides, waiting for pilgrims who no longer came. Everything was built in the Tibetan style and was painted red and white.

A few prayer flags were stretched here and there but otherwise the scene felt lifeless. Mongolian monks sat in the porches of the gloomy temple halls but only to check our entrance tickets. Wudang Zhao had formerly been a renowned stop on the pilgrim trail between Mongolia and Tibet. Now, however, the monastery seemed more a museum than a place of worship.

Only in the very last days of November, after three months in Baotou, did I meet my first ethnic Mongolian. In fact that girl, Rita, was a student in the city of Hohhot and was only in Baotou to see a friend. She was very amiable and I was struck by how Han Chinese her attitude to life was. She spoke flawless Mandarin, was studying economics and aspired to work on China's booming east coast. I had a poor eye for faces and did not even guess she was Mongolian until she told me.

I wondered whether Rita's approach was the only way in which a Mongolian could fit into Chinese society. Integration seemed to have come at the expense of a culturally-distinct identity. Other than her parents, there was very little Mongolian about Rita at all.

CHAPTER 4

Who's in Charge?

December came but no yuletide atmosphere accompanied it. The temperature continued dropping until there was barely a day it came above minus ten degrees, let alone the balmy heights of zero. There was not even any snow to liven things up. Baotou was dry and looked exactly the same as it had in the summer.

The absence of Christmas celebrations defied the fact that Christianity was popular in Baotou and in China as a whole. There was a church just around the corner from the school. It occupied an ugly red brick building and there were often people hovering around the entrance.

At the start of the month a friend asked a favour of me. His boss, a businessman named Zhao, wanted to be filmed speaking with a foreigner. I agreed and went to a restaurant in which a film crew from Baotou TV had also gathered. I held a conversation with Zhao while the cameraman circled around. He thought that this demonstration of his English speaking ability would be good for commercial purposes. We made small talk for fifteen minutes. During that time, Zhao told me that he was a Christian and I so asked how he had become so.

"I read the Bible for many years," Zhao explained. "Before I was lost and selfish but now I understand that my mission in life is to do God's Will."

If God's Will was for Zhao to make money then he was certainly fulfilling his earthly purpose. He had lots of investments around Baotou, including a training school. Christianity was one of the fastest growing religions in China and its rise was partly attributed to ambitious people associating western economic success with Christian values.

Not all converts I met were so narcissistic. I had one friend, Blue, who was a waitress at a restaurant. She was very quiet about her beliefs and never went to church. However, she read the Bible in her spare time and had developed a deep faith. The Bible's easily accessible nature made it an excellent gateway through which Chinese people could enter into Christianity. This was particularly so because organised religious communities could still not play a prominent public role.

*

Having been brought up in a society that protected children through all sorts of censorship and legislation, it came as a shock to discover that absolutely anybody in Baotou could buy alcohol. Central government legislation on alcohol purchase had been introduced a few years before, but what I saw suggested it was not being enforced.

I knew of some disturbing happenings. For example, a pair of dancers at 88 Bar admitted they were just seventeen, and judging by their tiny statures and flat chests they might well have been younger. It was not a job underage children should have been doing: being a dancer at 88 required the girls to flirt with paying clients.

Despite the absence of restrictions, these bad situations were few. My elder students at O'Sullivans explained that, although they could easily buy alcohol from shops, they never did so for fear of punishment from their parents. Government controls might not have existed but family controls were on the whole much stricter than in the West, particularly as parents only had one child to monitor. The home filled in where the state left gaps.

Denied social opportunities, my overworked students primarily turned to video games as the only readily available source of relaxation. They also spent a lot of time online. Primarily they used Chinese websites such as Baidu, Youku and Weibo. Many of these sites were blatant rip-offs of existing Western websites ideas. They swept to prominence and propelled their designers into the stratospheres of the world's most wealthy men on the back of the huge Chinese online population. These websites became dominant over their western competitors partly because they complied with the Government's internet censorship laws. These, in contrast to with the lax enforcement of child protection laws, wre rigorously upheld.

The internet was not a completely free place at the best of times in China. Typing 'Dalai Lama', 'Falun Gong' and other controversial key words into a search engine resulted in the browser becoming unresponsive for a few minutes. Facebook and YouTube were inaccessible except via a proxy. Activity on internet forums was closely watched. The online restrictions became particularly stringent for three days around December 10th 2010 because of the Nobel Prize Ceremony. Even the English language versions of the BBC, CNN and other websites were blocked.

A few days after the event I asked Bill, a student at Baotou University, whether he knew who Liu Xiaobo was. He thought for a moment. Then he paused, glanced around the street we were walking down and whispered, "Sshh. Don't talk about that here!"

I lowered my voice, even though I thought he was being over-dramatic, "So you do know?"

"Yes but very few people know about him."

I remarked that Bill was in fact to first person I had met who knew of Liu Xiaobo, to which he replied with a hint of arrogance, "I used to be in the Communist Party at Baotou University and so I know their secrets."

"Are you still in the Party?"

"No, not anymore. I now understand that it's a disgusting organisation."

The only way Bill had received access to the information that made him turn against the Chinese Communist Party had been to join it. For ordinary people it was not easy to get an insider's understanding of the CCP and for anybody wishing to join, a full vetting and education procedure accompanied the application. That was not to say that the Party was small—it had over eighty million members nationwide—but, with the rare exception of people like Bill, most members had a vested interest in perpetuating the system. The CCP could not stop people complaining privately but, by controlling access to information internally, it prevented isolated pockets of anger having a uniting focus.

*

Living in the school had become a problem. Students and parents lingered inside the building because of the cold outside. My room at the end of the corridor had lost any sense of privacy and it had become difficult to draw a distinction between work and home. In an effort to preserve my personal space, I spent every free moment away from O'Sullivans. Baotou's dirty underbelly hove into view.

One night in mid-December a cat fight kicked off inside a bar. Two girls were carried outside by security, still kicking, screaming and tugging each other's hair. A few minutes later, people started heading for the exit en masse. I joined the rush and squeezed my way outside to see a full scale brawl in progress. A swarm of men were scrapping in front of me and to my left men with baseball bats were chasing a departing car. They smashed up its rear windscreen before the driver managed to accelerate away.

I saw that Ryan, my Filipino friend, had got involved. When I found him afterwards, he had a stab wound in his side and another in his back. I was shocked and asked what had happened. Ryan tried to reassure me, "It's nothing. Don't ask. Don't worry about me, it's not deep . . . I think I stabbed someone. We had each other by the throat. He tried to stab me but luckily I stumbled backwards as he did and the knife only scratched me . . . I really stabbed him though."

He kept repeating this last refrain, his mind more focused on the harm he had done his opponent than on his own wound.

Once I realised he was not badly injured, I became angry. "What the fuck are you doing? Getting into a fight? Are you fucking stupid? Those girls who it started with; you don't even fucking know them do you?" I stormed, my adrenaline making its presence felt.

"You don't understand . . ." He replied. "It's not about the girls. I can't tell you anyway. I'm not allowed to tell anybody."

In the circumstances it was hard for him to stonewall and with persuasion he became less reticent. "You can't tell anyone what I tell you," he said. "Only a few people know. I'm in a gang. It's part of a Triad. I've been in it since I was a kid in the Philippines. When I came to China, to Jiangsu, it was the gang that watched out for me. I was young. I couldn't speak Chinese. The same when I came here to Baotou. I lost my Filipino passport two years ago. I don't have a visa. The gang looks after me; allows me to stay here; makes sure the police don't throw me out. I have to do stuff for the gang—little things. I'm just a worker. Like if there's a fight, I have to help out my brothers. This thing tonight was between two gangs."

At first I was incredulous but with this new perspective, subsequent events clicked into place. The police, for example, only arrived half an hour after the fight was over and then just stood around for a few minutes before departing. In the following days there were no legal repercussions either, because, as Ryan explained, one member of each gang had ended up in hospital. The two gangs, deeming a fair outcome, therefore brokered a deal between themselves and the authorities that a line should be drawn under the incident.

My scepticism hinged around Ryan's tendency to exaggerate and so I asked a few of his friends. Despite Ryan's mock secrecy, it became apparent on enquiry that lots of people knew about his situation. Absolutely he had no visa. Absolutely the police must know about it. Absolutely they did nothing.

Now I was 'in on the secret', many other gang members were pointed out to me. The common feature of the men indicated was tattoos. Mostly these were just small brands on the wrist but a couple of men had coiling dragons etched into their backs.

I began to recognise that the influence of the underworld was quite pervasive, particularly within the entertainment industry. A man I knew, the owner of a bar, explained that his establishment was used as a meeting point for gang members, some of whom had been former classmates. He did not seem particularly enamoured by the situation—not least because his staff kept quitting on account of the bar's bad reputation—but felt that he needed the gang's support if he wanted his venture to be a success.

The local authorities were apparently happy to go along with it all and had their own agenda. A fellow teacher, Jenny, told me that her boyfriend, whose 'job' was transporting goods for more senior gang members, had been arrested for drug possession a year previously. Jenny explained that the police took him to the station and consulted a sentencing manual. Then they summarily gave him a four year prison sentence. No lawyer; no court;

no judge. Shortly after the arrest, Jenny handed out tens of thousands of RMB to various officials. Her boyfriend was let out the next day.

*

Christmas Day came and went in a flurry of activity. The school was decorated with tinsel and fairy lights; sweets were bought; party games were designed and timetables were arranged. Being an English school, we threw parties all day on Christmas weekend. It might have been good fun, despite the hard work. The parties were indeed a great success. Unfortunately, I managed to fall out with two colleagues. It was the worst Christmas in living memory. Come Sunday evening I was exhausted, stiff from jumping up and down, and generally pissed off.

I went to the Haide Hotel for a massage and struck up a conversation with my masseuse as she pummelled my aching limbs and laid the ghost of Christmas present behind me. Her name was Li Mei and she was 28 years old. Like all the women who worked at the Haide, she was thin and attractive.

Li Mei explained that all the masseuses lived in large dormitories within the hotel. She said she worked twelve hour shifts and slept much of the rest of the time, so rarely left the artificially lit building. It seemed a fairly miserable lifestyle but Li Mei defended it, smiling resignedly as she said, "It's alright. I received free training in massage techniques when I started working here and I do enjoy my job. Also, I'm good friends with the other girls who work here. We receive free food and accommodation so it's possible to save money."

"How long have you been working here?" I asked.

"I came three years ago. I left my hometown of Xi'an and came to Baotou to find work."

It emerged that Li Mei still had a boyfriend in Xi'an who she saw only about once a year. Nonetheless she refused to be miserable about her lot. She knew that it could have been much worse.

Even at the plush Haide there was a separate group of masseuses for the clients who bought private rooms. Prostitution, though never called that, was everywhere. KTV bars had 'entertainment girls' for the clients to choose and the larger hotels provided 'mistresses.' Massage parlours were often not what they purported to be. The problem was not unique to Baotou. On one occasion I read in *China Daily* that police in a southern province had raided several hundred massage parlours and found that roughly two thirds were providing sexual services for clients. That statistic would probably have been matched in Baotou, but even so no coordinated effort was being to hinder the sex industry. As with the gangs, the attitude of the local authorities seemed to be, 'live and let live.'

The number of whorehouses providing temptation to married men must have placed considerable strain on family life. Chinese wives had a reputation for being dictatorial behind closed doors but they can hardly have had much control over their husbands when they were away for work. I met men in industrial jobs who spent on average only one night a week at home. Many women presumably turned a blind eye on what occured during these frequent and often lengthy absences.

I gathered that divorce, although not uncommon, was frowned upon. Of the university students I knew, both men and women took great care in choosing their partners and avoided casual relationships, often on the advice of their wise old mothers, who knew the challenges lying ahead.

A close friend, Viki, had split up with her boyfriend of three years shortly before I met her. As her mother explained to me, "He was a lovely young man. He treated Viki really well. He really loved Viki. He treated me well too. But he was a little lazy. He was a model, you know; taller than you and very handsome. But he just sat around all day. A man like that is no use . . . Viki let him go."

Viki said it was her mum who had pressured her to split up, though with hindsight she believed it had been the right decision. Now, however, her mum was encouraging her to think about getting married because she had turned twenty six. The balancing act between carefully choosing the right man and not missing the boat was a difficult one for her.

Although its implementation had relaxed compared to years gone by, especially in the wealthier parts of China, the One Child Policy complicated marriage even further. The intimate lives of couples had to suffer the indignities of state interference, with rumours of forced abortion and sterilisation still common.

*

It just kept getting colder. If I went outside after taking a shower, my damp hair became starchy within minutes. The hot burgers from the take away around the corner turned cold as I walked back to the school.

I celebrated New Year with a bunch of other foreign teachers. It was a lifeless affair. We just watched the television and waited for midnight. In order to liven things up, I suggested that we all go outside topless when the clock struck twelve. We did. It was minus 25 degrees outside. After dancing around singing Auld Lang Syne for a couple of minutes, we felt hypothermic and so went back inside. The next day I had a cold.

The whole city felt tired. I felt tired. Four months of teaching and two months of icy weather had worn me down. My exhaustion was nothing compared to what some of my students were suffering. They had been doing six-day school weeks for four straight months. Now, end of term public exams were coming up fast and everyone was preparing. For those in important exam years, their teachers were working them to the bone. My elder students stopped coming to my classes. I did not push them to attend; I felt they were having a hard enough time without yet another teacher on their back.

Yaming wanted our school to set end of term tests to assess how much progress pupils had made. I thought this a little unfair. After all, students came to our school primarily so that they could perform better in their public exams. If we overworked them too, they might end up underperforming across the board. Because Yaming insisted, however, I wrote a couple of tests for my younger students. In contrast to their public school exams, which were all multiple choice, I created tests that required them to write sentences in English. When it came to marking them, the expected pattern emerged. A handful of intelligent students came close to full marks, the majority got around seventy per cent and a couple failed to score fifty per cent.

Yaming asked to see the results before I returned them to the students. Her face darkened. "We can't have students getting fifty per cent! No . . . You have to remark the papers."

She showed me what to do. Obviously there had been some easy questions, which everyone had got right. I weighted these so that they made up seventy per cent of the total marks. The harder questions—the ones that distinguished the bright students from the less bright—now only counted for a small portion of the final score. Everyone's adjusted mark looked roughly the same. This is what Yaming wanted. She could not have parents questioning what they had spent their money on.

But from what I could see the same attitude existed in Baotou's public schools. Because tests were multiple-choice and because most questions were easy, I was told it was a poor result to get less than ninety per cent.

The absolute smartest students I taught and the absolute worst were sometimes only separated by fifteen percentage points in their public exams. In a society where everybody was told they could succeed by conforming and working hard, showing clearly that some people were more intelligent than others was not an option. Every single student had to feel themself a winner.

Of course Chinese students were separated out at some points down the line. This happened in part when middle school students' grades determined their high school and in part when high school students' grades determined their university. But in the end it happened after students graduated from university into life and found that there was no good job waiting for them.

I thought it was sad how hard students pushed themselves and how hard their parents pushed them, towards a hopeless cause. I was all for encouraging ambition but to me it was a no-brainer that not everybody could be successful at the same thing. A good education system would have encouraged a diverse variety of talents. Instead, in Baotou at least, children slaved away with tunnel vision at like-minded ambitions. With hard work, I saw fairly slow-minded children get ninety five per cent in their exams. No wonder their parents thought they were little Einsteins! It struck me that it would be fairer to give twelve year olds fifty per cent in a test than prolong their useless dreams for another ten years.

*

Professor Wang was the most senior teacher at O'Sullivans. He only taught the middle and high school students and specialised in preparing them for public examinations. The Professor was a shy man. Although he had been an English teacher for over twenty years, his spoken English was not good. He avoided speaking to me when we passed in the corridor.

In order to see what the students had to learn for their exams, I sat in on one of Professor Wang's classes. He distributed the old exam papers to every student in the class and gave them half an hour to make a start. I took a glance at the paper.

Most questions had a sentence in English. In some sentences a word or phrase was missed out; on others there was a spelling mistake; on others the word order was jumbled. The students had to choose the correct option: A,B,C or D.

Half an hour later, Professor Wang went through the first part of the test. Most questions were easy ones to which everyone knew the answer. Then there were a couple I could not do:

. . . . the night, the boy slept

A) In   B) On   C) At   D) During

I felt that both A) and D) were passable but the Professor said otherwise. "The only answer is D," he proclaimed, "because 'slept' is a verb of duration and so you should say 'during the night.'" All the students furiously scribbled this down, presumably each making a mental note to rote-learn the answer.

Another followed:

The man lived . . . the street

A) At   B) On   C) In   D) Over

The Professor only allowed B: "The man lived ON the street." Living IN a street or OVER a street was not allowed. Clearly no beggars or first floor lodgers were acknowledged in China.

I did not blame the Professor. He probably knew just as well as I did that the exam was a farce. But the students had to sit the exam and so he had to train them how to pass. It filled me with anger that the discriminating questions in English exams for which my students worked like Trojans could be so idiotic.

*

In protest at rising fuel prices, the taxi drivers went on strike. The strike was coordinated informally because taxi drivers had no union. Nonetheless it was a remarkably synchronised effort. One day Baotou's taxis, usually very abundant, disappeared from the streets and everyone had to take the bus. Because it was so cold, the strike was quite effective. Certainly I was disrupted by it. The drivers did not get what they wanted. Their fixed taxi meters remained the same.

Discontent hung in the life-sucking January air. I heard a succession of unpleasant stories: the Baotou father who had beheaded his son; the student who was institutionalised in a psychiatric hospital because of learning difficulties; the number of high school girls getting abortions. I wondered whether Baotou was just reflecting my own dark mood back at me.

Kris was feeling the same. One night I called him at 3am telling him to come home because we had to teach early the next morning. "I'll be home in a bit," he slurred down the phone.

"You've been drinking, haven't you?" I said, accusatorily.

"Yer . . . What the fuck else is there to do?"

He was right and I knew it. We all needed a break. Fortunately for me, a change of scene was forthcoming. After the end of term, my contract with

O'Sullivans completed, I packed my bags and went to the train station. I felt I had had given myself a good grounding in the realities of life in Baotou. Now it was time for me to move on and take a look at the rest of China. A tingle of excitement stirred in my belly.

CHAPTER 5

Capital Apathy

I went back to Beijing because I needed a new business visa, which would give me six months to stay in China. The only way for me to receive such a visa was to show proof of employment. I therefore needed a legitimate company to offer me a genuine job, get me my visa and then not expect me to turn up for work. Fortunately I had a contact who said he could provide me with the job title and paperwork in question. To reassure me, he said he knew people within the Public Security Bureau who would shoo through my application. I handed over a lot of cash and my contact proved as good as his word. He prepared all the necessary paperwork and the Chinese authorities did not challenge my credentials. After a week long wait I received my visa and started telling everyone I met that I was a sales rep for and import-export company, because I thought it would be wise to polish up my cover story in case I ever had to answer for myself.

Whilst I was waiting for the visa application to be processed, I checked into a hostel in a maze of hutongs near the Lama temple. The road outside this place of worship was lined with shops selling incense sticks and meditative Buddhist icons. The same soundtrack of chanting resounded from every direction: *Om mani padme hu-um, Om mani padme hum/ Om mani pamde hu-um, Om ma-a-ni pa-ad me hum.* After a couple of days walking down this street this lilting tune had rather lost its charm for me.

The hostel was located in a traditional courtyard house and was virtually empty. My room was on the ground floor and there was no central heating; just an air conditioning appliance. The thermometers in Beijing were recording temperatures of minus ten degrees and so the room was like an ice box. The manager would not allow me to change rooms without paying extra and would not refund me the seven nights I had foolishly paid in advance. I decided to stick it out. Every night I huddled under three blankets and tried to stop my teeth chattering.

I spent most of my time in Beijing walking; sticking where possible to the hutongs. These narrow alleyways had been everywhere in 'old Beijing' but few now remained. The blocks of ramshackle, cramped and atmospheric courtyard houses that the hutongs once wound between had been felled en masse to make way for wide boulevards and modern high rises.

Of the isolated pockets of hutongs that survived, many had been converted into tourist hubs. I tried to avoid these 'restored' areas, preferring the older hutongs where the smells of street food mixed gently with those of sewage. Finding these genuine stretches was becoming harder by the day. I had visited Beijing three years previously and had been able to buy branded clothes and outdoor equipment at miniscule prices in stalls lining the alleyways. Few such places now existed. New paving was advancing steadily into the mazes and commercial hotels, cafes and bars seemed to be opening on every corner.

I visited an exhibition to see what plans there were for Beijing's future development. I was dazzled by the huge projects in the pipeline: beautification, sustainable housing developments, public transport extensions, water supply safeguards . . . But everything was about the future; everything about improvement. No mention was made of what might be being lost in the process.

*

The heart of Beijing smacked of grandeur. The imperial magnificence of the Forbidden City was counterpointed by Soviet-style monuments, which paid awesome homage to the dominance of the Communist Party. At the centre of it all lay Tian'anmen Square. This huge patch of concrete paving had seen its fair share of iconic moments. The security guards who now guarded its access points bore witness to the most notorious of these. In 1989 the Communist government ordered the army to turn its guns on the Chinese people. The protestors in the Square—by that stage mostly reformist student who had outlasted the popular demonstrations—were killed indiscriminately. Hundreds if not thousands lost their lives during the night of June 4th, albeit mostly in the streets around Tian'anmen rather than in the Square itself. But times had changed since those heady times of public fervour. The Square, while impressive, was sterile. Policemen and tourists were the only people occupying it now.

In the chilly mornings, long lines of excited provincials queued up to see the mummified corpse of Chairman Mao in his Mausoleum. This concrete cube was situated in the middle of Tian'anmen Square and thus in the symbolic centre of China. In the centre of the building, sealed within a glass case, rested the Great Helmsman. As with mummified corpses everywhere, there was much speculation over whether it was a waxwork. One day I decided to take a look. I was directed through the various security checks and eventually found myself in the presence of the iconic leader. He was thirty five years dead and had aged well. His cheeks were a little sunken and his face had a strangely orange pallor, but otherwise he seemed in excellent health. I could not decide whether his appearance was a metaphor for China since his death: 'China now more orange than red,' seemed a little contrived. Anyway, I only got about ten seconds to look before a solemn looking security guard ushered me on. It was distinctly anticlimactic.

*

Apart from the cold, which had turned all of Beijing's lakes into ice-skating rinks, the weather during my stay could not have been better. Daily the blue sky stretched to infinity and relegated the legendary smog to memory. The city's hardy residents were not about to waste the conditions. People filled the streets, some buying and selling but many seemingly outside just for the enjoyment of it. I often stopped to watch men flying kites into the stratosphere and developed a great respect for the proficiency even the oldest Beijingers exhibited when playing sports.

Ringing the centre of Beijing, enclosed within the circumference where the capital's ancient walls had stood before their destruction at the hands of the Communists, was a vibrant and fast-changing area. Here the last hutongs survived; crystallised lakes shimmered in the sunshine and ancient pagodas glowered across at bold new architecture. I tramped this inner city ceaselessly until my feet were bruised and I felt I knew every patch of pavement within a mile radius of the Forbidden City.

I found Beijing an easy place to explore for hours on end because there were public toilets everywhere. Most I saw were clean and some even had prize certificates pinned to their doors awarded by some official whose job can hardly have been a fun one.

Convenience was a hallmark throughout the capital. The efforts to transform Beijing into an ultra-modern metropolis were visible across the city. The ever expanding metro system was shiny and slick. During my time I rarely had to wait more than a couple of minutes for a train, which was essential given that a couple of minutes was all it took for the platforms to fill up alarmingly. Beijing was over populated and commuters packed the trains throughout the day. At rush hour I even spotted attendants on some platforms whose job was to shove people into the bursting carriages.

The recycling bins I saw scattered about were another nod to modernity and demonstrated at least a superficial commitment on the part of the authorities to protect resources. Unfortunately, nobody seemed to have been educated in how to differentiate between recyclable and normal waste, and so the recycling bins overflowed with trash. Beijing's façade might have received a facelift—in huge measure because of the 2008 Olympics—but this manner of contradiction abounded. I witnessed massive development taking place but the Beijingers were struggling to keep up.

I was shocked as I walked past a new shopping mall one bright day to see a man who had suffered horrific burns. He had essentially been melted by whatever traumatic incident had caused his injuries. He was begging by the side of the street. I returned to the spot a number of times and he was always there. When I mentioned this to one local girl, she said he was probably forced by gangs to give them the money he collected. His case was the most alarming I saw but many of the beggars in Beijing were disabled. Blind, deaf, armless . . . It was paradoxical that in a city fast becoming a hub of world affairs there was such inadequate social security that cripples—if discarded as burdensome by their families—had to take to the streets.

*

China was a big place and travelling abroad was expensive, so the vast majority of Chinese people took holidays within their own country. At the time I was in Beijing, schools had broken up for the Spring Festival holiday and the city was filled with excited Han taking photos of their nation's heritage.

Foreign tourists were also numerous and a murky industry existed to exploit their disorientation. Most notorious was the 'tea scam,' whereby pretty girls were employed by semi-legitimate tea houses to bring along unwitting foreigners and trick them into paying exorbitant amounts of money.

Therefore, when one dark evening I was walking west along Chang'an Dajie, the boulevard slicing through the heart of Beijing, and a girl approached me, I was immediately on my guard.

"Hi," she said, "do you speak English?"

"Yes, what do you want?"

"Oh, it's just that I studied English and like to practise. Please can I talk with you?"

I had nothing else to do. The girl seemed maybe twenty five years old. I felt like an adventure so set off with her. She wasted no time in complimenting me on my handsomeness, which was a laying it on a bit thick seeing as my face was almost completely covered by the hat and scarf I was wearing.

"Do you want to go with me to drink some tea?" She asked out of the blue.

Alarm bells started ringing but I agreed to go. She guided me down a dark alley, clearly knowing where she was going. We went into a small building and were seated in a private room.

I insisted on seeing the menu. Yes, I was right. Every single pot of tea cost upward of 300RMB, massively more than its genuine value. I said it was too expensive.

The girl looked rattled. "Well this is what tea costs in Beijing. Well it doesn't matter. I'll buy a pot of tea and you can have something cheaper. Is that ok?"

I could spot nothing wrong with her suggestion and congratulated myself on having beaten the system. I ordered an over-priced but affordable coffee.

The tea and coffee came, and with them a bowl of biscuits and tangerines. The girl had taken her hat off and her black hair was strewn across her forehead. Occasionally she patted it self-consciously. I could not decide whether she was pretty or not. She kept up a relentless stream of small talk: "Where do you come from? . . . And what do you do? . . . A teacher, oh that's interesting . . . Where are you staying in Beijing?" While jabbering away, she unwrapped a biscuit, peeled a tangerine and gave both to me to eat. Then, after barely ten minutes, she said we should go.

"Already?" I asked in surprise. "But we've only just got here and you haven't even drunk any tea? Don't you want to chat a little longer?"

"I'm sorry but I've got to go. I've arranged to meet a friend. You can come too, if you like. I'm sure my friend would love to meet you." She called for the bill.

It totalled 700RMB. The 300RMB tea had been supplemented by my 50RMB coffee and an exorbitant 150RMB for the tangerines and biscuits. The room fee added another 200RMB. I had rejoiced prematurely; I had been convincingly outwitted.

"I'm only paying 50RMB," I blustered "I only ordered a coffee. I didn't want the tangerines anyway. I said it was too expensive. It was you who said you'd pay."

"I said I'd pay for the tea! You said ok! You ate a tangerine!" She shouted angrily. "This is what it costs in Beijing!"

I knew she was speaking rubbish but I could not drag myself away. She worked her way into hysterics. "What am I supposed to do?" She shrieked. "I can't afford this! I'm just a Chinese girl."

My resolve started to waver. What if I was wrong and she was not in fact a con-woman? I dropped 100RMB onto the table and hurried out before either she or the staff in the building could stop me.

*

Despite Beijing being the political capital of the world's most populous nation, there was remarkably little political activity visible. Posters, graffiti, lobbyists and anything else related to public opinion were notable by their absence, at least to the western eye.

The opaqueness of the governmental process was epitomised by the inaccessibility of the walled compound behind which the top CPC leaders lived. This site around the unspectacularly named Zhongnanhai—'Central South Lake' had been the centre of Chinese power since the Communists first took over; Chairman Mao had also resided on Central South Lake. China was greatly changed compared to the years of Mao's rule but monopoly of power and lack of openness, which had defined the political system during his time, was as alive as ever.

I found muted suggestions of protest at the 798 art district in an old industrial complex on the distant outskirts of the city. Some provocative artwork was exhibited but even that was targeted against Mao, who had been dead for over thirty years, and not directly against the present leaders. I knew the Chinese had a propensity to criticise present times through reference to history, and I also knew that overly direct criticism could meet with punishment, but nonetheless the efforts were tame. Political fervour was not in the air.

There might have been little sign of political activism among the locals but Beijing was also home to an enormous number of ex-pats. Through a friend I met several people who had long-term experience of living in

China. A slight sense of 'gentleman's club' hung over some, and I was sceptical of those who sipped café lattes and pontificated about what was wrong, but nonetheless I noted what a few said about the enormous challenges facing the country: the huge numbers of migrant workers; the inflation and unsustainable economic growth; the burden of energy production to sustain the new middle classes; the demographic nightmare caused by the One Child Policy and ageing population; the continuing problems with basic human rights . . . The list was a long one.

The government would probably have brushed off much of what I was told as exaggerated or would have claimed to be effectively dealing with the issues. The authorities liked to scoff at the opinions of outsiders and routinely denied the right of democratic foreign leaders to comment on China's internal affairs. A previous generation of leaders had even been prepared to murder those in Tian'anmen Square under the eyes of the world's media; an event that was vividly recounted to me by an English journalist who had witnessed the event. The recent incident with Liu Xiaobo had proved the current generation just as prepared to oppose international opinion. And so the smooth ex-pats could talk all they wanted but could make no difference to what they surveyed. Change in China can only come from within.

CHAPTER 6

Poverty, Tradition and Respect

For 'Chunjie'—'Spring Festival', known better in the West as the Chinese New Year, I went to a town in south west Shandong called Cao Xian. When Echo, my closest friend at Baotou University, had first invited me to spend the festive period there with her family, I had immediately jumped at the opportunity to experience the celebrations. Spring Festival was when every man, woman and child in China made an effort to return home. The weight of migrating humanity was visible at the railway station in Beijing and on the train itself. I had booked a full week in advance but still only received a standing ticket for the ten-hour journey. I was feeling tired when I finally disembarked.

Echo's house had one storey and was built around a small courtyard. It was simple, with three bedrooms, a kitchen, a living room, a bathroom and an outside toilet. A brick wall ringed the courtyard and just outside the gate was a small rubbish dump. I was given Echo's room; a room that during the day acted as a thoroughfare between the living room and one side of the house. Echo went to her little brother's room and her little brother went to stay with an aunt.

Because it was the eve of the Festival, everyone was busy. Food was being cooked, the house was being cleaned and red paper banners were being hung around every door. On the banners were gold or black characters with the meanings 'wealth', 'good luck' and 'happiness.' I participated in the making of 'jiaozi'-'boiled dumplings,' which are the traditional Spring Festival food. Minced pork was mixed together with diced greens and herbs, and then stuffed inside little parcels of dough. The stuffing was a conveyor belt process. One person kneaded the dough, another rolled it into flat circles and another used chopsticks to place the filling inside and seal the packages. At first I was more of a hindrance than a help, but it was a fun communal activity nonetheless.

I joined in elsewhere when possible but my assistance was not really needed. Everyone in the family knew what chores they had to do and got on with them efficiently. They did the same chores every year; Spring Festival was a time to stick with tradition. Echo's father, a kindly but withdrawn man of about fifty, told me that he had celebrated in exactly the same way when he was a child.

Other things had remained the same too. A fading picture of Chairman Mao hung on the wall above my bed and in the kitchen a large chart on the wall illustrated which foods went with which according to traditional Chinese culinary methods. Few things I saw in Cao Xian reflected the huge changes that had swept over China during the past generation.

*

At the turn of midnight and again at dawn on the day of the new lunar year, bangers were detonated. Echo's home lay outside the town proper but even so the noise was astonishing. The earth and sky shook with the reverberations. When her father lit the bangers in the courtyard, we all cowered inside with ears covered until the deafening explosions were over. There were no rockets or other colourful fireworks anywhere on the skyline. For the inventors of gunpowder, I thought it was a pretty poor show. All they bothered to do with their invention was make it go boom.

In the early morning gloom, Echo's mother lit incense sticks, offered moon cakes and burnt small denomination paper money for the two household gods; her father scattered symbolic sticks around the courtyard and then we all sat down for a breakfast of jiaozi.

In the afternoon Echo and I rode her scooter into town. Cao Xian was full of people. Everyone was milling around the dirty lake that swamped the town centre, munching on street food and bargaining for plastic toys with the stall vendors. I bought some sugar cane but found it fibrous and difficult to eat.

It was clear that the town was poor. The blocks of flats were flaky, the streets were dirty and people of all ages gawked unashamedly at me; a sure sign that modernisation had not swept in. I saw a school with windows missing and as I watched a pair of cats darted out from inside onto the street.

A crowd had gathered to the side of the lake. I stood on tiptoes to see what was going on. A miserable looking monkey with a rope tied to its neck was sitting on the ground. Its master kicked it to make it move. Then, when it started to slink away, he wrenched it back by the rope. Everyone watched on in fascination.

A hand grasped my elbow. I turned around and saw a swarthy looking man with a wad of notes in his hand. I shook my head. I had no money on me. The man did not let go of my arm. He looked aggressive. "You are looking at the monkey," he growled, "so you have to pay."

I pulled my arm away and turned to go. He tried to block my path. Echo stood to one side with a scared expression on her face. Although there were people everywhere, all were deliberately avoiding looking my way. After an unpleasant couple of moments I managed to dodge past him, smacking away his flailing arm.

*

Following the initial excitement, a status quo was quickly established. Spring Festival for Echo's household was essentially a long succession of social events. Some days friends came round to the house. Other days we all climbed into the rickety car and drove out into the countryside to visit family members. This was everyone's annual opportunity to catch up with friends and relatives, and though I was a stranger I was made to feel very welcome. At one meal I was introduced to a young boy as his, "waiguo shushu"—'foreign uncle.'

The region around Cao Xian was wheat farming territory. On the third day of the festival I saw small clusters of white robed people dotting the frost-hardened fields. They were burning incense and offering up prayers to the recently dead, who were buried in the very earth they had tilled while alive. Small hamlets stood in clusters between the fields. The dried stream beds around which they were built were choked with litter; a sure marker of poverty.

Because wheat was the local produce, it provided the staple of every meal I ate. Breads, dumplings, noodles as well as simple meat and vegetable dishes were served up in an endless cycle. What was not finished for breakfast was reheated at lunch; what was not finished at lunch was carried over to dinner, and what was not finished at dinner was served again the next morning. No distinction existed between the three meals. Nothing was wasted.

Many of the homes I visited in the countryside were dilapidated. Spring Festival was a misnomer because it was still the beginning of February. Everyone moved around with a thick coat on, even when inside. All the old houses had no heating and the temperatures stayed resiliently below freezing. Relief only came my way at night when I could retire to the welcoming warmth of an electric blanket.

It was difficult to get hot water so I went to a public bathhouse when I wanted to wash. This was a very different style of place from the spas I had graced in Baotou. It was dank and grimy, and there was one cloudy bathing pool. A few men wallowed somnolently inside the tub, perhaps fantasising about the black-and-white photo of a nude model, which was pasted to a wall above their heads.

*

Shandong was a coastal province and its major cities were economically booming. But Cao Xian, lying fatally inland, was poverty-stricken. Agricultural regions of course had fewer automatic opportunities for economic development but nonetheless the wealth inequalities were alarming. Deng Xiaoping, the architect of the market reforms that opened China up to foreign investment, famously promoted his policy by saying: "It is glorious to get rich . . . It does not matter if some people get rich first." Some people had got rich first. The problem was that they were the ones still getting richer. The gap between China's rich and poor was widening by the minute. Taxes were low and wealth redistribution from the cities to the countryside was not happening nearly fast enough. Of the Cao Xian residents I met, most said their best chance of making money was to move away, which many did. The men I had sat beside on the train down from Beijing had been returning home from their jobs working in the capital's factories.

Echo's mother and father, having never experienced better, were not infected by a sense of social injustice. Not even when, in the evenings, we huddled into the living room to watch the glitz and glamour of the Spring Festival Specials, did they seem concerned that the world shining out of their TV set was so far removed from their own.

I rarely watched TV myself because the speaking was too fast for me to follow properly. Even what I could understand did not inspire me. Chinese television as a whole struck me as tepid. It consisted of generic sitcoms, game shows and the endless war films on channel 7, where the heroes were chivalrous Chinese foot soldiers and the baddies were murderous Japanese generals.

The Spring Festival Specials I watched with Echo's family were evening long spectacles performed to live audiences and broadcast nationwide. Samey comic turns were broken up by musical acts, the most notable of which were traditional dances performed by ethnic minority troupes. These were fun to watch but propagated the impression that the only distinctive feature of minority cultures was the exotic way they dressed up.

*

On my penultimate day in Cao Xian, the local tax collector came to drink tea and smoke cigarettes with Echo's father, his former school classmate. He engaged me in conversation despite me struggling to understand his thick regional dialect. Being a CCP official, he had an air of self-righteous authority and preferred talking to listening.

He stated that China's policies under Chairman Mao had been mostly correct but occasionally misguided, praised the economic reforms of Deng Xiaoping, and said China wanted to be friends with everybody. He stated lots of other things that I could not understand and then praised me as 'brilliantly intelligent;' a compliment I had earned presumably by nodding along while he extolled the party line. Echo's parents praised me in similar terms, both looking slightly awestruck by the conversation. Their reaction was touching but more than anything it demonstrated their misplaced sense of inferiority to political ideas.

Echo seemed a little embarrassed by their enthusiasm. She had become increasingly anxious as my stay had gone on that I might not be enjoying myself. She apologised for everything about Cao Xian, particularly for the fact that there was very little to do. My constant reassurances that I was having a great time did not set her at ease, perhaps because she was not at ease anyway. Echo had enormous anxieties about how she should be leading her life. She felt loyalty to the conservative values of her parents but also understood their traditional attitude was dated in modern China.

I had met many girls in Baotou who were planning to return to their home towns after graduation, but Echo's inclination to do so struck me as especially limiting. I sensed that if Echo returned to Cao Xian, she would have little opportunity to build a better life for herself. Nonetheless that was what she planned to do. She was a shy girl and told me simply, "I do not want to make my father unhappy." I pitied her a little. Our lives were so impossibly remote.

After a week of heart-warming hospitality I decided to move on. I hoped that the length of my stay proved to Echo how much I appreciated her invite. At the station, before boarding by bus, I went to the public toilet. A line of squatting men gazed up at me, all crapping into an open furrow that ran the length of the room.

*

I had worked in Baotou, I had waited in Beijing for my visa and my Spring Festival had also been sedentary. Now I had complete independence and my travels could begin in earnest. My first stop was very appropriate: Qufu, the birthplace of Confucius.

Of all China's great thinkers, Confucius was the one who made the most profound impact. His ideas about human relations, governance and scholarship, conceived over two and a half millennia ago, were key features of imperial Chinese society. In fact a compulsory exam on the

Confucian classics existed in the Chinese civil service until 1908, just three years before the abdication of the last emperor.

Qufu was preserved throughout imperial times as a focal point for the worship of its famous son. Its present-day restoration existed less for worship and more for tourism. Grey bastions ringed the inner city and within these walls an unrivalled collection of imperial architecture—mostly Ming (1368-1644) and Qing (1644-1911)—stood intact. The atmosphere was that of a huge museum, but to me the solemn grandeur of former ages was still tangible.

Sprawling across the centre of town were the Confucius Mansions. Built for the descendants of Confucius, the size and luxuriousness of the residence was a symbol of the imperial patronage the family once received. Emperors of successive dynasties poured wealth and title onto the lords of Qufu in honour of their distinguished ancestor, and revered as a demi-god the teacher himself.

However, the retrospective worship of Confucius only served to highlight his lifetime failings. He sought hard for a state that would implement his ideas but gave up after years of frustration. Either rulers were corrupt or did not adequately understand him. Only after conceding failure did Confucius stop travelling and focus on teaching. He taught rich and poor, young and old; anyone who wanted to be educated. As much as anything else, this emphasis on the value of education was one of Confucius' most abiding contributions to Chinese society.

The Confucius Temple filled the site where the master had once delivered lessons. A dusting of snow flecked the ground as I strolled across bridges ornately carved with dragons and passed through halls that were paradigms of imperial architecture. Ancient trees and giant stone steles recording the visits of dignitaries were dotted around the courtyards. I found my way to the Apricot Pavilion; the very spot from which Confucius legendarily had lectured and tried to reach my mind across the millennia. A fleeting sense of time flitted across me, but I could not hold the feeling. The aeons of before were beyond my capacity to grasp.

But I did not need to look to the past to see the influence of Confucius. The Communists' original anathema to his thought—they considered it feudalistic—had been replaced by a pragmatic acceptance of its uses. Indeed one of the CPC's recent buzzwords had a very Confucian ring to it. After revolution, upheaval and general instability, what President Hu Jintao and the other leaders were looking to create was 'social harmony.'

I found this rather illusive terminology all over China. I saw the state media trumpet the importance of a 'harmonious society' via TV, newspapers, billboards and the internet. Some of the rhetoric focused on stamping out corruption, which was undermining the credibility of CPC rule. On other occasions the emphasis was more on encouraging ordinary civilians to cooperate with the Communists' vision for the country.

As I stood in the Confucian temple I wondered whether 'social harmony' was, in the great tradition of Confucian ideology, an honest call for responsible government acting in the interests of a cooperative populace. Or were there darker meanings hidden in the words? I was alone and China lay before me. And I had a quest. I left Qufu and set off in search of harmony.

CHAPTER 7

The Booming Yangtze Delta

Strange to any foreigner who looked at the map, the Chinese liked to refer to the area around the mouth of the Yangtze River as the 'south of China.' Centred on Shanghai but embracing several cities in the provinces of Jiangsu and Zhejiang, this geographically small chunk of the vast nation was to aspiring Chinese people its most superlative slice. Referred to as the Golden Triangle of the Yangtze; money, money and money was what it symbolised, but with a heavy dose of culture, style and sophistication thrown in. To the Western world, which was now investing heavily there both in financial and human terms—a large number of foreign students and ex-pat businessmen were based there—the Golden Triangle proved that China was a force to be reckoned with.

Getting there from Shandong proved difficult. Everyone was returning to work after the holiday and train tickets were hard to come by. I was forced to stand once more. When I got on the train in the early evening it was already full. Passengers were crammed into every available space. As the train drove on through the night, more and more people got on. I ended up in the aisle without even enough space to lean.

I was impressed by how well everyone around me dealt with the conditions. Because it was almost impossible to move, people who wanted hot water from the boiler at the end of the carriage just passed their cup to their neighbour. The neighbour then passed it to their neighbour and so on in a human relay until the cup reached the person nearest to the boiler. This person filled the cup and then relayed it back. The same principle worked with luggage and other more surprising 'objects.' A mother and father had ended up at opposite ends of the carriage. Their baby was with its father but was crying for its mother. The living conveyor belt kicked in action and the baby was passed hand to hand across the gap.

Universities, many of them among China's most prestigious, were very numerous around Shanghai. As it was the end of the holiday period, this was evidenced by the number of students around me, one of whom granted me temporary respite from my discomfort by offering me his seat.

Other than the twenty minutes following this act of kindness I was on my feet until I got off in Nanjing at three in the morning. I was feeling so dopey that I bought a Chinese map of the city from a hawker; a map that I obviously could not read. I dragged myself to the nearest twenty four hours restaurant, KFC, which was the most popular fast-food outlet in China. Unfortunately I was denied the opportunity of getting any free shut-eye because the restaurant was already full of people doing exactly that. There was no room at the inn so I had to grit my teeth and go to find a hotel in the city centre, first allowing myself to be ripped off by the taxi drivers in the rank, who all knew I was stranded and therefore coordinated in denying me a reasonable price. It was not the most auspicious start.

*

Over the three days I stayed in Nanjing I experienced balmy sunshine, pouring rain and a blizzard. Nanjing was known as one of China's 'three furnaces' for its summer temperatures but February evidently had it less good. Despite the variable conditions I largely ignored the new metro line. I firmly believed that walking was the best method to see a city properly.

Towering Ming-dynasty walls enclosed the city centre. They gave it a compact and orderly feel. Well-maintained temples and restored pagodas stood seamlessly besides rocketing skyscrapers and designer shopping malls. European style villas provided a contrast to the ugliness of the high rise apartment blocks. Outside the walls, urban sprawl spread out in many directions but not at the total expense of greenery. Most notable was the large forested area around Zijin Mountain, which served both as a nature reserve and as a treasure trove of historical monuments.

Nanjing was the capital of the Republic of China for the ten years before the notorious Japanese invasion of 1937. During this period the Government was ran by the Kuomintang, the Nationalist Party. After the Japanese lost the Second World War in 1945 and were expelled from China, Mao Zedong's Communists fought a bloody civil war with Chang Kai-shek's Kuomintang for supremacy. The Kuomintang lost and fled to Taiwan, which remained a thorn in China's side.

Contained within the trees of Zijin Mountain was the gargantuan tomb of the Kuomintang's original founder, Dr Sun Yatsen. His burial site was even grander than the nearby tomb of the Ming Emperor, Xiaoling. Dr Sun Yatsen's was the voice for reform that brought the last imperial dynasty, the Qing, to its end in 1911 and he briefly served as President of the Chinese Republic. After that promising start, things went awry and China fell under the controls of various warlords. Dr Sun Yatsen spent the rest of his life trying to raise armed forces and reunite China. He died in 1925 with his vision unrealised.

Considering that Dr Sun Yatsen was the progenitor of the enemy that came so close to defeating the CPC in its early years, I came to Nanjing expecting to find his legacy tarnished. Far from it: his mammoth mausoleum stretched down the mountainside like a river flowing from the sky. Looking up from the bottom I was faced with an intimidatingly long set of stairs; the climb broken up by various halls with navy tiled roofs. Hordes of people were slowly ascending, their determination proving them tougher than the usual tourists. The atmosphere was of a pilgrimage.

I made my way steadily upwards, stopping only to look into the various exhibitions extolling Dr Yatsen's lifetime achievements. They drew particular attention to his care for the Chinese people and his efforts to unite the nation, but his democratic ideals were also presented clearly. Compared to the obscurity and obfuscation with which I had seen democracy portrayed elsewhere, this came as a surprise.

By the time I had reached the top and paid my respects along with hundreds of others in the burial chamber itself, I found myself liking Nanjing. It seemed a self-confident city and mature city.

That maturity was hard-earned. The six weeks following the Japanese occupation of Nanjing on 13th December 1937 provided the backdrop to one of the worst war crimes in twentieth century world history. During that horrific time three hundred thousand innocent people were butchered by the Japanese forces. Thousands more were raped and mutilated. The atrocities were commemorated at the Memorial hall of the Nanjing Massacre, which had been built on the site of an unearthed mass grave.

On the day I visited the rain was lashing down against the black stone buildings. I winced at the brutality of the events, which were excruciatingly detailed in the exhibition rooms. There were vivid photographs of executions, footage of rapes by Japanese infantrymen, a large picture of a decapitated head placed on a fence with a cigarette in its mouth . . .

I could well understand why the Chinese still feel anger. But more powerful than disgust at what I saw, I felt ashamed that I had not known about the incident before I had come to China. The scale and horror of the massacre were comparable to the Holocaust and yet I had never really cared back home in England.

After walking through several harrowing halls, I found myself in the last exhibition room. Here were documented the efforts of the museum's Chinese and Japanese patrons to spread knowledge, build mutual understanding and foster forgiveness. I knew there was still much work to be done.

*

On the day I went to the Memorial Hall, I was driven around by Miumiu. She was very attractive, with a husky voice and a slight lisp. No doubt her looks were part of the reason I had agreed to spend the day with her. She had enrolled on an evening English course at Nanjing University and needed to read out a short presentation at the next class. Unfortunately her English was too poor to complete the task and so in frustration she had decided to seek out a Mandarin-speaking foreigner to help. She had approached me in a bar and offered to drive me around Nanjing if in the meantime I taught her English.

It worked out well from my point of view because the heavy rain would have made it a difficult day if I were not in her car. It also developed into a very strange experience. The oddities began when we went to a restaurant for lunch. It was a luxurious place and so I was careful not to order too much. As a man, I thought I would be expected to pick up the bill. After we had finished eating, Miumiu stood up and headed for the exit. I hurried after her and pointed out that I had not yet paid. She said it was no problem and we walked out. Nobody moved to stop us.

After eating she took me to a train ticket office. The tickets to my next destination, Suzhou, were sold out. Miumiu made a phone call and an hour later I had a ticket, free of charge.

In the evening we went to another expensive restaurant, this one a French-themed place. Miumiu ordered and she did not hold back. The piles of assorted meat and vegetables were delicious. Again we headed out without paying the bill. Again nobody stopped us. I was intrigued and asked her why we did not have to pay. "I have friends," she replied cryptically.

And then there was the fact that she had driven me around on a weekday despite being of working age. I asked her what job she did but she just smiled sweetly before adding, as if in explanation, that she had seven houses.

Miumiu wanted to learn English so that she could go to India and study meditation with a yogi. She was the sort of person it was impossible to meet away from the wealthy east coast.

*

Suzhou was one place my friends in Baotou dreamt of visiting. Nicknamed 'the Venice of the East;' its tinkling canals, poetic gardens and rich history made it for many Chinese people the model of culture and sophistication. It was once the centre of Chinese silk production and a first stop on the legendary Silk Road. It was the wealth from that industry that funded Suzhou's development into the paradigm of classical culture. When Marco Polo passed through in the thirteenth century he was awestruck by what he beheld.

The modern day Suzhou, as I quickly discovered, was more prosaic. Its GDP was among the highest in the whole of China and its development into a heaving metropolis was on-going. The suburbs were sprawling, with concrete towers shooting up and cranes dotting the landscape. Even in the centre, the dreamy gardens and pretty bridges were blighted by the number of tourists.

Wherever there were so many tourists there was inevitably a manipulative industry. Barely an hour after I arrived, a man stopped me in the street and invited me to the Suzhou Silk Factory. He told me that it still used traditional techniques and was a last relic of a forgotten age. I went along with a hint of scepticism and quickly discovered that the word 'factory' was an exaggeration. No production seemed to be going on. All that existed in the 'workshops' were a few rusting looms and broken silk cocoons. I followed the exit signs to a showroom where uniformed salesman tried to make me buy carpets. From here I followed more exit signs. I found myself back in the showroom. I tried a different direction with the same result. I retraced my steps to the entrance but the security guard standing there told me to follow the exit signs. They all led back to the showroom. I only got out by slipping through a side door with a large 'No Exit' sign above it.

*

That evening, I and three others took a taxi to Wumen, a large gate in the south of the city. It stood alone and forlorn, stranded by the destruction of the city wall of which it was once part. When we got there it transpired that we were not the only ones. Swarms of people—many of them young children—were gathered on the banks of a river. A massive police presence was trying to keep the crowds under control. In fairness the young men who made up the force were doing a good job; linking hands to form human barriers and guiding the weight of humanity through one-way channels.

Two boats pulled out into the current and then the fireworks began. They were the real deal. Everyone watched in awe as exploding rockets rained down droplets of colourful light. It was the Lantern Festival, the official end of the Chinese New Year celebrations. The eponymous lanterns were being lit all around. They rose up and drifted away with the wind, like a flock of firebirds migrating to warmer climes. Occasionally a lantern failed to make it and came drifting back down to earth. One bush caught fire and was hastily trampled by frantic officers.

After the fireworks were over I and my companions moved away from the crush. One of them was a woman of thirty who spoke excellent English. She told me that her English name was Tracy. She was from Shanghai and had an agitated manner. As we walked along, it was she who set the pace.

Tracy had just quit her job as a neurologist at a hospital in Shanghai. When I asked why, she did not answer directly but instead remarked that she had wanted to be a neurosurgeon. Then she continued on rapidly, seemingly wanting to get the words off her chest. "Sometimes you have to learn what you cannot do. I studied for many years to be a neurosurgeon. It was my dream. But I was not strong enough." She laughed harshly.

"Not strong enough in your mind?" I prompted.

"No: in my hands. One day my professor told me that I needed to be able to make a tiny hole in a skull with just a hand drill. We had electric drills but my professor said that I needed to be able to use a hand drill too. What if it was an emergency but the electric drill was not working? I tried and I tried but I could not do it! My hands were shaking. I kept trying for many months but I was not strong enough. All the neurosurgeons in China are men. But it was my dream!" She looked at her hands as if they were traitors and repeated hopelessly: "Sometimes you have to learn what you cannot do."

After her failure Tracy had become a neurologist. I asked once more why she had left that job and again she was evasive, "Oh . . . lots of reasons. I need a break." Then she remarked cautiously, "China can be very dark. How do you say it in English . . . Playing God."

I pressed for more detail and received a string of disjointed utterances: "Sometimes I have to choose whether a patient gets treatment . . . The pressure on me is so high: pressure on the conscience . . . Not everyone can afford it . . . Money for life."

I understood what she was getting at and asked, "Don't people have health insurance in China?"

"Oh yes the richer place do. There is insurance in Shanghai." She rallied her thoughts and went on the offensive, "All countries are the same. There are the same problems everywhere! The hospitals are very good in Shanghai!"

"But?"

"But some people don't meet the insurance criteria."

"And so they are left to die?"

"Yes."

Dark indeed. No wonder she needed a break.

*

I tried to find a quiet spot in Suzhou to relax and soak up the ambience. It was almost impossible to do because there were so many people around. One afternoon, when I was sitting by a canal and savouring a few moments' peace, a young man with black hair and glasses came over. He introduced himself as Michael and explained that he was a student at Suzhou University. I do not particularly feel like being used for English practice but my evasive answers were soon overwhelmed by Michael's friendliness and determination to talk. He was interested in my views on Chinese politics so I asked him whether he knew about the Tian'anmen Square massacre.

"Yes I do," he replied. "Everybody at the University has heard of it but nobody is exactly sure what happened. I know that many students were killed."

It had of course been impossible for the Chinese authorities to completely erase memories of Tian'anmen, though they had quite effectively propagated the impression that only students were involved in the protests. In reality people from all areas of society took part but this had been hushed up. I told Michael what I knew of what had happened and expressed my belief that a government killing its own people was just about the greatest problem that I could conceive of in a political system.

"Something like that could not happen now because so many people are watching," he said. "Also, I think history will say that the government made the right decision at Tian'anmen Square."

He must have seen my surprised look because he quickly explained himself. "Yes. Since then, China's opening-up has continued very successfully. Many people have profited. If the students had won, maybe it would not be so good now. The government had to protect Deng Xiaoping's reforms. I do not know how many people were killed but a very small number compared to China's population. There are over 1.3 billion people in China! Many people's lives have been improved by the reforms."

"So you like the Communist Party?"

"Oh no, I do not like it at all but I do support the reforms." Then he added with a defiant look, "At Suzhou University I discuss democracy with my friends."

Michael explained to me that there were local elections for some positions but that only people preapproved by the CPC were allowed to stand. He finished by saying, "So you see, it is not free."

As we were talking, Michael led me through an area of Suzhou I had not visited before. He clearly knew the city well and occasionally enthused about an aspect of its classical culture. We climbed onto an old gate tower, which straddled a main road. Michael bemoaned that traffic circulation was a greater priority than heritage. "Every day the leaders destroy old buildings to make way for new construction," he explained. "People are being forced to move out of their homes by the authorities. It makes me very sad."

"But at least you Han Chinese want modernisation," I pointed out, combatively. "It's much worse for ethnic minorities. Their cultures are being destroyed and they can't do anything about it."

"I am sad that you think that way," said Michael, looking thoughtful. "I have a great respect for their cultures. You must understand that China is a family of fifty six minorities. We are all brothers and all respect each other." His eyes glinted passionately; he clearly felt very strongly about what he what saying. "Yes, we are all one family and can only flourish if we are together."

I accompanied him to Soochow University. In the centre of the campus was a large lawn. The University was originally founded by Methodists in 1900 and a red-brick church drew attention to that heritage. Compared to other Chinese universities it was both old and beautiful.

"Do you discuss politics a lot here at the University?" I asked, picking him up on what he had said earlier.

"Yes we do. All my friends like talking about these things. There are even some professors who we can discuss with. Many of us write on blogs. Sometimes a blog is closed down but there are many more."

"And when you talk, do you and your friends want to change the system here in China?"

"We all think that the most important thing at the moment is continuing the economic growth. China must first become stronger and more stable.

Afterwards we definitely want democracy. Maybe it will take fifty years but I believe we will eventually have rights like you do in your country."

I questioned whether Michael was being naïve in thinking the CPC would just hand over democratic rights in the long run, even if that is what it was promising to do. I suggested that people should demand their rights rather than hope for them.

He turned to me and said, "Maybe you are right but what can we do? Chinese people are not the same as you in the West. We are like the moon: tranquil and reflective. We try to maintain harmony within our minds, with other people and with the universe. Look at the gardens here in Suzhou. The philosophy of the gardens is that a man can retreat to mountains and streams even when he is in the middle of the city. We do not seek conflict. In China we believe the only way to find peace is to withdraw from the world. You Westerners like to control everything around you. If there is something you do not like, you try to change it. You are strong and like action. I think that Western culture is like the sun."

Michael's ambition was to become a film maker. He wanted to make films that would help Westerners understand Chinese culture. He also had a patriotic wish to transform his country through the power of art. Interestingly, he told me that he had always got it into trouble as a schoolboy because he did not conform.

As we shook hands to part, Michael said: "Thank you for speaking with me today. You have helped me clarify many things in my mind. I did not tell you but I was thinking of joining the Communist Party. I thought it would be useful for my career. But after what you have said, I have decided not to join. The most important thing is to be honest with myself."

*

In an attempt to escape the rush of the city, I went to Tongli, a picturesque canal village not far from Suzhou. I had more luck finding a peaceful spot and was able to savour a couple of the smaller houses and gardens. Equilibrium was inherent in their construction. Gold fish and rockeries, bamboos and small waterfalls, pavilions and landscape paintings; I did not understand the mysterious laws that governed the relations between the features but I knew the goal of the architecture was an overall harmony, which the 'real world' fell short of.

Outside the various residences, in the narrow lanes and along the smooth-flowing canals, there were plenty of people milling around. I saw several models in traditional Chinese dresses and heavy make-up being photographed for promotional purposes.

The emptiest place was the Chinese Sex Culture Museum. A startling collection of objects relating to China's erotic history were displayed across three halls and a large courtyard. The museum's founders had the stated purpose of bringing an important part of culture into the open; no mean feat given the Communists' puritanical streak. Judging by the exhibitions, they also seemed to feel that every mountain was a phallic symbol and every cave a metaphor for the female genitals.

I found myself standing next to a young woman before a cabinet of ancient dildos. Obviously I was weighing up their cultural value. We both stared fixedly ahead. This was the sort of place where visitors avoided catching each other's eye.

*

The high speed rail link between Suzhou and Shanghai meant that I lapped up the distance in under an hour. The landscape flying past the window outside was almost exclusively urban; unsurprising given that the Yangtze Delta was one of the world's most heavily populated areas. More interesting was the train itself; a sleek and lightning fast meteor which was at that time the pin-up for China's development. The government frequently claimed they were the world leaders in high speed rail technology. They were laying down more and more tracks by the day, carving into travel times and linking up the nation's biggest cities. It was a hugely ambitious project and many commentators suggested it was happening too fast. The catastrophic rail accident at Wenzhou, which took place shortly after I left the country in the summer of 2011, gave further fuel to these critics.

As the train streaked smoothly onwards, I finished reading the *Tao Te Ch'ing.* This was the most important text in the Taoism, China's largest home-grown religion. Contained in the pages of the *Tao Te Ch'ing* were ideas that occupied the Chinese psyche as instinctively as those of Confucius. The legend of its authorship was almost as fascinating as the content of the book: The sage, Laozi, possessing of wisdom far beyond that of any other man and weary of the wars that consumed China around 500BCE, set off from his home and headed west. On reaching the furthest outpost of the Chinese world, he was stopped by a border guard who requested he communicate his wisdom. In one sitting, Laozi dictated the eighty one verses of the *Tao Te Ch'ing* and the simple soldier wrote it down. Then Laozi continued into the West and was never seen again.

I reflected on what Michael had told me about the Chinese character. Withdrawing from the problems of the world to cultivate one's inner self had a mighty precedent in Laozi. Was I the fool for thinking it was giving up?

*

Shanghai hit me. Hard. Immediately after I arrived I made my way to the Bund, a stretch of colonial-era buildings on the west bank of the Huangpu River. This was majestic for the stately architecture erected on it by the Western Powers but it is completely overshadowed by what now lay across the wide river. In the hazy afternoon light the futuristic spires of the Pudong New Area looked, well, futuristic. I felt like I had walked out of China and stepped onto another planet.

I crossed the Huangpu and walked beneath the skyscrapers. The vast metallic structures only served to emphasise the negative space between them. Empty air took on unimaginable bulk. I felt exhilaratingly small. Rewind ten years and the majority of the colossi had not been there. Rewind twenty and this incomparably lofty patch of real estate had been little more than marshland. If there was a symbol of China's burgeoning ambition, this was it. Concrete, steel, glass but no soul; the downside of such astronomically fast construction was that life had not caught up. I found a few bars scattered on the waterfront but otherwise the whole area lacked vitality. The streets were virtually empty.

I fled the no man's land of the pavements and entered the tallest of the towers. The World Financial Centre resembled an enormous bottle opener and the observation deck at the summit was, according to the blurb, at that time the highest in the world. From the one hundredth floor, perched almost five hundred metres into the sky, I gazed down on Shanghai. Dusk had settled and the lights had come on. Colourful electric blobs, each symbolising the presence of humanity, stretched to the horizon. The view was astounding but I was too far away to see anything clearly. I might as well have been in an aeroplane.

But the race for the stratosphere was not going to stop there. The latest plan, the Shanghai Tower, was already under construction and promised to add a further one hundred and fifty metres of height in the Babel-like ascendancy to heaven. It seemed a little hubristic. Those who rise quickly come down hard.

Back on the ground the next morning, I walked around the city. A hodge-podge of styles were represented. The stylish brick architecture of the French Concession mingled with traces of classical Chinese aesthetics, and also with the grotty legacy of the Communists' low rise building schemes. These greasy blocks were an endangered breed. Shanghai was the most glamorous place in China and wanted to look the part. They were being levelled en-masse and their residents were being forced to move elsewhere. It was a victory for attractiveness but not necessarily for the displaced families.

*

I met a university student in a Shanghai café. The ambience was cool and cosmopolitan. My companion, who called himself David, was also cool and cosmopolitan. His English was more American than the Queen's.

"I want to go into business after graduation," he told me. "My major is in economics. I have three semesters left and then I will try to find work here in Shanghai. I would like to work in a software company like IBM."

After a while I shifted the focus conversation and asked, "What do you think of the political system here?"

"I think it's terrible," he replied. "There are so many problems. I have a professor at my school who encourages us to talk about these things in class. He's a great guy. I really respect him."

I was interested to hear how openly critical he was, and my enthusiasm was perhaps apparent because David stopped me before I could get into my flow and said, "In fact I'm going to join the party. I know they're not good but it's important for my career." He looked almost apologetic as he told me.

I was not going to judge him for his own hard-headed choices. Pragmatism was in the air but at least people were well-educated, I reflected. David was well informed on the ins and outs of alternative political approaches, a product of his exposure to the world in a city that was China's most international.

Shanghai had an illustrious history of being China's gate to the outside world. It had been partly in the possession of the French until after the Second World War. This colonial legacy was still visible in the shape of the proud stone edifices on the Bund. It has also left a more profound mark, for it was in the French Concession that the First National Congress of The Chinese Communist Party took place.

I visited the small, windowless room where thirteen men, including a young Mao Zedong, first gathered in 1921. Although the Western powers were far from sympathetic to communism, it was less risky for the fledgling Party to meet in that French-administrated place than risk the ire of the vengeful warlords who dominated China at the time. From those fugitive beginnings the Party rose to unite China within thirty years, an outcome so unlikely that the feat was for years trumpeted from the rooftops by the CCP's propaganda machine.

However, the exhibitions within the museum were surprisingly muted. I came expecting to read about the CCP's 'glorious' past but everything proved rather low-key. The core ideas of uniting China and improving the livelihoods of the people were emphasised, but most of the ideas that might have distinguished the Communists' ideology from that of any other broadminded ruler's received little press.

Relaxing in Baotou

Christmas Day at O'Sullivans

The awesome spires of Pudong, Shanghai

The Dong Minority village of Ma'an

Miacimu briefly unveils herself

The Yubeng Valley

Puncture on the Sichuan-Tibet Highway

The Tibetan town of Litang

With a Tibetan couple collecting dung as fuel

I hypothesised that revolutionary folklore was being squeezed aside by the new priority of building a 'harmonious society.' The CCP's rise was the ultimate David and Goliath story and an inspiration to any underdog fighting against impossible odds. The leaders perhaps felt it wise not to rub their triumphs in people's faces anymore, lest the increasingly broad-minded population gets any ideas. Judging by my experience, even the CCP's own legendary Long March was no longer being flaunted.

*

Hidden away in a basement in the rear of a residential compound in the west of the French Concession was a gallery. Inside was a large collection of art produced during Mao's rule. Much of the art from that period had been eradicated or hidden. That the gallery in Shanghai was allowed to exist perhaps therefore indicated an increasing open-mindedness on the part of the authorities. Alternatively they might have allowed it on the basis that they could not stifle the content completely and thought better to have it in the open so that they could regulate it. The remote and inconvenient location of the museum suggested the latter. I was the only visitor for the whole hour that I was inside.

The vivid prints exhibited date from the period between the 1949 declaration of the People's Republic of China and the 1976 death of its founding father. Socialist realism was everywhere: huge farmers with un-Chinese features crushed spindly Americans beneath their mighty fists and smiling couples in blue overalls posed in front of belching factories. The biggest and most emotive images on show were the ones produced during the Cultural Revolution. Flocks of tiny figures with Little Red Books worshipped before a haloed Mao, who had become synonymous with the red Chinese sun.

The museum offered no criticism of Mao; the prints were not subversive and were merely a record of a period. Why the authorities might have wanted to prevent people seeing them was an interesting question. Obviously they would have liked the horrors of Mao's rule such as the Cultural Revolution to be forgotten, but it was less clear why they would seek to obscure the better periods.

I got a clue as to a possible reason behind this in a government white paper that I bought. The policies described inside were made to sound as if they had existed continuously from 1949 to the present day. Among other things, the reforms of Deng Xiaoping—twice condemned as a capitalist roader during Mao's rule—were implied to have been just an extension of Mao's original socialist plan. In reality the CCP's rule had been marked by endless changes of direction and internal divisions, but this was not alluded to.

The problem for today's generation of Chinese leaders was clear. Their rhetoric was all about slow but continuous reform and so they could not have people thinking a major policy shift might happen at any moment. If they wanted people to wait long years for the final result, they could not have them imagine that it could all change tomorrow. They needed people to think that China under the Communists had always followed a smooth path and to do that they needed to hide a few facts. And so the details of Mao's rule were not discussed openly. Maybe one day Chinese children would walk into KFC and imagine that was what Mao led the revolution for.

*

In the north of Shanghai lay the Moganshan Art District. A disused factory had been commandeered by the local artistic community and now every workshop was a studio. Most of the artists seemed to be playing on their laptops when I walked around but the fruits of their more constructive labours were on display. Dotted amongst the more harmless selections were paintings of Mao in armbands swimming with babies waving Little

Red Books, and of drooling Red Guards with dummies in their mouths. There was also some erotic art, which if anything revealed more blatant protest than those with political themes: under communism sexual expression had long been censored just like political expression.

I spoke to an artist with the unusual name of Mutt. He was wearing jeans, a hoody and slippers, and had unshaved stubble around his jaws. I commented on the open subversion in some of the art I had seen. I said that, in Shanghai, the CPC's attempt to open up society for economic reasons while trying to carefully control its monopoly on political power had the potential to spiral out of control.

Mutt, while seemingly energised by what I said, remarked, "No, there is nothing we can do to remove the Communist Party. They are too strong. I know people who have tried over many years to change the situation. It is impossible."

I tried not to be disheartened and spoke passionately about how, with conviction, anything could be achieved. I cited the meteoric rise of the CPC itself as proof that change could succeed against seemingly impossible odds.

Mutt's eyes sparkled as I spoke but when he opened his mouth his mocking words deflated my bubble: "You, me, now!"

Then he went on more kindly, "Maybe if young people felt like you then things could change but all that Chinese people your age are interested in is money. When they are older and have more life experience, then they start to think about political things. By then it is too late for them to be able to make a difference because they have families and jobs to worry about."

*

After a few days I decided to leave Shanghai. From my backpacking point of view it was too big and too commercial. In one nightclub I visited, all the girls gravitated towards suited men with bottomless wallets. I was not a suited man with a bottomless wallet and so I did not have much fun.

Worst was the East Nanjing Road, the shopping street in the very centre of the city. Every time I walked down it I was bothered by touts. A man would draw up and shiftily mutter: "Watch? DVD? Lady bar? Massage? Hash? Marihuana?" With each word the volume would drop slightly so that by the time the man was finished, I could barely make out what he was saying.

Then another man would draw up and offer identical 'goods.' It appeared that every scrawny man on the street had not only a harem but also a drugs den just a phone call away. Probably they were all working for the same organisation.

Out of curiosity I started negotiating prices for 'massage.' After getting a sense of the price from one man I would say, "Sorry, it's too expensive," and then wait for the next person to come and bother me. A consensus emerged. A genuine massage would cost 100RMB whereas extras would push up the price to between 300RMB and 500RMB. I did not try negotiating prices for the drugs. Seeing as I had no intention of buying any, I thought I might seriously piss the dealers off. After all, selling drugs in China was a risky business, with execution a potential penalty for the most serious cases.

I was also frequently pestered by 'tea girls.' I told one group that I knew their game so they could leave me alone. The three of them grinned conspiratorially and then, like harpies onto sailors, descended on two middle aged white men who had just walked past.

In a bid for solitude I boarded a passenger boat and sailed out of the mouth of the Yangtze on a late February evening. The ferry passed huge container ships and silent shipyards in the darkness. By the time we met the rolling waves of the open sea, the mighty river was several miles wide. Then I descended into the belly of the ship, to the bottom deck where over fifty bunks were spaced around and where ladies with harsh voices passed the time playing cards. I slept poorly in my cramped berth and was drowsy when I disembarked early the next morning at Putuoshan.

This holy island in the East China Sea was the earthly residence of Guanyin, Bodhisattva of Mercy and China's most popular deity. I went in the hope of finding a contemplative spot. Instead I found tourists. Scattered across the island were several notable temples. Whenever I entered one, cameras would turn my way and the shutters would start clicking. Teenage girls frequently came over and asked to have their picture taken with me, and I smiled sheepishly while they struck poses. Eventually, and most uncharitably in that Buddhist place, I started refusing the requests. I chastised myself for visiting on a Saturday. So much for peace of mind.

I climbed up a forested hillside in an attempt to be alone but, just as I thought I had left the crowds behind, I was chased by a vicious looking dog. I had ventured too close to the military control tower that stood at the isle's uppermost point and a malevolent-looking soldier appeared to shoo me away.

My mood darkened and the world started to reflect my grumpiness back at me. The ubiquitous goldfish in the lily-filled ponds looked bored and lifeless; the weather turned grey and cold; the tourist buses whizzing around were all trying to run me over, and the food seemed ridiculously overpriced even by touristic standards.

Only when the light started to fail did things improve. The tourists disappeared back to their hotels for dinner and I went to the west of the island. I stretched out on a rock and watched a magnificent sunset settle over the archipelago. Even the military vessels in the sheltered coves below me took on a peaceful aspect.

I saw two toads copulating—a reminder that early spring was approaching—and reflected that nature was losing out in a big way to China's urbanisation. From Nanjing all the way to Shanghai I had barely seen a break in the built-up landscape. The weight of humanity had left little room for anything else.

*

With hindsight it was unsurprising that Putuoshan was so full of tourists because it lay within striking distance of one of the world's most densely populated urban areas. Quite how easily accessible it was from the mainland I discovered the next morning. An hour was all it took to be back in China proper. From where I disembarked from a passenger ferry on the nearby island of Zhoushan, it was possible to catch a bus to the coastal city of Ningbo via a succession of colossal bridges. Just like the high speed rail link, which then propelled me from Ningbo to Hangzhou, that bridge network was one of the pin-up infrastructure developments that were fuelling the economy and binding that part of China together.

Like Suzhou, Hangzhou had a special place in the cultural heart of all Chinese people. The main attraction was West Lake. Scattered around it were temples and gardens of such beauty that they had for centuries been held up as models of classical Chinese aesthetics, and a selection of Chinese history's greatest painters and poets had given West Lake mythical status. The body of water itself had been continuously dredged for over a thousand years in order keep it as West Lake and stop it reverting to nature as West Marsh. Artificial preservation was inherent in the identity of the place.

I was not surprised, therefore, when artificial preservation, or complete restoration, was what I saw. As I learnt, much of West Lake's original architecture had been destroyed when the city was sacked during a revolt in the nineteenth century. Nonetheless I could not deny the beauty: the works of man and nature stood in exquisite balance. Unfortunately I was unable to appreciate anything beyond its visual appearance. To the Chinese tourists jabbering excitedly around me, *this* was the room where the great poet, so and so, had worked and *that* was where the mythological white snake, whatshername, transformed into a beautiful girl. But I just did not possess any of the knowledge to bring this icon of classical culture to life. Beyond wandering around it a couple of times, the huge significance of the lake was lost on me.

I understood better what was going on in the city east of the lake, though it seemed particularly ugly by comparison to its illustrious watery neighbour. Hangzhou was booming and, as with elsewhere in the country, that meant concrete high rises, multi-lane roads and grey overpasses. This might have been hailed as economic success but it was bloody ugly.

*

I stayed in a hostel near the lake and was approached one evening by a member of staff who offered me a beer. "How long have you been working here?" I asked him.

"Just a few months. It's only an evening job. During the day I'm a law student."

"I didn't think there was any law in China," I said jokingly.

He laughed and said: "Yes you're partly right. There are written laws but the legal system's completely corrupt. For example judges and barristers are often good friends. If you want to win a case you have to pay a lot of money to hire the right barrister. Then you're guaranteed to get the outcome you want."

"If it's so bad then why are you studying it?"

"A few reasons. If I or my family ever gets into trouble, the only way to be sure of getting good representation in court is to represent myself."

I had heard this argument before and it worried me how little confidence people expressed in the legal system. I asked him whether, as a budding lawyer, it was helpful to be a Party member and whether he himself was.

"No I'm not in the party at the moment," he replied. "I probably will try to join but I doubt they'll let me in. You have to get good exam results and then you have to do nothing controversial for two years whilst they consider your suitability. Not everybody can make it."

We started talking about my travels and then another man came over. He was a fellow guest in the hostel. "I do a lot of travelling," he said, joining in with the conversation. "I'm from the North East of China, from Jilin province. Do you know it? We people from the North East tend to travel widely. I've done business all over China."

"Have you ever been abroad?"

"No, but I want to. My dream is to go to Africa. There are lots of business opportunities there."

"Really?"

"Don't you watch the news? You know all the instability at the moment in North Africa, in Egypt, Libya, those places? Well the government's bringing a lot of Chinese workers back home. They were all doing construction work over there."

Because I was about to leave Hangzhou and put the Golden Triangle behind me, I tried to understand how it fitted into the scheme of the 'social harmony' that I was searching for. During my time there I had heard many complaints about the political system but on a personal level most people had seemed content with how their own lives were going. Some individuals had worried about what rights they lacked compared to the West but, in comparison to what they had experienced before, each knew that their current lot was a great improvement. While China was getting richer these people were going to shelve their scruples. But if there was an economic turn for the worse then I sensed a lot of problems lying in wait.

CHAPTER 8

Back to the Sun

Huangshan, the Yellow Mountain, lay in the south of Anhui province. Wealth from the East Coast was struggling to make its way inland. I had already observed this during Spring Festival, and judging by what I saw on the drive there, the problem applied to Anhui too. I spotted large numbers of men and women working in the paddy fields. There were considerably more oxen than tractors.

I just received a snapshot impression of Anhui, however, because I only went to climb the Yellow Mountain, and it had a micro-economy all of its own. When I got off the bus in Tangkou, the town at the base of the mountain, I was immediately accosted by Mr Hu. He offered me accommodation, food, a guide and a lot of other things that I did not need. I evaded his advances and went into town to buy some food. Virtually every building seemed to be a hotel, a restaurant or a shop. The streets and the facades of the houses were clean. The town was clearly flourishing entirely on the back of tourism but then again, as I was about to experience first-hand, the Yellow Mountain had an incomparable fascination.

My wallet feeling considerably lighter for the crippling entrance fee, I climbed the mountain in the afternoon mist. Tour groups came to the mountain in hordes but—mother of all blessings!—there was a cable car. Because all the Chinese visitors were taking the lazy option, I was literally the only climber on the path. In the gloom the vertical rock formations around me took on an unearthly quality. I followed the path up some precipitous columns and found myself perched in the clouds; bottomless drops just a step away.

I slept a night at the summit in a hotel, and awoke the next morning to a spectacular panorama. The morning sunlight illuminated the innumerable yellow crags, which rose like islands from the clouds tumbling far below. The ethereal beauty was stunning. I could well appreciate the mystique that has inspired artists over the ages.

On the descent the path was again virtually deserted. I passed an occasional porter with supplies balanced at both ends of a pole on his back, and a solitary monkey disappeared into the undergrowth as I approached.

*

By the beginning of March, I was utterly fed up with the cold. I had barely taken my jumper off in five months and had spent most of that time in tight thermal vest and itchy long-johns. I wanted to get as far south as possible as quickly as possible.

I sat on the train to Xiamen for twenty four hours and met Swallow, an art student from Anhui province. She was travelling alone with just a backpack and guitar; not a usual thing for a twenty one year old girl to do in China. But as she explained to me, she was used to being independent. Because of an exemption to the One Child Policy granted to countryside communities from the very beginning, farming households were allowed two children. Swallow and her younger sister, however, were the third and fourth children in the family. They were packed off from birth to live with distant relatives so her parents would escape a crippling fine. It was a sad situation but it did not seem to have adversely affected Swallow in the long run.

She was very animated and spent much of the time chatting with a mother returning to her Xiamen home. It seemed to me that these two women were just as interested in each other as I was in them. China was a big place and major cultural differences exist between people in different areas, even among the ethnically Han.

Featuring prominently in their conversations was the exorbitant cost of property on China's East Coast. Apparently the average cost of renting a small flat in Xiamen then stood at 3000RMB per month, which was well out of an average young person's price range. They said city house prices were going up so rapidly that many young people had to save for years before being able to buy a mid-range flat. During the intervening period the majority lived with parents. Swallow summed it all up by saying, "China is rich but the Chinese people are poor."

When I got off the train in Xiamen, a warm breeze stroked my face and I removed my jumper, which I had pessimistically kept on. Then Swallow and I set off to find a youth hostel.

Because of the unfamiliar heat, I quickly became sweaty and suggested we stop for a rest. We put down our luggage and sat on a stone wall. "You know what annoys me the most?" She said, her attention attracted by the police station across the road from where we are sitting, "Corruption."

"Yes, it's everywhere," I remarked, knowingly.

"Yes, but it's not the corruption that bothers me so much. I mean, it bothers me too, but what really bothers me is how the government pretends they don't know about it. Did you hear about the Li Gang incident?"

I confirmed that I had. In the aftermath of that outrageous illustration of official corruption it had become a popular joke to answer every criticism with the phrase, 'my father's Li Gang.'

"You know the government tried to hush it all up until they realised they couldn't keep it a secret any longer?" Swallow said. "Then they made a huge scene about it, saying they would punish the son severely and so on. I mean, every time corruption gets discovered by the public—it usually happens online—the government says that they are trying hard to stamp it out and make a big show of punishing the bad guy, but really they knew about it all along."

"So you think corruption happens because of the system, not in spite of it?" I suggested, leadingly.

"Yes that's exactly what I think. The officials are all in it together. It makes me sick. Anyway, I don't get involved with that stuff. I just want to have a fun life and get rich."

An old man hobbled over to where we were sitting. His clothes were ragged and he had no teeth. I thought he was a beggar and shook my head. He did not go away but rather scribbled something down in a notebook with a blunt pencil he was holding. He showed it to Swallow.

She turned to me in surprise and said excitedly: "He's from my home province." She spoke to the old man but he appeared to be deaf so she took the notebook and scribbled something down in return.

The old man smiled warmly, his eyes twinkling, and wrote another sentence. Swallow smiled too. They made mute conversation for about fifteen minutes. I did not know what was being communicated because I could not read the characters but I watched on in fascination.

Eventually Swallow turned to me and said, "He likes collecting foreign currencies, just like me! Do you have any on you?"

I pulled out a one dollar bill from my money belt and handed it over. Swallow also gave some coins she had in her pack; a few Hong Kong dollars and Japanese Yen. We moved off cheerfully.

*

Xiamen was quite small and had a very different atmosphere from the bigger cities I had left behind. It sat in a green and hilly location on the edge of a bay opening into the East China Sea. There was still bustle and the suburbs were seeing construction, but there was none of the frenetic pace that defined Shanghai and its surrounds.

Xiamen's nineteenth century history as a British-administrated port rankled with Chinese national pride but the British architectural influence had undoubtedly contributed to the city's pleasant ambience. The island of Gulangyu, which squatted in the bay, typified this. It was a charming amalgamation of beaches, jungle and colonial villas. Clearly the Chinese liked it too because it was overrun with tourists.

I would have found it hard to guess from the vibe but Xiamen was situated at the closest point to a very tense frontier. From a beach near the spacious campus of Xiamen University, Jinmen Island, which belonged to Taiwan, was clearly visible. The CPC believed Taiwan was an inalienable part of Chinese territory but the Taiwanese claimed they were an independent nation. The relationship between the Beijing government and its Taipei equivalent was thawing but only at a glacially-slow pace. Many mainland Chinese were still confidently predicting that Taiwan would 'return to the fold' in the near future.

As I sat one evening facing Jinmen and watching the waves splashing on the sand, consecutive explosions resounded across the water. It sounded like the rapport of two enormous balloons being popped. I looked along the beach but nobody else seemed particularly startled by the noise. Ten minutes later another double boom echoed from the island across the sea. I suspected I was listening to the music of American military might. It was they who provided the muscle that gave the Taiwanese their mojo.

On Saturday night, a couple of days after arriving in Xiamen, I went to a bar with a mix of locals and foreigners. We all sat outside drinking beers and cocktails. It might not have been the most important economic centre on the East Coast but Xiamen was more expensive than I had planned for. The bar had a Cuban theme and my wallet was fast draining to the sound of salsa.

A Taiwanese man was one of the people at the table. "Why don't you go and argue with the Taiwanese guy?" I asked Qing, a sexy girl sitting next to me. I was a little drunk.

"Why would I do that?"

"Because you Chinese don't like Taiwanese."

She looked at me coldly. "You're right, they do annoy me."

"Why?"

"Mainly because they say 'I'm Taiwanese' as if they're better than us but then make all their money out of China. Most of their stars do that. The actors come here to make their movies; the singers sell their records here . . . But then the same actors and singers criticise us."

"They criticise the government, not you Chinese people."

"You're wrong. They just say 'China' like we're all bad."

"Maybe they've got a point," I said sharply. Qing had been giving me the cold shoulder all evening and I was feeling combative.

"What?"

"Well if you don't try to change your government then you deserve what you get."

Qing looked hurt and snapped back. "You're speaking rubbish. How can we change the government?"

"You're all just useless. You just sit there saying, 'there's no way to change,' but you don't even try."

"What do you think we should do then?"

"I don't know," I mumbled, scrapping around for a clear thought, "You could try criticising the government publically for a start."

"Do you know who Zhao Ziyang is?" She asked abruptly.

Zhao Ziyang was the General Secretary of the CCP when the Tian'anmen Square massacre took place. He sided with the reformist cause of the students against other powerful figures within the party. After the massacre, Zhao Ziyang was removed completely from public life.

"Yes, I know who he is."

"Well his son is a friend of the family . . ."

"What? You know Zhao Ziyang's son?" I asked, sitting up.

"Yes I do. Do you know what happened to Zhao Ziyang?"

"No. What happened?"

"He died in 2005 in Beijing. He was under house arrest."

"Yes well I assumed that sort . . ."

"He was the leader of the whole country and look what happened! That's why we can't change anything! Get it!"

I stayed quiet. I knew I had been a fool.

*

Despite my drunken behaviour I managed to patch things up with Qing and took her out the next day for lunch. I quickly discovered that she had expensive western tastes. She insisted on drinking a smoothie, eating pizza and washing it all down with fresh French yoghurt.Qing was in fact from Shanghai but was working for the American computer firm Dell in its Xiamen office. She moaned about how Xiamen was boring compared to her home city and about how the people were considerably more small-minded. I thought that she was exaggerating slightly; probably she just felt home-sick. She also complained about the cost of living in the city. By the standard of most Chinese people aged 25, her 7000RMB per month was quite good but she spent almost half of it on renting a flat.

After lunch I accompanied Qing to a hospital because she wanted to pick up some medicine. I had not been into a Chinese hospital before and was keen to take a look. First we went to a lobby on the ground floor where long lines of men and women were waiting in front of counters. We joined a queue and fifteen minutes later reached the front. Qing handed over her medical card, paid some money and received three forms.

"Are we done?"

"No, we've just started," she replied ominously.

We went over to a table and filled in the forms, pushed back in at the front of the queue and had them quickly stamped. Then we climbed up a flight of stairs to the second floor. A smell of detergent pervaded throughout. We walked into a waiting area where a large number of people were standing around. Qing ignored the crowd and made for one of the examination rooms behind. They had fancy names like 'laser treatment' and 'magnetic scanner.' Qing opened the various doors until she found a room with doctors inside. One took off his white plastic gloves and completed a section of her form as if he was well used to that style of interruption. Qing took the form and made for the third floor. She collected a number from a dispenser on the wall and then went back to the second floor. She queued in a line behind a counter and once more handed over her medical card and forms. They were stapled together and stamped once more. Then she climbed back up to the third floor and at last saw a doctor.

I stood in the waiting area while she had the appointment and watched the other patients. It was stuffy inside and so everybody was sweating. One man rasped up phlegm from his throat every ten seconds and deposited globules of yellow mucus into a waste paper basket. None of the nurses standing around seemed to be doing anything other than supervising.

"Done?" I asked when Qing re-emerged.

"Almost."

Qing went to another counter on the same floor, handed over a new piece of paper she was holding and had it checked. Then she paid for the medicine and received a receipt. She returned to the doctor she had just seen and collected the medicine. We went back down to the second floor. Qing barged in on a room where a doctor was seeing another patient. The doctor stopped what she was doing, told her patient to wait and quickly scribbled something on another form. We returned to the ground floor, made our way to a final counter and Qing handed over all the paperwork.

After an hour we finally got back out into the open air. For her troubles Qing had a pack of twenty four pills.

"Why did it take so long?"

"It is always like that."

"But why don't you just go to a pharmacy?"

"It is because of my health insurance. This is the only way I can claim the cost of the medicine back."

*

The local bus to Liulian, although just a few hours away from wealthy Xiamen, felt anything but wealthy. Men and women in well-worn clothes scrambled on and off in the middle of nowhere; the man next to me lit a cigarette and periodically spat onto the bus floor; the ruddy-faced female bus conductor barked out greetings to people in the street and twice climbed down to hand parcels of newspapers to shop owners. The bus was much more than a transport service; it was the area's only link to the outside world.

That was changing, however. A huge amount of road and bridge building was going on. I saw teams of workmen and heavy machinery everywhere I looked. The terrain made construction difficult because hills with wooded slopes rose up on all sides. The forests were being cleared and the exposed clay hillsides were being steadily covered in asphalt. Large billboards stood erect by the sides of the road. Many of them showed Hu Jintao clad in a dark overcoat and shaking hands with a well-wrapped-up local baby. Others showed three Chinese servicemen saluting beside a tulou—an earth roundhouse peculiar to the area—with a Chinese flag fluttering artificially behind.

It was the tulou that I had come to see. I hired a driver to take me around the surrounding area for an afternoon. She was of the Hakka people; a sub-group of the Han whose origins were obscure but who had occupied the region for centuries. She therefore spoke a dialect I could not understand. Different dialects were spoken in every part of China and some of them bore almost no link to Mandarin at all. However, because the Communists had standardised Mandarin as the national language—the word for Mandarin in Chinese, 'putonghua,' meant 'common speech'—I was able to communicate somewhat fluently wherever I went.

My driver managed to answer some of my questions in heavily-accented Mandarin. When I enquired about the road building I only understood a small part of her response: "Hu Jintao came here in 2009. He said the roads were bad." That was it. The leader of the nation made a comment and now this astonishing development. No delay; just action. I was unable to learn what she felt about changes because of the language barrier. I guessed, particularly given that less than two years had passed since President Hu's inspection, that few local people had had a say in the matter

The tulou themselves were very numerous. Over thirty thousand were scattered across that part of south-east China. Made from compacted earth and stone, with wooden beams providing structural support, they were astonishing feats of architecture and engineering. Inside, a central courtyard was usually ringed by rooms cut into the earthen walls. The ground floor provided space for cooking and keeping livestock; the second floor was for eating and the third was for sleeping. Some tulou were so large that they could house entire communities.

I was driven to a few especially photogenic specimens. Old ladies stood about and tried to sell me local tea leaves, and young children peered at me curiously. Men were notable by their absence and there were not many young women either. I guessed, foolishly, that they were working in the fields. A woman I spoke to in the evening told me otherwise: "The men have gone," she explained. "Many of the women, too. There is no work for them here. Most have gone to the towns to earn money. My husband is working elsewhere. Most of the tulou now stand empty."

I spent the night in one of the earth houses. It was very cozy and I was woken in the morning by a cock crowing. But other than me there was only one creaky old man in the fortress and the central courtyard was full of litter.

*

Revamping my wardrobe was my first priority when I reached Guangzhou, better known in the West as Canton. The weather there was rainy but there was no need for the thermal clothing still weighing down my backpack. Out went the vests, jumpers and some old jeans. Then I went to buy a couple of shirts. There was no shortage of options but, unbelievably, the markets in the very centre of the city only sold wholesale. I ran into intransigent shop keepers who refused to sell just one item at a time. I had no need for twenty identical shirts. In fact I did not even want two identical shirts.

The Guangzhou locals spoke Cantonese and had notorious problems with Mandarin pronunciation. My speaking bordered on toneless too. The effect as I negotiated was of an international trade fair with Mandarin as the common language. It was a fascinating glimpse of a possible world future, but at the time I had bigger concerns than to reflect on such abstract matters.

I looked in another market but found the same wholesale problem. Huge numbers of people were selling clothes but the only people buying were doing so in bulk so that they could resell at a profit. A shopkeeper agreed to sell me one shirt but only if I paid for the price of three. I told him that if I paid for the price of three shirts I would expect to receive three shirts. He looked at me like I was from Mars and said that he would happily give me three shirts for the price of three shirts but that I was causing the problem by only asking for one. I saw that I had been outfoxed and moved on. Eventually I did manage to buy one shirt, but only after I had tried the patience of a female shopkeeper so severely that she gave me the item just to get rid of me.

All around Guangzhou large markets were prominent. There were markets for stationary, markets for books, markets for drills and DIY equipment . . . The hordes of people I saw selling identical things reminded me of the under-employment in Baotou, but the difference was that here there were large numbers of people buying too. Guangzhou was one of China's most important ports and was a key centre of trade.

Aside from all the bulk retail items available in Guangzhou, the city was notable for its food. As I was walking around, many halls drew me in with their powerful stenches and I found such assorted delicacies as scorpions, live snakes, bull frogs and eels squirming in plastic containers. Snack food outlets were everywhere. Steamed buns, sweet cakes, seafood and sticky rice stuffed with pork were served up alongside noodles, various mushrooms, dried fish . . . The aroma of the world-famous Cantonese food filled my nostrils.

On the roads, which were heavily congested because of the bad weather, drivers weaved in and out of lanes looking for openings. On the pavements, pedestrians barged past each other with their eyes fixed firmly ahead, only stopping at pelican crossings where men with red flags and whistles blocked their path. These men seemed to have a pointless job. Their only purpose was to wait for the green man and then allow people to cross the road. Surely people could understand the meaning of the green man themselves? But were it not for the presence of these workers, I guessed that the relentless locals would never bother to stop, even for the cars.

As I was relieving myself in a public toilet, the man on my left leaned in to size mine up. Following suit, the man on my right also leaned in. To my chagrin, their faces did not light up in astonishment and awe. Even so, the incident said a lot about Guangzhou. Anything went; the only thing was how well one's own 'goods' compared to one's neighbour's.

Relaxing at my hostel that evening, I met a Malaysian man who had come to pick up computer hardware to export to America. Shortly afterwards I spoke to a German man, stereotypically named Herr Boesselmann, who told me he came regularly to Guangzhou in order to buy huge batches of trainers, which he then shipped back to Europe and sold at ten times the price. The costs of shipping and trade tariffs were minimal, he informed me, before offering me a job. I turned him down but reflected that there was still big money to be made in that line of business. The Pearl River Delta, in which Guangzhou was the largest city, was the home of 'made in China.' And it was no longer just cheap plastic goods that were produced there.

*

I met Joey, a local girl, in a restaurant one afternoon. She claimed to be thirty four years old but she looked much younger; though admittedly I was never a good judge of Chinese ages. Reflecting Guangzhou's internationalism, Joey spoke excellent English. She also had a confidence when discussing political issues that I had rarely witnessed among Chinese people. Despite her age, she still lived with her parents because buying her own place was too expensive. And anyway, she explained, she liked her mum's cooking.

We spoke about the differences between England and China, especially about the different attitudes of the respective governments. The question of democracy quickly came up."

We couldn't have a democracy in China," explained Joey. "The people are too uneducated. If there was democracy then crazy people would be given power. First people need to be educated about what is right and wrong,"

"But if you wait until a government says that ordinary people are 'educated enough' to make their own political decisions, you might be waiting for a very long time!" I replied. "Ok, I grant that people often don't vote wisely even in developed countries, and yes there'd probably be lots of mistakes made in the immediate aftermath of China becoming a democratic country, but in the long run people would get the hang of it. Also, to vote well I don't think that people need to be more 'educated' in a schooling sense. If you allow an existing government to decide if and when it gives democratic rights to its people, you're handing it a free pass for dictatorship."

Joey listened closely to what I said but stuck to her point. "What you say is fine in theory but think about how big China is. I don't want uneducated people thousands of miles away choosing my rulers. At least I know what I'm getting with the situation we have now. The current leaders know how to rule. If we had a democracy all sorts of people with no understanding of government might be elected. I don't want to risk that"

I tried arguing that in a society where all people and political ideas were allowed to compete freely, the best rose to the top, and that even if bad rulers came to power, the whole point of democratic elections was that they could be voted out after a term in office. I stated my opinion that the worst case scenario in any country was not being able to get rid of one's rulers, regardless of whether they were benevolent or not. Joey did not see it that way at all; in fact benevolent dictatorship struck her as quite a positive thing.

*

Guangzhou had a long history of being an east-Asian commercial centre. In 1840 the British sent military vessels up the Pearl River and, in the aftermath, forcibly opened the port to trade. European architecture was still dotted around the city. Especially notable was the French-designed Sacred Heart Cathedral, whose twin spires rose above the centre. Recently, however, the Chinese had sought to outshine the colonial heritage with their own buildings and had achieved this in some style. The elegant Canton Tower, which was completed in 2005, stretched an astonishing 600m into the sky.

I took a ferry down the Pearl River to the customs house from which the British had governed the port. I saw Chinese naval vessels moored to the riverbanks and large freight ships were making their way slowly towards the ocean. The customs house occupied a discreet yellow building. It had once been a link in the mighty network that incorporated the British Empire. The museum on the site had an exhibition on the British administration of the harbour but it was primarily concerned with the custom house's later and more celebrated purpose. In 1924 Dr Sun Yatsen, the Nationalist leader, opened the Whampoa Military Academy on the site. There the officers and soldiers were trained who would later fight to defeat the war lords of the time and reunify China. Some of the money used to fund the academy came from supportive foreigners and Chinese ex-pats who had made their fortunes abroad. More importantly, much of the project was paid for by the Russians, whose support for the reunification of China at that time fitted into their larger strategy of communist takeover. In the long run their patronage did help to propel the CPC to power, but in the aftermath of victory Mao destroyed China's relationship with the Soviet Union.

Guangzhou's remoteness from the power centres to the north and its international influences had at that time made it a launching pad for political change, but that sort of change was not on the agenda now. The shift was visible in the city's stylishly designed sky-scrapers and its flashy sports cars. Guangzhou was China's third largest city; an economic hot-shot; a place where fortunes were made. The people I spoke to had never had it so good. It might have drizzled steadily for the entire time I visited but there was no escaping that optimism was in the air.

*

On the Chinese side of the Hong Kong border glowed Shenzhen, the richest city in China. This former fishing village saw its spell in the limelight begin in 1979, when Deng Xiaoping, the leader who came to the fore after the death of Mao, was looking around for places to experiment with market reforms. Five enclaves along the Guangdong coastline, far away from China's traditional centres of power, were chosen so that the possible failure of the reforms would not be politically catastrophic. As it turned out the reforms were an astonishing success and Shenzhen's position cuddling up close to Hong Kong meant that its star shone the brightest. Men and women frustrated with the restrictions of communism flocked there and foreign investors leapt at the opportunity to access the previously-closed Chinese economy.

The figures were grotesque: the population had risen from barely thirty thousand to over ten million and there were now almost thirty buildings over two hundred metres high; an enormous amount given that the highest building in the city in 1979 had been just five stories high.

Although Shenzhen still belied statistics, in my experience its iconic status appeared to have faded in the eyes of the Chinese people. The traditional power brokers of the Chinese world, the Beijings and the Shanghais, had caught up and reasserted their cultural dominance. I made the decision not to stop off.

Looking out of the bus' window as it streaked past the endless concrete high rises of Shenzhen's suburbs, I reflected that I had made the correct call. In Guangzhou I had met a group of British architects based in Shenzhen who had talked of its soulless-ness and wealth inequalities. They described how millionaires employed underpaid factory hands while leaving their kids in the care of underpaid domestic servants. To my mind there was something sinister about a city that only existed for money. Capitalism gone mad was not a pleasant outcome, even if it happened in a communist country.

*

The first thing I noticed on arriving in Hong Kong was that a bag of crisps cost three times more than on the mainland. I soon realised that almost everything was different. In 1997 the British returned the territory to the Chinese but by the terms of the handover agreement, the CPC have to leave the British-inherited political and economic systems in place for at least fifty years. More quirky relics lived on too, including driving on the left-hand side of the road.

Because I was still feeling a hangover from the long winter, I stayed in Hong Kong for several days. As I was travelling for an extended period of time I occasionally found it difficult to keep taking stuff in. When I reached Hong Kong I was feeling saturated. Therefore, I relaxed, drank, soaked up the March sun and explored the natural beauty of the bay. It was just the break I needed to recharge.

In the very centre of the territory, in the built-up centres on Hong Kong Island and Kowloon, it was just as likely to see a foreigner as a Chinese person in the street. The whole world milled about and the number of nationalities on show gave the simple experience of walking down the road an incomparable vibrancy. Sight and smell received a thorough bombardment from the diversely-themed restaurants.

The large British ex-pat population behaved like they still owned the place, and many employed domestic servants to see to their house-keeping. Quite how many servants there were becomes very apparent every Sunday, when they all got a day off. I saw hordes of Filipinos and Malaysians picnicking and playing cards on carpets stretched out across the pavements by the waterfront.

Despite the international feel and a system that meant even visas treated Hong Kong as a separate country—going back into mainland saw me get an entry stamp in my passport—the territory was now unequivocally part of China. How 'social harmony' might be brought to bear on Hong Kong, however, was difficult to see.

On the one hand the freedom of the press meant many of the outrages that were stifled in China proper received prominent coverage. For example, down by the Kowloon pier of the famous Star Ferry I saw several posters criticising the actions of the Beijing government over their violent suppression Falun Gong, a quasi-religious group with a huge following. Press freedoms such as this made it hard to imagine that the people of Hong Kong would ever swallow the Communists' governance as unquestioningly as the mainlanders.

But on the other hand, as one of the terms of the handover agreement, the CPC had negotiated that Hong Kong's schools should align to the mainland model. Of the elder Han people who served me in restaurants, the order of languages spoken often ran Cantonese, English and then Mandarin. Younger people, however, spoke good Mandarin; a key feature of the CPC's efforts to harmonise the country.

I received ambivalent impressions of how Hong Kong Chinese perceived their identity. One evening I met a group of Han students who turned up their noses at the very mention of China. They sneered at the nominal authority of Beijing, laughed at the CCP and talked about 'the mainland Chinese' as if they were separate and marginally inferior. Many seemed to think of themselves as half European and gave anecdotes about their most recent trips to London.

But by chance I got an alternative view while having a beer with a girl from Taiwan called Hiko. "I bet everybody asks you this but do you feel Chinese or Taiwanese?" I asked as a conversation starter.

"Taiwanese, of course," she replied with a strong American accent.

"But where were your grandparents from?"

"I don't know."

"Haven't you ever asked them?"

"No. I'm not interested in knowing."

"Fair enough. What are you doing here?"

"Just passing through. I'm going home soon but I've just been travelling in mainland China. I didn't enjoy it much. It's just not as good as Taiwan. It's poorer, uglier and the people aren't as friendly."

"Most of the people I've met have been pretty friendly."

Hiko's retort was bitter: "Yeah, but you're not Taiwanese. Everyone who hears I'm Taiwanese says: 'Hey, welcome back to the homeland. When are you going to re-join us? We're all brothers,' and all that shit! I just want to say 'No I'm not! I'm not Chinese, I'm Taiwanese and I'll never be part of your country!"

"But you don't say it?"

"No, because I don't want to start an argument. But it's a pain in the arse."

True to form, in a moment so well-timed it could almost have been scripted, a middle-aged local who had heard us talking waded into the conversation.

"You're wrong," she said to Hiko, "We are all the Chinese people. We are all one family."

Hiko came back loudly, clearly deciding to lay her former un-argumentative policy aside: "No we're not one family. How can you tell me we're one family?"

"But we have always been one homeland! Look at yourself. You are Han Chinese!"

"I am Taiwanese!"

"Your blood is Chinese. I am from Hong Kong but I do not say that I am not Chinese. How can you not see that we are all the Chinese people?"

"I am not Chinese!"

"But we are all brothers!"

"No I am not your brother!"

"Your history is Chinese!"

"I don't care about history! I care about the future!"

"Taiwan has always been part of China!"

"Well, not anymore! Taiwan is an independent country!"

"You cannot deny your history! Our culture is the same!"

"Our culture is not the same now!"

"We are all one family!"

Remarkably, they held this entire shouting match in English. It was fascinating to witness the differences in opinion of the two, both of whom were ethnically Han but neither of whom had ever lived in mainland China. The argument only ended when the lady from Hong Kong stood up and stormed away. By that point, both looked close to tears.

*

Before crossing back over the border, I decided to take in Macau. This formerly Portuguese territory followed a similar trajectory to its big brother, Hong Kong, and was returned to China in 1999. I spent an afternoon exploring its Portuguese heritage, though ultimately that was not what I had come for.

Macau was synonymous with gambling. In fact Macau's casinos had a gross income surpassing that of Las Vegas'. Many of the names dotted around were identical to those in America's Sin City. Venetian, Quinn and MGM had all set up shop in this historic trade port and fishing centre. Inside these 'hotels', time and space were so twisted that it was possible to eat a lunch of spaghetti in 'Venice,' while outside in Macau the darkness of night prevailed.

I found my way to the Hotel Lisboa, the first casino ever established in the territory. It hailed from a time before the glitz of the Vegas brands swept in and inside I still found a hint of that old grunginess. On the casino floor the mood was serious. There was no laughing, no smiles and no glamour. The dealers looked tired; the players, dressed plainly, looked focused. I joined a blackjack table. I was playing minimum stakes but around me the Chinese men and women were dropping big money. If they won they looked grim, if they lost they looked grim and if I caught their eyes they looked at me grimly. Despite blackjack being a game of everyone against the dealer, no camaraderie existed on the tables; no friendly remarks of 'good hand' or 'bad luck'. Etiquette was largely forgotten and everyone played as if they were alone in a darkened room. To one side of the casino floor, courtesy drinks were served. Coffee or coke in a polystyrene cup was the choice. No exotic cocktails were served; in fact there was no alcohol at all.

I took a walk into the bowels of the hotel. The marble floor felt cold and hard, and the corridors were poorly lit. There was none of the plush carpeted comfort I had seen in the other casinos. Sitting around in a canteen I found the hotel's whores. They wore blank expressions on their faces. Most were dressed in mini-skirts and caked in make-up. They looked more like street walkers than show girls. None fluttered an eyelash as I passed. All, it seemed, were just waiting to be sent to a room.

Compared to the surreal glamour of the American casinos I thought the atmosphere was considerably less pretentious and more recognisably Chinese. But whether either model embodied the society the Chinese Government envisaged, I seriously doubted.

CHAPTER 9

Towards the Ethnic Minorities

Chinese trains were invariably social places. Distances were so huge and journey times so long that the rail network was the easiest place in the country to meet people. In hard sleeper carriages, open compartments with two tiers of three beds were the norm. The upper berths were the cheapest and gave very little space to move; the middle berths were more expensive and more spacious, and the lower berths were the most expensive, very spacious but had the drawback of becoming a sofa for all six people in the compartment during the daytime.

On the train to Guilin, while sitting on somebody else's bottom bunk, I started chatting to four girls, including one with a championship-winning 'English name' of YKK. They were heading out of Guangdong province for the very first time and were both excited and nervous. All four sold train tickets and said this was exhausting because the stations they, worked at were packed throughout the day. Although they moaned about the hard work, they recognised they would be unable to find a job elsewhere. Two worked in Guangzhou and two in Shenzhen, but even in those cites they explained there was not enough good employment to go around. Working at the train station, despite being low paid, was steady and allowed them to pay their bills.

The Chinese rail network was nationalised. Because so many people took the trains, considerable profits must have been turned over but, from what the girls said, little of this was leaking down to the employees. Instead, most of the profits were being reinvested in infrastructure developments like high-speed rail.

Guilin was an unsurprising choice for the girls' first trip. It was one of the most popular tourist destinations in south-west China and had a large enough tourist industry to see to a traveller's every need. As with other of China's popular destinations, much of this industry was unpleasant. I experienced this straight after arriving when I ordered a bowl of rice noodles for lunch. The price of the noodles—a cheap local staple—was double what I was used to paying and so I asked whether it was a particularly large bowl. The boss replied in the affirmative. When the food was brought, it was indeed an enormous bowl but the noodles barely covered the base. There were literally four mouthfuls inside.

It was likely that I was overcharged because I was a foreigner. Plenty of international tourists loitered around Guilin, particularly in the nearby jam-packed town of Yangshuo. The draw of the region was its stunning natural beauty but I found it hard to appreciate the scenery when every second person in the street was trying to hawk off souvenirs.

Only when I hired a bike and cycled aimlessly into the surrounding countryside did I truly understand the attraction of the area. Innumerable green peaks, rising like watchtowers from the ground, were threaded by somnolent rivers. Soaking rice paddies and muddy paths squelched around crumbling hamlets. Using the lazy Yulong River as my only reference point, I passed water buffalo, usually with a farmer in a wide brimmed straw hat trudging dreamily behind, and occasionally had to swerve to avoid running over chickens. The low cloud contributed to the eerie beauty and untouched mystery of the scene.

The next day I hiked along the banks of the Li River. This stretch of water was so pretty that its stylised image had made it onto the back of the 20RMB note. Again I found rural life continuing in all its manifestations, some of which were more bizarre than others. Notably, I saw a headless dog being blowtorched by an old woman so that the fur would be singed off ahead of cooking and was offered baijiu—fifty per cent proof rice liquor—from a petrol can while eating my breakfast at nine o'clock in the morning. I was not sure whether the alcohol was to prevent the dirty food upsetting my stomach or was simply recreational.

After a few hours' gentle walking I took a rest on a patch of lush grass beside the pale blue river. Leafy green escarpments rose like hedgehog quills from the banks opposite me. A few water buffalo grazed away to my left. Every now and then a tour boat from Guilin passed downstream and the silence was disturbed by the babble of awestruck day trippers. Otherwise it was silent.

An old man came over and sat beside me. For a long time he said nothing, allowing me time to gorge my eyes on the scenery in silence. Then he cleared his throat and asked in English, "Bamboo?"

"I can speak Chinese," I replied.

"I thought you were a foreigner."

"I am a foreigner."

"Oh," he said, lapsing into thought. "Well, do you want to ride my bamboo raft down the river?"

"I'm sorry but I prefer walking."

He considered for a while and then persisted: "Only 100RMB. The scenery is so beautiful. You will enjoy it."

"Yes, the scenery is incredibly beautiful," I said. "Have you lived here your whole life?"

He nodded and pointed to a small collection of brown houses a few hundred yards from where we were sat. "I was born just there. I have lived in the same house since I was a child. I am fifty nine this year."

"You are fifty nine? You look much younger!" I remarked, politely. The wrinkles in his face in reality showed every one of those fifty nine years.

He smiled weakly and fell back into silence. After a while he remarked, sorrowfully, "Your life must be so comfortable. You are rich. I have very little money. Please take my bamboo raft . . ."

I could not help him and did not want him to humiliate himself. I stood up and walked away. Another cruise boat chugged down the river beside me. I doubted that the owner of the cruise company was a local man.

*

I had heard repeatedly about China's 'family' of fifty six 'brothers.' I had even bought a white paper on government policy to the ethnic minorities. It stated that: "(The state's priority in ethnic minority areas is to promote) economic development, political stability, cultural prosperity and social harmony." In another section it added: "(According to the constitution) all ethnic groups in the People's Republic of China are equal." Given my upbringing in England, where the press rarely reported anything positive about China's treatment of its minorities, I had an instinctive scepticism about words of that sort. I thought it best to go and see what it was like on the ground.

To the north of Guilin sat the village of Ma'an, whose native people were the Dong minority. The village rested on the inside bend of a river and was reachable via a bridge which the Dong people had built one hundred years before. It was a large and symmetrical structure with five towers along its length. The result was hugely impressive, particularly given the absence of machines at the time of the construction. Having got off the bus from Guilin, I handed some money to a smiling woman in a long black skirt and colourfully embroidered coat, and in return received an entrance ticket to the village. Then I stepped onto the bridge and was immediately accosted by another smiling woman in similar clothing who invited me stay in her house. The warmth of her welcome was touching.

After dropping my bags, I headed up a mountainside and did some improvised Tai Chi in the wind on the summit. From my high vantage point I could see that the land around was mountainous and forested. It was the inaccessible terrain which had traditionally guaranteed the Dong their isolation and autonomy. But isolation had now been relegated to memory—especially with the tourism hub of Guilin so close by—and genuine autonomy had gone with it.

When I descended into the village I found a beautiful sense of community. It was early evening and the narrow paved lanes between the pine houses were filled with villagers. Children were running around with their school packs on, women were carrying baskets and men with muddied hands were talking together. The obvious absentees were teenage student. Ma'an was too small to have a middle school and so all students above primary-school age had to study elsewhere.

As I strolled through the narrow passageways that separated the houses, I was scrutinised curiously by faces that were invariably full of smiles. One old man beckoned me into a tall pagoda with an eleven tiered roof. It was a Drum Tower, the traditional centre of Dong villages. In one corner a group of men were sitting around a fire warming their hands and in another a gaggle of children were watching a program about dinosaurs on an old TV set. I sat for a few minutes with the men while they gazed at me. I could not understand the language they were speaking. After a while the man who had invited me in, who seemed to be a village elder, mimed that I should donate some money to the upkeep of the building.

Later in the evening a Chinese tour group arrived in the village and a traditional performance was put on to entertain them. I perched on one of the wooden benches, which had been placed around the small central square. The young men and women of the village arrived wearing traditional clothing. They danced around and sang to the accompaniment of wind instruments and drums. Old ladies moved between the benches, trying to sell their embroidery.

A little girl with a cheeky grin came over and climbed onto my lap. She spoke Mandarin and lisped that she was five years old. When I asked whether it was past her bed time she threw me a contemptuous look and started singing along to the music.

"Do you know this song?" I asked.

"Yes I know all the songs and I can do the dances too," she boasted proudly.

I asked for a demonstration so she hopped from my knee and started skipping and twirling. She could not move her legs fast enough to keep up with the adult performers but it was unmistakably the same dance. Her enthusiasm quickly made her tired and so she scrambled back onto my lap. I was fired with questions. "Where are you from?" she asked, showering me with spittle.

"England. Do you know where that is?"

"No . . . Do you speak Chinese there?"

"We speak English. Can you speak the Dong language?"

"Yes of course I can," she stated, looking at me like I was stupid.

She taught me to say 'nyalai' which meant 'hello.' Unfortunately my pronunciation did not impress her and I eventually gave up trying. One Chinese language was enough for me.

The darkness was complete by the time the main performance came to a close but a fire cast flickering shadows over the faces in the crowd. The members of the tour group were extremely appreciative and applauded the Dong performers wildly. They then chanted for their tour guide to sing a song, which she reluctantly did. When she had finished, clearly eager to take revenge on someone, she gestured to me. I judged I would look stupid if I did not get up and I was by that point in such a state of ease that I was more than happy to oblige. I sang Adel Weiss to the fifty or so onlookers. It was a memorable few moments.

I knew I was not the first Western city dweller to have felt humbled by the affectionate simplicity of a rural people. All the same I could not help but feel a twinge of disquiet as I returned through the blackness to my guesthouse. The traditional Dong culture was evidently still surviving but how far its preservation now depended on tourism I could not be sure. The micro-economy of the village had come to rely on the money of visitors such as myself. But tourism, I reflected, was a fickle saviour and had the potential to destroy the very thing that made Ma'an so special.

*

A few hours bus drive from Ma'an was Dazhai, a Yao minority village perched among the spectacular Dragon's Backbone Rice Terraces. Because picturesque rice terraces were such a draw in south-west China, the local tourism bureau had moved in. A large tourist centre blocked the narrow road a few miles before the 'scenic spot' and I had to splash out on an entrance ticket.

I used Dazhai as a base for climbing the steep mountainsides around. I discovered little hamlets perched in the vales of hills. Many of the wooden huts were balanced on stone stilts rather than built into the ground. There was little activity around them and guard dogs were often the only sign of life. I did make way for occasional men driving pack horses and saw a few old ladies scything the old stalks in the rice paddies but other than that the area seemed virtually unpopulated. Just as in Yongding, I guessed that many people had left for the city to work.

Litter clogged some of the streams but that eyesore paled into irrelevance compared to the spectacular terraces. They had been carved out over many centuries and now looked like staircases rising up the sheer mountain slopes. The cloudy weather hindered the view but I was still staggered by their scale. I had known nothing about either the Dong or the Yao before coming to the area and could not help noticing that they placed more emphasis on living amidst beauty than their Han compatriots.

After spending the night at the home of a man who I had encountered on a path in Dazhai, I descended from the village back to the road, where a local bus was standing. Occasionally a person sauntered down from the village and climbed on. Most of the passengers were middle aged women in traditional clothing. They beautified their black base layers with sky blue cardigans and shawls, but incongruously wore trainers. Many of them were whiling the time doing embroidery. The last seats were filled by three young women. To contrast with their elders they wore jeans and brand jumpers. They did, however, have Yao-style wicker baskets, which they left at the front of the bus. They came to the available seats next to me and then the driver set off.

A female conductor walked up the rickety bus collecting the fare. It was 9RMB and I was embarrassed to only have a 100RMB bill. Everybody else had the exact money. When the conductor had finished counting out my change, she handed me a thick wad of notes back. Most were 1RMB bills. Clearly that denomination of money was what most Yao people had cause to use in their daily lives.

"Where did you stay last night?" One of the women next to me asked.

"At the home of a man I met in the street."

"How much did it cost?"

"Erm. About 30RMB," I lied. In reality it had cost 60RMB but I was feeling self-conscious. I guessed some of the people around me did not earn more than a few RMB per day.

Her response woke me up from my pitying stupor, "That little! I would have charged you 100RMB for staying in my house!"

"Really?" I said, warming to the edge in her voice, "What makes you think I'd pay that much?"

"Because you foreigners are rich!"

"Not all of us. I know it's much richer than China but some people in England—that's my country—are quite poor."

"Yeah, right!" She snorted.

Another woman perked up, "Do you have a girlfriend?"

"Err, not at the moment."

Many of the elder women on the bus could not understand Mandarin but when my response was translated to them, they looked at each other with knowing glints in their eyes.

"What are the girls like in England?" I was asked. "Are they beautiful?"

"Some are and some aren't," I replied to chuckles.

"It's best that you don't try to get too beautiful a girlfriend," remarked the first woman, "because she probably wouldn't have you!"

CHAPTER 10

Yunnan

Even within the context of China's south-west, the number of ethnic groups in Yunnan was startling. Twenty five entirely distinct cultures coexisted within the one province. Geography was the main reason for the diversity. Yunnan rose gradually from jungles in the south to the Himalayas in the north and this terrain had traditionally made it a difficult place to get around. Since the Communists had taken power in 1949, a number of ethnic groups from other areas of the south-west had also been herded into the province. Yunnan was now the pin-up for ethnic relations in China.

On my train journey there I fell into conversation with a middle-aged travelling salesman. He said he had travelled widely in China and recited a strange anecdote over a smoked cigarette in the noisy intersection of two carriages: "Some of Yunnan's ethnic minorities live in very remote areas. Many years ago, when I was a young man, I travelled extensively in those parts for my work. During my wanderings I came across an isolated village. The local tradition was for all the men and women to bathe naked together in a warm mountain spring. Beautiful women with long dark hair and large eyes washed themselves in public without embarrassment. You maybe do not believe me but I assure you, I saw it."

My first stop in Yunna, the Yuanyang Rice Terraces, were not nearly as remote as the tantalising spring the salesman described to me, but they were still hard to reach. Situated in lush but rugged terrain in the south of Yunnan, they were only accessible via one twisting mountain road. The driver of my bus maintained a frightening pace no matter how winding the tarmac became. He seemed oblivious to the precipitous drops that lay just feet away. Most nerve-wracking were the moments when he pulled out to overtake slow-moving trucks. I and everyone else on the bus held our collective breath and prayed for survival.

It was evening by the time the bus pulled into Xijie, the one-road town at the access point to the Yuanyang region. A thick mist obscured everything and I could find no driver prepared to take me onwards in the treacherous conditions. I checked into the dank hotel opposite the bus station.

The next morning the mist was still impenetrable but I managed to make my way to Duoyishu. This village was situated only twenty five kilometres outside Xijie but it took me almost most two hours to get there. At sections the road was little more than a dirt track and was littered with pot holes. As we drove through roadside villages my driver pointed out the arrow-shaped coattails that distinguished the dresses of the Yi minority women from those of the Hani women.

Duoyishu was a Hani village sitting directly above one of the most spectacularly beautiful man-made sights in China. Unfortunately, when I first got there, I was completely unable to see anything further than ten metres in front of my face so the great accomplishment of the Hani people was hidden from view.

Despite the spine chilling dampness of the air, I went for a walk through the village. The houses were solidly built with stone walls and thatched roofs. I saw overweight pigs and other livestock living on the ground floors of the houses. Then I left the village behind and set off down past the water filled rice paddies. I walked downhill for well over an hour but I had not yet reached the bottom of the terraces when I decided to give up and turn back. I quickly lost any sense of direction in the mist and failed to find the way back to my original path. Fortunately I came across a huddle of men and women in wide straw hats but when I asked them for directions, none understood. I was only saved by the translation of a boy who looked no older than ten. His parents might not have understood Mandarin but he clearly studied it at school just like every other child in the country.

I checked in to a guesthouse, which was run by a Han Chinese woman. She was from Hunan province but had gone to Shenzhen after graduating from high school. Hers was a typical story of someone from a relatively poor province moving to the big city in search of fortune. However, she had soon tired of Shenzhen's aggressive atmosphere and had decided to relocate to Yuanyang. Now she spent her days tending a wood—burning stove in a house with a thatched roof and cooking meals for herself and any guests. When I asked her why she had come to the area, she answered, "Because it is so beautiful and peaceful. I like the quiet life. Here I am cut off from the rest of China."

Only in the late evening did I get a glimpse of the beauty that she alluded to. The clouds retreated down the mountainside and revealed the water-filled paddies in all their glory. There were literally thousands of individual pools. The water reflected the colours of the land and sky: green, blue, grey and brown. I was awed by the panorama. But within minutes the clouds rolled back up the valley and the scene was lost from view.

That was the only window I got because the next morning, the mist as claustrophobic as ever, I caught a minivan away from Duoyishu. The driver picked up several people along the road including a man with a basket packed full of live chickens. The van only had seats for seven passengers but in no time at all there were nine of us squashed inside.

Back in Xijie I noticed that new shops selling mobile phones lined many streets. There was a weak signal from a recently erected mobile tower nearby. Next I guessed there would be a new road.

*

The linking up of its most far-reached western provinces was a key priority for the Chinese Government. Yunnan, for example, was almost two thousand miles from Beijing and its native people lived their lives largely oblivious to the distant capital city. To bring it more into the fold, investment was being poured into the province. As I went from Yuanyang to the provincial capital, Kunming, the road became progressively better and eventually widened to two lanes. Not far from Kunming the bus passed through a new tunnel in a mountain. It certainly made things quicker.

Kunming was known as a convenient and relaxed city with a great climate, and during my brief stop-over it justified its reputation. The clean streets and pruned green spaces contributed to the liveable vibe and gave a comforting sense of affluence. From a traveller's point of view it was ideal. I came across many backpackers who, like me, were using Kunming as the starting point for trips deep into Yunnan.

Despite being the nerve centre of the most ethnically varied province in the whole of China, Kunming was a city dominated by the Han Chinese. I did, however, see great variety in the faces of the people at the city's main bus station. Some of the people waiting patiently had features that were dark and seemed almost Indian. I sat down beside a girl whose long hair, soft features and willowy figure were strikingly different from those of the Han. She was strikingly beautiful.

"Excuse me but you're not Han Chinese, are you?" I asked, turning to her and asking my question without much subtlety.

She looked up in surprise once she realised I was addressing her and when she spoke her voice was very light. "Why do you say that?"

"Oh, well, well I suppose your face doesn't look Han," I mumbled.

"You're right. I'm Bai."

I knew that the Bai people were one of Yunnan's largest native minorities and had possessed a major empire a thousand years before.

When I asked where she was headed she replied, "I'm going back home for a few days. My home is in a village far from here. I miss my family very much."

I felt like giving her a hug but instead enquired about what she did in Kunming.

"I study medicine," she said. "During the day I train as a nurse at the hospital and in the evenings I go to classes. It is very busy and I feel lonely here but there is no other way for me to become qualified."

"Isn't there a place where you can study nearer your home?"

"No there are no universities over there. After finishing high school three years ago I came to Kunming. I only go home about once a year because the rest of the time I have work. Even when there are holidays I must earn money to pay my expenses."

I asked whether she could speak the Bai language but she replied that she could not, explaining, "My parents can speak Bai but chose to speak Mandarin with me from when I was a child. They thought that it would be better for my life."

*

Dali had been the capital of the Bai kingdom until it was wiped out by the Mongol hordes in 1253. In modern times it had suffered the mixed blessing of becoming one of Yunnan's most popular tourist destinations. Chinese tour groups flooded the town and provided custom to the endless shops selling identikit souvenirs. Foreign backpackers, who moaned that Dali was 'theirs' before the tourists came, loafed around the streets, smoked cannabis and knocked back milkshakes in blaring Western bars.

I hired a bike and pedalled into the countryside outside Dali, alongside the tranquil Erhai Lake. Very early in the ride it started to rain but I pressed on in the optimistic hope that it would prove nothing more than a spring shower, passing through several white-washed Bai villages. In the green fields men and women were cultivating the various crops by hand, as if oblivious to the bustle in the town just a couple of miles away. I gave up further exploration because the rain became torrential. But when I cycled to the main road heading back towards Dali I soon regretted the decision. The road was narrow and the conditions awful. Worst was when cars came to overtake the trucks that were ploughing slowly along. In the face of oncoming traffic the overtaking car would pull out and force the drivers on the opposite side of the road to steer to the very edge of the tarmac. I found myself repeatedly squeezed out in this way and often had to brake violently. Just outside Dali I came across the scene of an accident. A wrecked scooter lay in the middle of the road. A single glove on the road beside it brought home the human reality of the incident. It might have been me.

Back in the Dali I invested in a new waterproof. Most of the shops I looked into before settling on my purchase were attended by Han people. Relentless tourism within areas of natural beauty was a pet hate of mine, even if it was hypocritical for me to visit and then moan about everyone else. The more tourists visited Dali the less atmospheric it became, and little of the money was even going to the native population.

*

The well-trodden Yunnan tourist trail continued on up from Dali to Lijiang but I took a small diversion to Shaxi, a village that existed in a time warp. In years gone by it had been a notable stop on the Ancient Tea Route, by which goods were transported out of China, over Yunnan's mountains and then down through Burma into India.

I found quiet cobbled streets lined with quiet old buildings. The village was virtually deserted and I was told it only filled up on market day when people flocked in from the surrounding area. People moved slowly and seemed content just to watch life go by.

The Bai occupants might have been living in peace but I quickly learnt that their 'idyllic' lifestyle was fragile. Although it was only now that tourists were coming to Yunnan en masse, over forty years ago Shaxi suffered the ravages of an entirely different Chinese wave. I discovered a temple that was looted during the Cultural Revolution. Its Buddhist icons had still not been replaced and it felt painfully empty.

In one of the bare side rooms was a small exhibition on Bai culture. There were English captions, which described how, at that point in time, China's benchmark for poverty stood at 625RMB per year; over three times less than the worldwide recognised benchmark of $1 per day. The Bai average income allegedly sat between the two figures, at $120 per year. In China, they did not count as an ethnic group in dire poverty. The exhibition implied that dire poverty was exactly what many Bai were suffering.

Scattered piles of litter lay beside the paths leading out of the small village. Trash dumps were a hallmark of impoverishment in all the most deprived areas I visited. Stray dogs sniffed at the discarded plastic and one pregnant bitch followed me around the winding lanes.

The obvious way for local people to rise out of poverty in Shaxi's neck of the woods was to embrace tourism and I saw signs that the more savvy villagers were doings so. In the large guesthouse where I stayed the potential wealth from hosting travellers was evident: a huge TV screen was prominent in one of the comfortably furnished living rooms. The daughter of the owners, aged probably three, seemed happy with life and spent hours on end singing a Chinese version of 'Old Macdonald had a farm': "la la la la la la la EEAY EEAY Oh!"

Shaxi gave me cause for pause. Up to that point the minority areas I had visited had either fully adjusted to tourism and lost some of their soul or else had remained poor but culturally 'pure.' My white paper on the ethnic minorities talked of the state improving economic conditions but also guaranteeing the preservation of cultural heritage. I had not yet seen a place that had managed both. I wondered how Shaxi would deal with the dilemma in the future.

*

The Naxi minority, who built Lijiang, were now barely visible because tourism had taken over their town. Indeed the only Naxi I met were those trying to capitalise on their expert local knowledge to cash in on the visitors. Both the people who offered me their services had the same calling card.

The first, a middle-aged woman, said, "Do you know Ralph Fiennes? Yes, well he came here in 2003. I was his guide."

The second, a ragged looking man, said, "Do you know Ralph Fiennes? Yes, well he came here in 2003. I was his guide." Seeing that his opening chat-up line had not dazzled me and possibly suspecting that I had heard the same thing previously, he went on, "Do you know Oxford University?

I was also the personal guide to a professor from there!" Finally, looking exasperated, he shouted, "You are making a mistake if you don't have me as your guide. Trust me, I'm the best!"

I did not accept his offer but I could sympathise with his frustration. After all, the vast majority of the people collecting the tourist dollars in his town were outsiders. I saw the Han tour groups from Kunming eating in Han-owned restaurants; drinking in Han-owned bars and sleeping in Han-owned hotels. Although I the traditional architecture of the centre had been preserved, the atmosphere could hardly have been described as traditional when the entire main street was occupied by raucous nightclubs pulsing away into the early hours. One evening I saw a couple of Buddhist monks in flowing robes peering into one such place. They looked extremely tempted by the enticements on offer inside, but ultimately their resolve won through and they continued on without stopping.

Billboards showing idyllic pictures of the Naxi people dancing in mountain fields were dotted around Lijiang. As I judged it, the Naxi could have done with slightly less celebration of their 'heritage'—especially as it was presented in a way that more reflected the tourism bureau's kitsch imagination than any reality—and slightly more substantive action to safeguard that heritage. It struck me as ironic that minority cultures such as the Naxi were being steadily diluted by the Han pouring in and yet were simultaneously being idealised, at least superficially, by those same people.

In relation to this paradoxical situation, one paragraph in my white paper on ethnic minorities seemed to me especially pertinent: "The state also pays great attention to relevant training for those working in press and publishing . . . Meanwhile the state pays attention to strengthen management over publications, radio and TV programs and video-film products and the use of the Internet to bar any contents hurting ethnic feelings and damaging ethnic unity." I reflected that the state could be spending more time actually protecting China's ethnic groups from assimilation than worrying about whether their 'feelings' would be hurt on the way down.

However, I also could not help noticing that the Naxi—and the people of south-west China in general—were seemingly not making any attempt to claim autonomy. Since arriving in the south-west, no one I had met had breached the subject of politics with me, in sharp contrast to what I had experienced on the east coast. I knew people had their own lives to contend with and perhaps did not feel they could influence the actions of a government based several thousand miles away, but all the same the absence of political dissent or even political interest was disconcerting. I reflected that either the ethnic peoples had given up hope of self-preservation or else were genuinely satisfied with the efforts being made to protect them. The latter seemed implausible but I could not rule out the possibility that I was just too cynical.

*

In spite of all my concerns, I had an enjoyable time in Lijiang. The reason was simple: it lay in a stunningly beautiful setting. To the north was Mount Satseto, a peak standing majestically at the gate to the Himalaya. I saw the mountain up close from the spectacular topography of Tiger Leaping Gorge, by some definitions the world's deepest river canyon. From the rapids in its depths to Satseto's summit far above, there was a height difference of roughly three kilometres. I trekked through pine woods and bamboo thickets; passed grazing goats and pack horses, and feasted my eyes on sheer mountain walls, snow-capped peaks and the rushing torrent of the 'Jinsha Jiang'—'Golden Sands River', which was a tributary of the Yangtze. I was the sole walker on the path for much of the time, only occasionally being pestered by local Naxi women to ride their horses or smoke the marihuana that mysteriously grew in the area.

After a day and night of natural bliss, I emerged at the end of the Gorge and smelt fresh tarmac. The roar of heavy machinery broke the stillness and the landscape was scarred by blasting. Lying just to the north of Lijiang, Tiger Leaping Gorge had been hard to access not so long before but it was being increasingly integrated into the tourist route. The road I watched being built was going to allow increasing number of people to be bussed in to experience the Gorge from the sterility of tourist centres and observation platforms.

After finishing my trek, I hopped onto a bus and with no warning whatsoever found myself in a new world. The road climbed into the mountains and suddenly I was in Tibet. Wooded slopes disappeared away from the side of the bus and then rose up again to glimmering white peaks. From the road I saw log huts, yaks and Buddhist stupas wreathed in prayer flags.

But when I got off the bus in Shangri-la, I found that it too was strongly influenced by the Han; replete with a Bank of China, cosy guesthouses and several internet cafes. The remote town had a very short history in its present incarnation. A few years previously, the local Chinese authorities had decided to change its name from Zhongdian to that of the elusive paradise described in the novel *Lost Horizon*. Their plan had been to lure tourists further north from where they were already well entrenched in Lijiang. Their ruse appeared to have worked because plenty of travellers were now heading to Shangri-la. On the flip side, the prospect of finding nirvana in the town was reducing in direct proportion to the number of people coming to seek it.

Shangri-la sat at an altitude of over 3000m but as I walked around I saw the traditional plateau lifestyle of the Tibetans in fast retreat and the forces of commerce taking hold. In the old town virtually every building seemed to be occupied by a shop selling 'genuine Tibetan souvenirs.'

However, away from the centre I came across areas that were still relatively untouched. The major attraction in Shangri-La was the Ganden

Sumtseling, a Tibetan monastery with a population of seven hundred monks. I explored it on a chilly but brilliantly clear day and was drawn in by halls resonant with the sound of chanting. I was impressed by how flourishing the monastery seemed to be. The vivid artwork painted on the inside walls of the prayer halls was freshly painted and the shining-gold roofs glinted miraculously in the sun. But I nonetheless feared for its future. Already there were souvenir stores and English-language sign posts dotted around the monastery.

The new opportunities in Shangri-la were causing increasing numbers of Han Chinese people to move there to set up business. On an individual level each of these émigrés was leaving behind the over-population and limited employment opportunities of the Chinese heartlands. While I recognised that every one of them had the right to improve their life, the cumulative effect of all these immigrants—although just a miniscule proportion of the overall Han population—risked overwhelming the culture of their new home. The result of such 'Hanification' had been plain for me to see in Dali and Lijiang. Shangri-la was almost certainly bound for a similar fate.

*

It took a full day for me to get to Deqin. The bus had to climb over a pass at almost 5000m; an ice world in early April. Teams of workers with trucks and diggers were both trying to clear the road of the winter snows and repair its decimated surface. For any vehicles it was slow going. Along the route, painted onto any available rock surface, were advertisements for China Mobile. A phone signal was a clear trail-blazer for infrastructure development.

Next to me on the bus sat a sinewy Han Chinese man in scuffed black shoes, worn trousers, a shirt and a loose blazer. He was on his way to join a road-building team and planned to stay in Deqin for at least six months. He only had one bag and the phone number of his work unit manager. Middle-aged and weathered, without wife or children, he said that he went where the work took him.

"Did you come to China for the hotel attendants?" He asked me in a thick accent.

"Attendants?"

"Yes . . . *attendants.*"

I was a little drowsy, perhaps because of the altitude, and did not latch on.

"You know," he said, before changing to English: "Fuck fuck."

I laughed and commented that it was not my primary reason for coming.

The construction worker, who had barely half his teeth, said, "The hotel attendants are the best thing in China. Before, with Mao, it was very difficult to find a woman but now . . ." he broke off with a dirty look on his face before remarking. "It was Deng Xiaoping who did it. He was a very clever leader."

I smiled at what Deng Xiaoping might have thought about that legacy.

The man got off the bus at about 4000m and stood alone in the white wilderness. His clothes seemed hopelessly inadequate to the conditions.

He was trying to screw girls when Mao was leader? My mind suddenly clicked. That was over thirty five years ago! Clearly he was older than he looked and yet he was still doing extremely tough manual work to make a living.

*

Deqin lay not far from the upper reaches of the Mekong River; already brown and with a long journey to go before it exited the sea in Vietnam. Beyond the mighty river, beneath the towering mountains of the Kawa Karpo range, hid a last place of solitude.

Deqin itself, however, was an ugly smudge in the cleft of a rocky mountainside. When I came out of the bus station, drivers jostled for my attention. There were five times more drivers than people looking to take a taxi. Rows of cheap restaurants lined the streets and I glimpsed a school nestled in a gap between apartment blocks. Other than that there was very little. Most people living in Deqin at that time were linked to one employment: construction.

I hoisted my backpack, crossed the Mekong and set off towards the mountains, ignoring the advice of those who said I ought not to trek alone. After my first day's walking I stopped for the night in a grimy building belonging to a scowling Tibetan man. The wind howled outside and light snow floated down from the angry sky. I ate dinner sitting on a lumpy sofa in a gloomy living room. There with me were three Han Chinese drivers, who were waiting in that miserable but cheap place for their clients. Each had brought a minivan load of intrepid travellers, who had now gone off with local guides into the mountains.

As we ate noodles together, the three drivers started talking about Lhasa. I pricked up my ears because the holy capital of the Tibetan religion had long exerted a powerful pull on my imagination. But the men were more interested in discussing Lhasa's business opportunities and house prices. I was faced with the reality that the city of my dreams was now a major Chinese economic centre.

The next morning I rose early and headed up through a forest of pine trees. I climbed for many hours into the snowline. Eventually I reached the top of this frontal range and could do nothing but gasp at what I beheld. Before me, so close I felt I could touch it, stood Miacimu. The Tibetans believed this peak was the goddess wife to the larger mountain further down the range, the god Kawa Karpo. At just over 6000m Miacimu might not have been as tall as her spouse, but her arrow-point sharpness lent her a celestial aspect. Usually she was enveloped in cloud but that day she granted that I see her naked. I stood in awe.

Between me and the mountain lay a place I had heard tales of. The green Yubeng valley twinkled magically beneath me, utterly cut off from the world. I descended in excitement but soon felt compelled to sit down on a rock and feast my eyes uninhibitedly on the view. As I gazed a horse trotted down the path in front of me. A few minutes later its owner came by. He was very slight, had a sharp nose and walked with a slight limp. He was wearing patched blue trousers and his beige coat was filthy. He sat down next to me and offered a cigarette. I offered him a biscuit in return and he accepted with a yellow-toothed smile.

"Do you speak Mandarin?" I asked.

"You can speak Mandarin?" He uttered in surprise, and immediately asked me to ride his horse.

I declined but he seemed in no hurry to go anywhere and stayed sat. I asked him where he was from.

"Ninong. It is a village down the valley. I am on my way back there now. This morning I guided a Chinese traveller who was riding my horse." He spoke slowly with frequent long pauses. Mandarin was no more natural for him than it was for me. After a few moments of silence he asked hopefully, "Do you have a guide?"

"No, but I plan to walk around by myself," I replied nonchalantly.

"Don't do that!" He said with an anguished look. "You must always be with somebody in this area. It can be very dangerous. Just last year a lady died because she slipped off a path and fell very far. Safety is the most important thing. Safety first. Promise me that you will not walk around alone."

"Ok, I promise," I lied. I had no intention of surrendering my precious solitude.

I gestured towards where the summits to the right of Miacimu were obscured and asked whether Kawa Karpo lay in clouds. I received confirmation and the instruction that Kawa Karpo was a powerful god so I must pay my respects. I dutifully bowed in the manner he demonstrated. As I did so he spotted the watch on my wrist and leant in for a closer look. He removed the fake watch he was wearing and offered to trade.

"No. I'm sorry but I can't," I said, scratching around desperately for a polite excuse, "Because, you see, well, my mum gave it to me."

His reaction astonished me. He grovelled backwards and started bowing his head up and down. "I'm sorry. I'm sorry. I'm really sorry."

I said was no problem and, touched by his humility, set off down the path with him. I asked whether he was married.

"Yes I am married. I have two elder brothers. We all share one wife." As I digested this evidence of polyandry, which was indicative of the area's remoteness, he continued, "I am on my way home now but will probably return to this area this evening. I will come to find you, is that ok?"

"What do you want to do? Do you like drinking?" I asked.

"Yes! Very much."

"What do you drink?"

"Pepsi," he said, which was not quite the response I expected!

*

A few of the log houses scattered around the Yubeng villages doubled up as guesthouses for any travellers who passed through. Aside from a small number who acted as guides, the Tibetan natives kept yaks and horses, and cultivated what few hardy vegetables they could.

In my guesthouse were a group of travellers; perhaps the same people who the drivers were waiting for on the other side of the range. I ate a large evening meal together with them by the light of some candles. After we had all eaten our fill, we went to sit around a stove and warmed our hands. A few of the local Tibetan men were with us, one of whom had a remarkable appearance. He stood over six feet tall, with long black hair and a powerful build. A long knife in an ornate scabbard was strapped to his waist, and prayer beads coiled around his wrist. He was strikingly handsome and was treated with smitten admiration by all the girls sitting around him.

The evening grew late and we all became increasingly drunk, with the exception of my friend of earlier in the day, who was indeed teetotal. After a while the handsome Tibetan performed a rap and from then on the floodgates opened. The flames from the stove flickered on our faces as we swayed and sang and laughed.

Outside, a universe of stars illuminated the heavens and I felt a glow that I knew would be gone in the cold light of day. Ethnicity, including my own, did not matter then. Han, Tibetan and English lived together in harmony.

*

Against the repeated warnings I continued to trek alone. I left Yubeng and headed down the valley, following a roaring stream. The path passed down the canyon, rising all the time until I was on a mountain ledge with a precipitous drop away to my right. A gusty wind knocked me off balance and I came alarmingly close to falling. Thereafter I focused my mind and placed my steps with extreme care. The concentration brought stillness upon me. I passed one Tibetan man during the whole day. In contrast to my sturdy boots, he wore little more than pumps but still moved more easily than me across the treacherous ground.

My peace was shattered, however, when I reached the Mekong. Across the river from where I stood, the brown mountainside was being smashed and a new road was being built. Broken rocks and scree bounced down the sheer cliffs and crashed into the water below. To the north of me lay the border with the Tibetan Autonomous Region; that was where the road was leading. The tentacles of Beijing were creeping ever further.

I stayed the night beside the Mekong, in Ninong village, in the house of a friendly Tibetan lady. Her home seemed affluent by comparison to some I had seen. In a small yard on the ground floor were two yaks, a horse and a couple of pigs, and upstairs the large rooms were furnished with clean couches and tables. The toilet even had plumbing, presumably because of the proximity of the river.

In the living room were several shrines and pictures of famous Tibetan Monasteries. A postcard photo of the Dalai Lama, the exiled head of the Tibetan religion, took pride of place on the mantelpiece. I went for a closer look and found the inscription: "Liebe und Mitgefuhl sind fur mich das Wesen der Religion. Um solches zu entwickeln must du allerdings nicht irgend einer Religion angehoren."

The German might have been meaningless to my hostess but I doubted she wanted the text translated. The mystery of the words was greatly enhanced as they were. In the context of the surroundings it was pertinent to observe that some things were better off left alone.

*

Two evenings and lots of driving later I found myself back in Shangri-la. At eight o'clock music resonated from big public speakers in the old town. A hard-core group of middle-aged Chinese ladies started dancing. They knew the steps to all the dances and led the way: Right foot forward, left foot forward, kick, twirl, hop, skip . . .

The Han women were clearly the regulars but lots of other people joined in. Several Tibetan women moved gracefully in time to the music and a handful of tourists stumbled around. The only people not represented were those perennial no hopers: men.

It was enjoyable to watch everybody having fun. I had my reservations about the collateral damage to minority cultures caused by the relentless infrastructure building and tourism drive in Yunnan, but I could see that it was not all negative. What I had seen in the province had unsurprisingly demonstrated both sides of the modernisation coin, I reflected, but at least I had seen no expressions of anger.

I spoke my thoughts to an American man who had lived in Shangri-la for several years and had married a Tibetan woman.

"Yunnan's different from other places," he said. "It's the poster province for ethnic relations. Fifty six minorities but all one family; all that stuff: here in Yunnan it works ok. Everyone speaks Mandarin and doesn't cause trouble, and in return they get to keep some of their culture, their religious freedom and things like that . . . You go up to parts of Tibet though and it's a different story."

CHAPTER 11

Shattered Illusions in Kham

I could not go into the Tibet Autonomous Region. By an unforeseen consequence of getting a business visa, I needed extra paperwork to be allowed in. I cursed the motives behind the regulations and then decided to take the positives. Although the Tibetan religion's most important sites lay in and around Lhasa, travelling in those parts could not be independent because every excursion required the accompaniment of a tour guide. I wanted to see how the Tibetan people really lived and, to get an impression of that, I needed to get off the beaten track.

To Tibetans, Western Sichuan was part of the Kham region. This eastern section of the Tibetan plateau was known for its deep-wooded valleys and high mountain passes. Encompassing most of the area were counties and townships that were nominally governed by 'autonomous' Tibetan administrations. The rough and dangerous Sichuan-Tibet highway traversed the precipitous terrain but few travelled along it. I hoped its remoteness would make Kham the perfect area to see how 'social harmony' applied to the Tibetans; to see how the CPC treated them in insolation; to see whether the Tibetan people were really given equality as one of China's 'fifty six brothers.'

Not knowing what I would find, I caught a bus from Shangri-la early in the morning. At the border with Sichuan a group of sinister looking policemen climbed on. They ordered everybody off, collected passports and ID cards, and unpacked a few bags. I did not know what they were looking for and did not ask. It was half an hour before we were allowed to continue. Later in the day we passed another checkpoint. Again passports were collected but that time no bags were searched.

Even without the stops the driving was slow-going. The steepness of the mountains meant that the road had to wind up them like spaghetti; only rising at a gradient that ordinary vehicles could manage. My bus spent ages coiling its way slowly up ascents before taking similar amounts of time descending on the other side. The endless corners meant that straight line distance lost all relevance. Xiangcheng, where the bus terminated, was only about two hundred kilometres from Shangri-la but it took the better part of eight hours to get there.

In Xiangcheng I discovered that there were no public buses travelling onwards for a couple of days. I did not want to linger and therefore immediately hired a minivan with another Englishman and two monks who were heading in the same direction.

The scenery heading out of Xiangcheng was sublimely beautiful. The highest point of the road came at over four and a half thousand metres on a plateau strewn with ice and boulders. Sublime it might have been but harsh and cold it certainly was too. The driver was nervous because it was already late afternoon by the time we set off and he doubted we would reach Litang, our destination, by nightfall. It was not wise to attempt the route in the dark.

His efforts to drive quickly in order to make up time were stymied by circumstance. The road surface was uneven and very early on we got a puncture. The driver had no jack and so we had to rock the van and place stones underneath in order to prop it up. Fortunately he had a spare wheel because we would otherwise have been stranded on an almost deserted road at four kilometres in the sky.

Even after we got going again we were frequently slowed down by yaks; herds of which were scattered on sparse grassland to the side of the road. Yaks were the Plateau's most abundant large animal and had long been herded by Tibetan nomads. They had hunched backs and long shaggy fur. The latter was an essential survival feature at the altitude but other than that the yaks we passed did not show much instinct for self-preservation. There were evidently too few cars for them to have developed any road sense and their behaviour bordered on both the suicidal and the murderous. Individuals would saunter out into the minivan's path, bringing us all to a bone shuddering halt as the driver hit the brakes. Then the recalcitrant beasts would often not move until the driver used his bumper to nudge them out of the way.

I paid close attention to the two monks who I was sharing the lift with. One was elderly while the other was perhaps forty years old. From what this younger man told me in slow Mandarin, I surmised that the two of them were returning to their home monastery after a winter spent at a monastery in Yunnan. Neither spoke much. They seemed to enjoy the sound of silence.

At one point the senior of the two took out some prayer beads and started humming throatily. This serene old monk was a mine of contradictory impressions. After chanting for a long time, he took a few swigs from a bottle of water. When he had finished, to my astonishment, he casually tossed the empty bottle out of the window. He had a fake Tissot wristwatch, an electric razor and a mobile phone on which he took my photo. But when we stopped for a toilet break he had to squat down just to urinate because his maroon robes had no opening.

At the most beautiful section of the drive I unwound my window and tried to capture the panorama on camera. I was so enthralled by the spectacular terrain that I failed to notice the inside temperature of the car, which within a short time started to resemble an ice box. I was only alerted to the problem when the elder monk started coughing quietly into his robes. He had not uttered a word of complaint. I thought that he probably should have.

The driver was similarly hard to read. He drove recklessly and chain-smoked, and yet had a Buddhist icon on his dashboard. On one occasion, the road was bisected by a Buddhist stupa. The Tibetan tradition was for all religious buildings to be passed in a clockwise direction. The driver did so, even though this act took him onto the wrong side of the road.

Night had indeed descended by the time we pulled into Litang. I could only find one place in which the local police authorised foreigners to stay. I felt exhausted and a little dazed by the time I finally laid my head down on a knobbly pillow.

*

Litang was a small town rising up a hillside on a long brown plateau. Quiet snow-capped peaks shimmered in the distance but in the streets there was great bustle. A modern district had been built at the lowest point of the town, in contrast with the older houses that filled the higher ground. Both areas were dominated by Tibetan people. On the pavements I made way for men of wild appearance. They were kitted out in high boots and wore long robes belted at the waist. Many had long hair and their smiles flashed with gold teeth. The women wore long dresses layered one on top of the other. It was early April and at four thousand metres in the sky it was still very cold. Motorbikes roared down the streets with monks on the back; their red robes fluttering. Stray dogs roamed and sniffed at me as I walked by. I stood out like a sore thumb but felt welcomed by everyone. I could say the Tibetan greeting, "Tashi Delek!" and received glowing smiles when I did so.

A few shop owners were selling distinctly Tibetan amenities such as yak skins, knives, clothes and prayer beads, but many people were doing no work. The traditional Tibetan lifestyle was centred on agriculture and livestock but the season was too early for those pursuits. Amid all the colour and activity, there was a strong sense of poverty. Dignified-looking ladies waited for me to draw up and then held out their hands to beg. A small girl with tangled black hair and a dirty face screamed out an English word; probably the only one she knew: "Money!"

On a grassy slope outside town an old couple were collecting dried yak dung. Few trees could grow at Litang's altitude and so dung was used as fuel. The man gestured me over. He had a weathered face and deep set eyes. Prayer beads hung from his neck. He examined my walking boots intently, gave me an appreciative thumbs-up and then mimed for me to give money to his wife. I was taken aback by their lack of shame. It showed desperation. They were clearly penniless.

Before I walked away the man rose and pointed north-eastwards along the plateau that stretched away from Litang. Then he brought his arm in a sweeping curve, moving imaginarily behind mountain ranges until he was pointing westwards. "Lhasa," he said.

Later in the day a young man invited me into his home. I sat down in a low room held up by wooden beams. Four couches were placed facing towards a shrine in the corner. A photo of the Dalai Lama took pride of place. My host offered me yak butter tea and tsampa, the local snack made from barley mixed with yak milk and hot water. He wore jeans and a black sports jacket. He also spoke rudimentary Mandarin. As I chatted with him he took out a photo album.

"Look," he said, pointing at one photo of a man in red robes, "My big brother."

"Your brother is a monk?"

"Yes. In India. In Dharamsala . . . Look this one me in Lhasa," he said, indicating a slightly younger version of himself standing in the car park of the Potala Palace, the former seat of the Dalai Lama.

"Very nice," I commented. "Lhasa looks very beautiful."

"Yes it is. Where you from?"

"England."

"India?" He repeated hopefully.

"No, England."

He shaped the word on his lips and then asked: "You go India?"

"No I am staying in China."

"You take me to India?"

"I'm sorry, I'm not going to India."

He caught sight of my watch and looked closely. Well-made items were cherished considerably more than cash. He requested that I give it to him.

"No, I can't," I replied, surprised by his directness.

"Give me watch so I can go India."

"I'm sorry it's not possible."

"How much it cost go India?"

"I don't know. Maybe 2000RMB"

"2000RMB? You give me money? You take me India?"

Although I could not help him I understood what vexed him so. The Dalai Lama, together with the cream of the Tibetan leadership, was in exile in Dharamsala, in northern India. Tibetan Buddhism was oriented around monastic communities and around lamas; holy men believed to be reincarnations of Buddhist deities. The bulk of Tibet's monasteries had been destroyed under the Communists and many of the lamas had been forced into exile, severely weakening Buddhism on the Plateau. But to the Tibetans, Buddhism was not just a past-time; it was the heart of their culture. In Dharamsala lay the Tibetan soul.

Quite how integral the Buddhist religion was could be seen in the monastery, which stood on the hillside above Litang. Inside were scattered earthen huts for the monks to live in and at the highest point, looking down over the town, were three temples. The golden roofs glinted whenever a shaft of sunlight slipped through the clouded sky. Repair works were underway inside the monastery. Every single one of the workers, be it carpenters, brick layers or lackeys, was Tibetan. Inside one hall a statue of Sakyamuni Buddha was being meticulously chiselled from wood by a sculptor. The dancing frescoes on the walls were vivid with fresh colour. As I was looking around a shout of glee resonated from one prayer hall and streams of monks—some of them young boys—started emerging after the end of a prayer session. Now that the service had finished, one of the carpenters working nearby started up his chainsaw and continued the work that he had respectfully put on hold.

Outside the monastery walls the atmosphere was similarly religious. For laypeople, the focus of Buddhist worship was the 'kora;' the act of walking clockwise around holy sites. Women were particularly numerous on the kora path around Litang's monastery. In Tibet, only men were allowed to become monks and so women had no outlet for their piety other than this insatiable walking. I saw a steady stream of women moving along with their backs hunched and with their excess clothing bunched around their waists to stop them getting too warm. They fingered rosaries, span prayer maces and muttered incessant sutras. I was struck by the devotion and joined in.

In the early evening, tired from a long day of walking, I descended back into the town. The air was cold and dark clouds were gathering above. A disturbance in a side street caught my eye so I went to take a closer look. A crowd of Tibetan men in cowboy hats were hemmed in by a line of police with riot shields.

I hurried away before my presence was noticed and entered an internet bar. The worker asked for my Chinese ID card. When I offered him my passport instead, he refused to accept it. I thought he was being unreasonable and persisted.

Eventually he shouted, "There's no way! I can't let you online. It's the police's rules. You need Chinese ID! If you want to complain then go to the police station."

Instead of popping in on the authorities I entered a restaurant, which promised Wi-Fi on the door. Unfortunately the owner explained that the Public Security Bureau had recently ordered him to remove the facility. The only way to access the internet in Litang was to submit to being watched.

Now I looked more closely there were police boxes on many street corners. In contrast with the locals, the vast majority of the uniformed men around them were Han.

A power-cut occurred in the night and the town was plunged into blackness. My electric blanket, which was my main defence against the outside cold, did not work. I slept with several layers of clothes on and dreamt lucidly. Dogs barked all through the night.

*

The scenery on the road from Litang to Kangding was magnificent. The southern branch of the Sichuan-Tibet Highway had a glowing reputation and it did not let me down. Although the grasslands were more brown than green after a long winter buried under snow, the beauty was still exceptional. The towering peaks all around and the untouched snow gave a palpable sense of being in the sky.

I had plenty of time to appreciate the view because I sat on the bus for over ten hours. There was one long wait while I and a couple of other foreigners registered at a checkpoint. The policeman did not know what he was doing and ended up writing all our details down on the back of a scrap piece of paper. Other than this delay the only thing lengthening the drive was the ruggedness of the terrain. The driver certainly could not have driven faster. In fact I would have preferred him to have taken it a little slower. He spent the whole journey steering one handed whilst on his mobile phone, used his horn every three seconds and on one occasion had to swerve violently to avoid crashing into another bus. When I got off in Kangding, I was relieved to have made it.

I found a lively but recognisable town. Apartment blocks were creeping up, several banks lined the roads and small canteens served up the Chinese culinary staples. Chengdu, the provincial capital of Sichuan, was just a day's bus ride away and its proximity was apparent. I had seen the influence of Han culture on native population several times previously but here it was different. In Yunnan the changes had been at times regrettable but they had been taking place without visible tensions. Kangding, however, was indefinably uncomfortable and I felt tense.

Perhaps it was just that, as a Westerner, I had been indoctrinated with the Tibetan cause since childhood. Perhaps it was because I had recently learnt that Ai WeiWei, a prominent dissident, had been arrested at Beijing airport. Perhaps it was the fact that my hostel stood next to a hospital of traditional Tibetan medicine, a golden-roofed monastery and a military barracks. I was confronted with the possibility that all the talk of social harmony might be an elaborate façade for oppression. Did the Tibetans stand a chance?

At 8pm, just like in Shangri-la, public speakers started booming out music in Kangding's main square. A huge crowd of people—I estimated over two hundred strong—rotated in front of me. Right foot forward, left foot forward, kick, twirl, hop, skip . . . I watched in fascination but this time I experienced no enjoyment. Again there were Tibetan people mixed in with the majority Han but something about the dancing was sinister. I could see the puppets but not the puppet master.

*

From Kangding I changed direction and set off on the northern branch of the Sichuan-Tibet highway. I caught an early bus in the direction of Ganzi. The other passengers were a mixed bag. There were Tibetans but also a number of Han migrant workers. They were all heading towards Qinghai, Sichuan Province's northern neighbour. Near the border, in the remote town of Yushu, a massive earthquake had occurred the year before. My fellow passengers were heading for the destroyed region to seek work.

The Han workers all wore similar clothing: dark trousers, shirts and coats. Most had their luggage in huge rice bags. It took considerable guts for someone to come to those harsh mountainous areas in search of low-paid work. Really it implied poverty. The various habits of the workers reflected their social status. One drank baijiu from a plastic bottle in the early morning. Several chain-smoked. Spit, melon seed husks and chicken bones covered the bus floor. My seat was cramped and hard but I was becoming used to the hardships of the road.

During the drive there were a couple of toilet stops. At the first, everyone walked into a barn and did their business on an empty patch of ground. Shit lined the earth and only a cracked wooden screen separated the sexes. The second was at a bus station. Inside the reeking gents' toilet were a couple of buckets. Four people could cluster around a bucket at any one time. A man who did not feel like waiting pissed onto the floor.

The going was slow and the scenery less exciting than on the southern highway. Prayer flags and carved Tibetan script covered the brown hills but there were fewer breath-taking mountain panoramas. Sometimes the road deteriorated to little more than a dirt track and became too narrow for vehicles to pass side by side at speed. The bus was held up for a long time in the early afternoon when a military convoy drove by. The driver guided the bus into a ditch on the side of the road to make way for it. I counted over seventy trucks go past, each driven by a young Han soldier.

Later on we came to another halt. The sun was blazing down and the inside of the bus became uncomfortably hot. Only after two hours did we start moving again. Everyone craned their necks to see what had caused the disruption. A long line of cars stretched along one side of the road. Roughly fifty policemen were standing about. Several had riot shields and I saw two with shotguns. A number of motorbikes were also parked on the verge. Their Tibetan riders were sat down in huddles on the grass. I could make out nothing more.

In total the journey took fifteen hours. My tiredness can have been nothing compared to that of the bus driver. I knew he would do the same route again the next day.

*

Ganzi was the capital of the surrounding prefecture and had a similar layout to Litang. Its monastery surveyed the surroundings from a hillside, while down in the centre of the market town the streets were hives of activity. Men flashed their gold-toothed smiles as I passed and joyously responded to my "Tashi delek!" Gangs of children followed me around chirping, "Money?" Middle-aged women sat in shops and called for me to buy their beads and amulets. Motorbikes roared down the roads, dodging the stray dogs that yielded to no one.

The oldest part of the town lay just below the monastery. The walls of the cuboid homes were made from a mix of materials: earth, stone, bricks, wood and straw. Clearly they had first been built with whatever was at hand. I saw one man repairing the roof of his home by sprinkling mud on the weak patches and trampling it in.

Down one narrow alley I spotted two donkeys rutting. The female seemed less eager and pulled away. The male trotted after her, his member still primed to go. Two minutes later the female came cantering back up the street with a young boy on her back. He was smacking her haunches for all he was worth. The poor jenny was having a rough day.

In a different street a monk was chanting at the side of a truck. A large catch of river fish was flapping in a shallow pool of water in the back of the vehicle. They were slowly suffocating and the monk was saying prayers to help their souls take flight in peace.

The religious devotion was most prominent around the monastery. Having already completed the lengthy kora once, I unintentionally found myself back on the kora path while looking for the entrance to a temple. I retraced my steps but was stopped by a Tibetan man who pointed out that I was walking in the wrong direction. He did not allow me to walk anti-clockwise relative to the monastery, and so I had to complete the whole circuit once more.

At dusk I walked along the road out of town and stopped to admire the beauty of the scene. Across the valley in front of me crawled a wide river and white-tipped mountains were silhouetted beyond. My attention was drawn by the approach of a military convoy. There were exactly eighty in total. Like I had seen on the previous day, each was driven by a young Han Chinese soldier. Many of the drivers waved cheerfully at me and a couple of soldiers leant out of the passenger side windows to take pictures of me on their mobile phones. It might have seemed friendly but it was a stark reminder of who was in charge.

As I went up to my hotel room in the evening I met a Tibetan man on the stairs. He asked whether I was on my way to Lhasa, to which I replied that the government's regulations did not allow me to go.

He nodded knowingly and asked, "Where are you from?"

"England."

"That is good," he said loudly. "I like foreigners. I don't like the Han." He paused for breath, his face contorted and then went on, "Americans, Germans, French, English: I like them all. But I hate the Han! They are crushing us!" To confirm his point he brought his hands together in a sharp slap, as if squashing a fly. His anger was helpless.

*

Manigango was situated in lush grassland. Yaks grazed, prayer flags quivered on the hills and monasteries could be seen wherever I turned my eyes. The village itself was just a cluster of homes dropped unceremoniously in the middle of the plain. It felt as though Tibetan nomads had put up their tents one day and never bothered to move on. The homes were now made from logs and stone but the atmosphere was still wild. A dirt track comprised the main street. Stray dogs roamed freely and ventured through open doors into canteens; yaks moved somnolently about and wandered in front of motorbikes; loose horses cantered up and down the track, and hawks hovered in the skies above scanning for prey.

I hired a driver to take me to a nearby lake. On arrival I saw that 'lake' was a gross understatement. Half of it was frozen and where the ice had thawed the turquoise waters twinkled in the sunlight. On the far side from where I stood, shining mountains stretched up from the water's edge and reached for the sun. A grey stupa lay in the trees on one end of the lake, wreathed in prayer flags. The beauty was astonishing. It was the sort of place that could only exist in the imagination. But there it was. I would happily have stayed there for hours, days, months. To be able to retreat from daily life and search for enlightenment in a place such as that seemed a tempting option. With such extraordinary scenery providing the backdrop to their world; I thought it no wonder that the Tibetan people were so religiously inspired.

On the way back to Manigango I engaged my driver in conversation. "How long have you been a driver for?" I enquired as an ice breaker.

"More than twenty years. How old do you guess I am?" He replied, and then when I had guessed wrongly he said he was forty three years old. He explained that he was married with three children. The One Child Policy did not apply to ethnic minorities.

"Are you married?" He asked, turning the tables on me.

"No, I'm too young."

"Are you Buddhist?"

I decided to keep things simple and replied in the affirmative.

"That is good," he said. "Do you study the teachings of the Dalai Lama?"

"I try," I replied, "but there is of course much I do not understand."

My response clearly pleased him. "You should find a Tibetan wife," he said. "Tibetan women are beautiful. My eldest daughter is very pretty. She is only sixteen now but when she is a little older then . . ."

I was flattered to be considered an eligible Tibetan husband. A herd of yaks was blocking the road in front. As he eased the car through, I asked my prospective father-in-law about his work. He told me that he drove all around the Tibetan plateau, even as far afield as Lhasa if his clients wanted to travel that way. The Tibetan holy city was one and a half thousand kilometres to the west.

He enquired where I was headed. "Up to Yushu in Qinghai," I replied. "I heard there was an earthquake there last year?"

His face became very solemn, "Yes, it was terrible. Everything was destroyed . . . I went to help; to dig in the rubble . . . It was terrible . . ." He trailed off.

*

That evening I ate a dinner of noodles before going to sit beside a stream. The tinkling of the brook was the only sound in the empty air. I sat down and listened. My mind became very clear. I melted into the world around me. There was something in the Tibetan air that made those peaceful moments especially profound. Afterwards, in a slightly less spiritual mood, I bought a beer and sat down to drink it on Manigango's one street. A policeman approached. He had a boyish face and short hair.

"Hello," he said, "Do you speak English?"

"Yes," I replied warily. "But I can also speak Mandarin."

He commented on how much easier that made things before inviting me along to the police station. When I asked what he wanted, he smiled and told me that, as a foreigner, I needed to register. I was slightly nervous of whether he would question my visa but I need not have been. He did not even check my passport and just asked me to fill in a few boxes on a form. Seeing as the policeman seemed not only unthreatening but positively friendly, I asked a few questions.

"How long have you worked here?"

"About two years. I'm from Chengdu, the capital of Sichuan, but got sent up here when I finished my police training. It's a bit of an unfortunate posting to be honest. Travellers like you come here and say, 'Wow isn't it beautiful,' but they don't really understand the difficulties."

I pressed him for more and he obliged. "There are a lot of factors that make it difficult. For a start the altitude and thin air are hard to get used to. Then there's the winter weather. It's alright now but in winter the temperatures go incredibly low." He broke off talking and I was about to leave when he said "By the way, please can you not drink beer in the street."

"Why not? Is it because the Tibetans are Buddhist?" I guessed.

"No, that's not the reason," he replied. "In fact the Tibetans like alcohol but they're not allowed to drink outside by law."

That was not a law I had come across in other areas so I asked about it.

"You're right it's only a local law," he said indiscreetly. "You see, when the Tibetan men drink they like get very drunk. If they are in public places they start fights. They all have knives. It is very dangerous!"

"They fight with the police?"

"No, with each other. We police have to break it up. Because they all have knives we all have to carry guns. There are only sixteen policemen in the whole of Manigango so it would not be safe for us otherwise . . . I have heard that in Beijing the police do not carry guns but here it is necessary. I want to go to Beijing very much. I think every man should visit his capital city."

But his capital city and that of the people he watched over were two different places.

*

I woke late the next morning and went to the toilet at the end of the corridor. Three squat toilets were built into the floor. The plumbing had broken and piles of human excrement were sitting in all three. I gulped, cursed myself for waking up so late and then contributed to the problem. It was an inauspicious start to a day that ended much more enjoyably.

I spent the afternoon visiting a historical monastery. However, the real interest came when I was back in Manigango and was sitting not far from the spot where the policeman had approached me. A monk came over. Aside from the red robes, he wore a black hat pulled low over his forehead. The visual effect was part gangster, part holy man. He addressed me in English, in a soft and nervous voice.

"Do you want to speak with me?" He asked. "I would like to practise my English. I studied English in Lhasa but I do not have many chances to speak it now."

I asked him when he had been in Lhasa.

"I came back last year. I studied at a Tibetan college there. I studied English, Chinese and Tibetan," he said. He struggled slightly with his grammar, particularly with his past tense verbs, but I could still understand what he was saying.

"Are there problems between the Tibetan and Chinese people?" I enquired, taking the opportunity to ask the obvious question.

"No, no,no," he said, hurriedly. "In two oh oh eight lots of problems. Now no problems."

"But do you like the Chinese?"

"Nooo, no, no. In two oh oh eight in Lhasa they killed many Tibetans. I was at college. I saw the soldiers like this . . ." he said, miming using a machine gun.

"Did they kill monks?"

"Monks and normal Tibetans."

He looked upset so I did not press him for more information. We walked up to his monastery, which sat on a quiet hillside a short walk from Manigango. Around it there was no surrounding wall. The central monastic prayer hall was under scaffolding. My new friend gestured me inside with a proud look on his face. Tall tree trunks acted as structural columns and propped up the roof high above our heads. Some of the columns had fresh carvings cut into them. Elephants, tigers and monkeys emerged from the pine; their incongruousness to the surroundings harking back to the Indian origins of Buddhism.

"How long have you been building the hall?" I asked.

"It started in 2008. Maybe next year it will be finished," he replied, a tad optimistically.

"Who is building it? The monks?"

"No, the Tibetans. They get 200RMB per day." Then he added, with a hint of pride and defiance, "There are no Chinese workers."

I asked where the money come from and was told that Tibetan donors supplemented the monastery's own savings. No state funding had been offered. Nor, I suspected, had it been asked for.

At the back of the monastery was a small building on the edge of a forest. "In there are eight monks. They have been in there for two years," explained my new friend, and then murmured with a slight laugh, "I think their beards must be very long by now!"

"Do you want to go in?" I asked. "It must be very lonely inside."

"Not lonely: peaceful. I will go in next year. I am very happy about it. Inside there are no problems, no difficulties . . ." He smiled at the thought.

I empathised with his search for enlightenment but I could not help thinking that he was running away from the problems of his people, particularly seeing as he had witnessed their sufferings at first hand in Lhasa. His search for internal harmony was doomed if the world around him was not compliant. The alternative 'harmony' being dictated to his people from afar threatened to destroy everything he stood for.

Before we left the monastery, I was introduced to a little boy who had run over in excitement: "This is one of my two students. I teach him Tibetan language. He wants to join this monastery."

The boy can hardly have been eight years old. He seemed a little young to be making that sort of life decision. But then again Tibetan monasteries also functioned as schools for young children. As well as being religious sites they were the traditional political and educational centres of Tibetan culture. Or at least they had been.

*

Dege was extremely hard to reach. The principal way to get there was to cross the Chola pass, which towers at over five thousand metres. The prospect did not deter me nor did it deter the female pilgrims who I saw on the road. But while I was in a bus, they were walking through the snow; while I was just going to Dege, they were heading for Lhasa a thousand miles further west. Their zeal was remarkable. If they succeeded, the journey would take them months. I feared that the end of their pilgrimage would bring them face to face with the disappointment of concrete high rises in Lhasa. My own detour contained a small measure of that disappointment because, by comparison to the wild and vibrant Tibetan towns I had visited, Dege proved quite sterile.

New construction was crammed into the narrow canyon that held the town. I saw a couple of new schools and shopping malls. The modernity did at least make things considerably more comfortable. For the first time in a long time I had a toilet and shower with hot water attached to my room.

Shortly after arriving I ate in a restaurant owned by a couple from Shandong. They had been lured away from their home province by the business incentives and tax breaks available to businesspeople in developing areas such Dege. Even so the situation brought difficulties for them. They missed their teenage son, who still lived in Shandong with his grandparents, and they seemed weary after the brutal Tibetan winter.

In the centre of Dege was a large square fortress. Its red walls were thick and only one small door led inside. This was the Bakong Scripture Printing Lamasery, a hugely significant site in the Tibetan religion. The building held the largest collection of Buddhist scriptures of any site on the Tibetan plateau. Inside, shelves upon shelves of wooden tablets filled every available space. It was not just a storehouse, however. On the top floor I found eight men printing scriptures in the traditional style. They inked the wooden tablets, placed thin sheets of paper on top and then pressed the paper down with rollers. The men worked in pairs and the speed was phenomenal. It had to be because orders for Bakong's scriptures came from monasteries all over the Tibetan world.

Outside, crowds of Tibetans were doing endless laps around the building. Their appearances were varied. Some had features which looked almost Middle-Eastern. It was clear that people came from all over the plateau to make a pilgrimage at this holy place. I wondered whether that was why the government encouraged Han Chinese to move to Dege: to mitigate the effect of so many united Tibetans in one place.

I laid aside my worries and joined in with the devotion. None of the Tibetans batted an eyelid. "Of course the foreigner wants to walk the kora," their faces seemed to say. "For what other purpose to life is there?"

After walking away from the Lamasery, I was approached by a little girl. "Hello," she said in English, "What is your name?"

"My name is Nico," I responded, recognising the intonation in her voice from my teaching days. "What is your name?"

"My name is Mary. How are you today?"

"I'm fine, thanks. What about you?"

"I'm fine." She stopped to think for a moment, trying to remember what came next in the textbook.

I prompted her: "How old are you?"

"I am eleven years old. What do you do?"

"I am a businessman. What about you?"

"I am a student."

After a while I tired of this formulaic English and addressed her in Mandarin. She spoke it fluently and told me that she preferred it to her native Tibetan. Her parents spoke both languages with her at home, Mary explained, but her school classes were all taught in Mandarin. I asked what her parents did and received the reply, "My father is a doctor and my mother owns some shops."

I went through the town with Mary, making for her school. She was very sociable and seemed to know everybody she bumped into in the streets. Sometimes she spoke Tibetan but more often than not she used Mandarin, even with the other little Tibetan girl who came to walk with us. She was clearly a clever and quite worldly girl. She told me that she wanted to go to America. Most of the Tibetans I had spoken to previously had seemed relatively uneducated, but not Mary.

When I left her at the school gates, she offered to sing me a song, which she had learnt in class: "Hand in hand . . . We are all family . . . Walk one thousand miles and meet in Beijing."

I applauded but felt troubled. I could see it all so clearly. Mary was well equipped to succeed in life. Her upbringing in an ambitious family and good school would set her ahead of her fellow people. The cost, however, was a high one: she was to all extents and purposes Chinese. It appeared to me an inescapable Catch Twenty Two that a Tibetan could succeed in Chinese society but only by stopping being Tibetan.

*

Dege sat on the border with the Tibetan Autonomous Region so the way west was closed to me. Another road was impassable because of the season. In order to continue my journey I was forced to retrace my steps to Ganzi.

Snow had fallen during the night. The pristine white landscape was only tainted by the dirty fumes emanating from the aged bus I was on. For a few hours progress was smooth. Then we started to climb up to the Chola Pass. I had crossed this on the way to Dege but then the way had been clear. Now the road surface was essentially sheet ice. The bus continued slowly on up until, fatally, the driver was forced to stop because of traffic ahead. Then, all forward momentum gone, we began to slide back down the slope. Fortunately, the driver seemed well used to this scenario and guided the bus expertly into a snow drift at the side of the road. Then he used a shovel to dig into the ice and laid tracks of earth in front of the wheels. After a couple of failed attempts, we finally managed to get some traction and pulled away. Just over the top of the pass I looked down and saw the shell of a burnt out truck lying in the snow. In case I had forgotten, it was a reminder of the dangers.

Prayer flags at one end of a mountain lake near Manigango

Stuck in the snow near the top of the Chola Pass

Earthquake Devastation in Yushu

Uighur butcher in the bazaar at Qiemo

Uighur women at work in a carpet factory outside Hotan

The Livestock Market outside Kashgar

Jiayuguan, the fortress on the western end of the Great Wall

Pupils of the Number 1 High School, built after the 2008
Sichuan Earthquake

The Three Gorges Dam in the rain

The Longmen Caves outside Luoyang

I had already seen Ganzi so, after arriving, I walked away from the town towards a distant monastery. When I got there it was deserted and the heavy wooden door to the main hall was locked. I turned away and was about to leave when a middle-aged monk appeared. He could speak excellent Mandarin and said that he would go to fetch the key from upstairs. He invited me to go up with him and led me into a large room. Then he offered me a cup of salty butter tea poured from a kettle on the stove.

"You have prayer beads," he said, spotting them. "Do you mind if I take a look?"

I handed them over. Many Tibetans had expressed an interest in my beads. They were a cheap set which I had bought at a shop in Shangri-la but he examined them respectfully.

"What do you say whilst you turn them?" He asked.

"Om mani padme hum."

"Yes, that is correct," he nodded approvingly.

After this ice-breaker, conversation flowed more naturally. He explained that he had been a monk for twenty five years and that he was now forty years old. "Many conditions have changed in my lifetime," he said without prompting. "There are so many pressures. Our Tibetan culture is being destroyed. It is happening very slowly but steadily. I fear that in fifty years there will be nothing left."

His words gave me a strange sense of deja-vu. Michael, the Suzhou University student, had spoken of 'fifty years' as the point in the indiscernible future when he would have his rights. For the monk I was not speaking to, however, that same fifty years was a symbol of despair, not hope.

I asked how it was happening and the monk replied, speaking slowly but determinedly, "The Tibetan people are not like you from Western countries. I think maybe seventy five per cent of people from your countries have some knowledge of their own culture. Of the Tibetans maybe only twenty five per cent do. The traditional centres of Tibetan education have always been the monasteries but now the Chinese government insists that everyone studies at one of their schools. Do you see?"

"So the monasteries are no longer allowed to educate Tibetan children?" I asked for clarification.

"Yes, that is right," he confirmed. "In Ganzi, if a policeman sees a monk talking to a child on the street, he tells the monk to move off. Children therefore have no choice but to study at Chinese schools. They must speak in Mandarin and learn Chinese characters. There are many young Tibetans now who take their names, transform them into Chinese sounds and write their signatures in Chinese characters. Maybe in fifty years' time not a single person will be able to write their name in Tibetan anymore!" As he spoke his face was passive, like that of all monks, but his voice quivered.

"I don't agree that the Chinese are forcing you to do this," I said, trying to gather my thoughts. "Just yesterday I met a little girl—a Tibetan girl—whose parents spoke Mandarin with her. That's what's destroying your culture."

"You are right that the Tibetans are doing it themselves but don't you see that they have no alternative," he responded. "I told you that only about twenty five per cent of Tibetan people have cultural knowledge. Many do not understand that they must protect their Tibetan heritage. They just watch Chinese television and hear about getting rich, and so think they must try to get rich too."

I was thinking hard, trying to keep up with what he was saying. Probably he saw my pensive expression because he explained further. "Look at it like this: the Chinese government does not allow Tibetans to study their own culture and so they think the only possible sort of good life is the sort of life the Chinese have. The Tibetan people cannot protect their heritage if they are not educated in what their heritage is. For example, twenty years ago there were over two hundred monks at this monastery but now there are fifty six. Just last year some monks wanted to open a school in Ganzi but the authorities immediately closed it . . ."

His phone rang as we were talking. He answered and spoke in a hushed voice for a few minutes. "Sorry," he said when he was finished, "Sometimes there is no signal here so it is best not to waste the opportunity to answer a call. Sometimes the authorities cut off the signal to prevent people communicating. I do not think they do that in your country, am I right?" He said with a hint of sarcasm.

"No of course not," I muttered.

"Here we must always be careful on the phone. They have a listening post in Kangding. Also in Chamdo and Lhasa."

"It's that bad?"

"Yes it is. We have no rights. Look there," he said, indicating a photo of the Dalai Lama, which stood at the end of the room. "Today that photo is allowed but tomorrow it could be taken away. If a Tibetan opens a business and there is a picture of the Dalai Lama inside, the police close it. The lives of Tibetan people are awful."

His sincere manner left me in no doubt of the truth of what he was saying but I questioned it anyway, noting that the lives of Tibetans I had met had not seemed quite as difficult as he was suggesting.

"But you only visit where the road leads," he said, fixing me with his dark eyes. "In the towns, in Ganzi and Dege, it is ok." He waggled his index and middle fingers; a Tibetan extension of the 'thumbs-up' principle. "But in the countryside, in the places where the road does not lead, it is incredibly poor." He waggled his little finger. "The houses do not even have roofs. During winter many people die. You foreigners do not see these things. The road only leads to where the government wants something, to towns and to places for mining. They come for gold, silver, iron, coal, wood, and then they build roads so the trucks can take it away."

We both mulled over what he had just said. I asked him whether there was any hope for his people.

"My dream is that one day there will be a Tibetan nation again. We have all the characteristics of a nation you know: our own language, history, script, clothing, architecture, food, religion . . ." He said before adding sorrowfully, "But that dream is impossible. The Chinese military is so powerful. Amongst all the Tibetans there is not one who has a gun . . . No, I just hope that we Tibetans can get some rights, some fair laws. Also I hope one day to have a conversation with a foreigner in Tibetan, like we are speaking Mandarin now . . ." He trailed off, lost in thought.

Although it was not his intention, I felt embarrassed by my inadequacy. Of course I had chosen to learn Mandarin above Tibetan. It was more *useful* after all. And that was just the problem. "Can countries in the West do anything to help your people?" I asked.

"You must support our right to be an independent nation. That is what the Dalai Lama says. Listen to the Dalai Lama. Some Tibetans want to fight the Chinese but the Dalai Lama calls for peace. Listen to the Dalai Lama. Support the Dalai Lama."

I asked about all the lamas and monks who had gone to Dharamsala. It seemed to me that they could make a huge difference to life on the Plateau if they returned from India.

"The monks who have been to India are not allowed to come back," he replied. "The Chinese government prevents it. My own cousin went to Dharamsala but when he tried to return to Tibet he could not. He even went to Malaysia and tried to catch a flight to China from there. He told the officials at the border that he had been on holiday but they did not believe him. They knew who he was and said that he could not possibly have taken a holiday because monks are not allowed to carry money."

We stood up and he led me to the door. A lady was waiting for him outside and she lovingly handed him 8RMB, one bill at a time. He thanked her quietly. In explanation he turned to me and said, "The government does not give our monastery any money. Everything we must raise ourselves. If we want to buy something it takes a very long time."

We descended to the gloomy prayer hall. Along the back wall were several gold-coloured statues, while the side walls were lined with yak butter Buddhist figurines. Indicating the benches for the monks to sit on, my friend repeated what he had already said about the falling numbers of the monastic community and added with pain in his voice, "Our pressure is so great. There are so many factors . . . In 2008, in Lhasa, they killed many people."

"I know," I said quietly.

"You do not really know . . . they did not allow journalists. In your country they report earthquakes, government mistakes: critical things. I know this because sometimes we can get the BBC World Service here. But in China the media are not allowed to report the bad things that happen. Last year, when Liu Xiaobo won the Nobel Peace Prize, it was not in the news."

I contained my astonishment. How on earth did he know about Liu Xiaobo?

"Also, last year in Yushu there was a huge earthquake," he went on. "Again there were no journalists. It makes me so sad . . ." His eyes welled with tears. "Very many houses fell down and so many people died."

There was nothing to be said. We shook hands. "We Tibetans have always known that happiness lies within the heart anyway, not in the outside world," he remarked pathetically, and allowed his face to smile.

"I will tell people about what you have said when I get home," I promised. It was a vow I knew I must keep.

*

As I sat in a minivan waiting to depart Ganzi the next morning, a yellow-robed monk opened the door and begged for alms. The Tibetan passenger next to me looked agitated and at first refused to give anything. The monk said a few words, clearly guilt-tricking, and eventually my neighbour threw some money over. I felt compelled to follow suit.

"That monk looked different from the others. Why was he in yellow robes?" I asked after he had gone.

"Because he is just a travelling monk; not attached to a monastery," muttered my neighbour with an angry look on his face. "The monks at the monastery are good: they do not ask for money; they help other people; they give food and clothes to children. That man is different. Monks like him are selfish and just help themselves."

I did not fully understand the various statuses of Buddhist monks. However, his comments betrayed the fragile current relationship between the ordinary Tibetan people and the holy men who they were traditionally expected to revere. Divided they would fall.

My minivan was one of eight that drove north in convoy. Each had a young Tibetan driver and the effect was predictable. We bombed along at a frightening pace; all the boy racers determined to overtake each other as many times as possible.

All of my fellow passengers bar one were Han Chinese workers heading for Yushu. Four were men and one was a woman. None of them were under the age of forty, which suggested they had come because they could not find work elsewhere. None of them enjoyed the ride much, particularly when visibility dropped and the road became icy. Whenever our driver pulled out to zip past yet another lorry, or braked sharply to avoid ploughing into a yak, they all held their breaths and muttered, "Slowly, slowly."

Unsurprisingly given the reckless driving, one of the minivans got a severe puncture in the afternoon. It took the combined efforts of all the drivers over an hour to repair it. During the delay, one of the other minivan's drivers climbed into the passenger seat to warm up. He pointed at the photo of the Dalai Lama on the dashboard and tested, "Who's this."

"I don't know," replied each of the Han passengers in turn.

*

I arrived at Shiqu in the evening. The town was covered by mist and thick snow lay on the ground. It was bitterly cold. The women driving their yak herds back from the hills wore face masks and their eyes looked at me suspiciously. Even the monks milling on the road leading up to the large monastery did not smile when I caught their eyes.

I slipped into a dark restaurant and ate a bowl of noodles. The owners were a Han couple from Chengdu, the capital of Sichuan. The thick accent of the man was hard to understand but one bit was perfectly clear: "Why have you come here? Summer is different. Summer is green and warm. But in winter and even now, in early spring, this is the worst place in China."

I laughed to myself contemptuously. I thought he was being soft and it was hard to be sympathetic to the moaning of a Han man in Tibet. If he did not like the place then he could go home.

After eating I walked over the slushy ground to the monastery. Dogs were everywhere; black, large and long-furred. Most were coiled up in little hollows in the snow. I set off walking around the kora path. The dogs ignored me until I stopped to take a photo and then three suddenly appeared in front, barking in fury. I hastily concealed my camera and hurried on. I saw a troupe of dogs racing after a motorbike, snapping at the ankles of the intimidated driver. Another pack harassed a horse, which had been tied by its owner to a post in the snow. They were like wolves. Fortunately they seemed used to people doing the kora so, after I had sheathed my camera, they left me alone.

I completed the circuit and entered the monastery complex. No monks were around. I saw light emanating from the main assembly hall and peered inside. Rows upon rows of robed figures sat in the shadows. I watched for a couple of minutes and then headed back across the courtyard to the front gate. A growl told me that I had been found. An intruder. I tried to ignore the spectre behind me. Never let a dog see that you are afraid, I thought. But more were coming. Jet black hounds were tearing across the snow towards me, barking ecstatically. Animal instinct took over. I wheeled around to face the beasts behind me. Five hell-phantoms glared back, not barking now. Four had milky-white eyes and the fifths were glowing red. I heard more pounding behind me. I was being cut off.

And then two monks ran out from a grey building to my side. "Shh," is all they said "Shh."

The dogs cantered away. And only then did my heart start pounding.

CHAPTER 12

The Way to the Holy Mountain

I was driven across the pass that separated Sichuan from Qinghai the next morning. I left the sharp terrain of Kham lay behind me and entered the Tibetan region of Amdo, which was known for rolling plateau that rarely dipped below two miles high. Near the border the white mist was the same shade as the white snow. The world became one smooth and dark continuum. I saw a nomad driving his yaks across the wilderness; a speck in the unyielding emptiness.

My minibus descended down out of the snow line and passed heavy trucks on the road. A tell-tale sign of destruction started to appear: blue canvas tents. I had been hearing about Yushu since I first found myself among the Tibetans. All the roads had been leading there and now I had arrived. The earthquake that struck Yushu in April 2010 decimated the old Tibetan town and—according to an official figure that had been disputed because of the absence of independent journalists in the region—killed 2698 people. Before the quake, Yushu's population had been ninety seven per cent Tibetan and its position on the borders of Tibet, Qinghai and Sichuan had made it one of China's most remote regions. I wanted to see what the authorities were doing to rebuild the town. The true test of a government was how it looks after its people in times of need.

When I disembarked from the minibus I found rubble. A huge bronze statue of King Gezar, the Tibetans' most famous folk hero, towered defiantly in the main square but all around him lay a swathe of destruction. Barely a wall stood undamaged. And everywhere were the same blue tents. They were pitched in the wreckage of houses, in the main square, by the river . . . Every aspect of life was covered inside them. They functioned as homes, canteens, grocery stores, antique dealers, paint shops and medical clinics.

I set off walking through the town. The streets were hives of activity. Almost every person I saw was working in one reconstruction capacity or another. Among others there were men driving diggers to clear away the bricks left by destroyed houses, electricians unravelling long coils of wire and lackeys hoisting supplies. The faces of the workers were varied. Tibetans beamed at me, a clean shaven Hui Muslim in a white cap watched me carefully and several Han Chinese gawped unashamedly as I passed. Few foreigners can have passed through since the quake. Although it was over a year since the event, the area had been closed off in the aftermath and then the long winter had made the region hard to access. It was now late April but the weather was still harsh. Even when I was walking around a sudden blizzard whipped up and sent everybody running for cover.

It was difficult to estimate what proportion of people doing the work were Han Chinese but I guessed about half. I spoke to several, including four workers from Lanzhou who had come to build houses; an electrician from Chengdu who was working on wiring; and a man from Xi'an, who was selling steamed buns. All had come for the work opportunities presented by the catastrophe and all planned to stay in Yushu for several months at the very least. Their help was of course indispensable but I wondered what would happen when the work was finished and Yushu stood reconstructed. Where would they all go?

Having climbed up to what had been Yushu's monastery, I surveyed the devastated valley from above. Poking out from the destruction were several electrical pylons. They were the most prominent signs of the reconstruction work being done. I was no judge of what constituted an effective response to an earthquake but it did seem that progress was slow. Everybody was still living in tents and having to use unhygienic communal toilets, which stank unimaginably.

Back into the centre of town I entered a small restaurant inside a tent. The owner had been working out of the canvas structure for almost a year and had partially decorated it. There was a stove attached to a chimney, and a light bulb cast shadows around the tiled interior. A Tibetan man was eating on the table adjacent to mine. I guessed from the lines around his small eyes that he was over fifty years old. I asked him what job he did.

"I do business; I sell yak butter," he replied in a slow voice.

"Was your home destroyed in the quake?" I asked, trying to sound as sensitive as possible.

"Yes. My home used to be below the monastery. Everything up there was destroyed."

"Is your home going to be rebuilt?"

"They are going to build new homes there but the Government will not give me the land back. They say they will provide a house for me in a different area. I do not want to live in a different area. That land is mine!"

I asked him where his future house would be but he said that he had not yet been told. He did, however, tell me of the plans for the area where his previous home had been, saying, "They are going build apartments. Then they will sell the homes to Han people with money."

Outside again, I continued looking around. Fluttering wherever construction was on-going were red Chinese flags. Artists' impressions on large billboards depicted the future developments. There was something disturbingly familiar about the regimented town that was going to be slung up.

I knew that remote enclaves removed from central authority were not what the CPC wanted. I could not help but reflect on how long it would have taken the Government to send the wrecking ball into Yushu themselves if the earthquake had not done the dirty work for them.

I followed the road out of town to a famous pile of stones; an enormous pile of stones. Each individual one had sacred Tibetan texts carved into it and there were an estimated two billion stones in total. This, the Seng-ze Gyanak Mani, was one of the largest such sacred sites on the entire Plateau. And here, though blue tents lay just across the road, crowds of Tibetans were continuing undaunted. Walking, walking, walking. Amid all devastation, I could not help but feel a twinkle of admiration for the resilience of their religious faith. For when everything was reduced to piles of stones, what more appropriate thing was there than to worship at a pile of stones? The Tibetans smiled as I joined them and together we did the kora. They understood that nothing was permanent anyway. They were wonderful people but their greatest strength was also their greatest weakness. They could not help themselves if all they wanted to do was worship.

*

The next morning I stood by the side of the road outside Yushu and tried to flag down buses heading north. All the new buses that streaked past were empty but all the drivers refused to stop. After a long wait, one Han driver did come to a halt and I climbed on. A second driver was dozing in the back but otherwise the fifty-seat bus had no passengers. I asked why all the previous drivers had not stopped.

"We are not allowed to take passengers," replied the driver. "Every second day we drive full buses of workers from Xining but when we drive back we cannot take anyone. There is a checkpoint ahead. Because you are a foreigner, it should be ok."

Further down the road several people, mostly Tibetans, tried to signal the bus as we sailed by. The driver did not stop for them. On the opposite side of the road, heading towards Yushu, I saw full sleeper buses. They had travelled over night from Xining, the provincial capital of Qinghai, with their cargo of workers. A couple of moments after we had passed one such bus, I looked back and saw it launching into a full three hundred and sixty degree spin as it caught the ice on a hairpin corner. Remarkably all four wheels were still on the tarmac when it ground to a halt. I shuddered to think of the carnage that might easily have ensued.

After a couple of hours we reached the checkpoint at Qingshui and the driver climbed down, looking anxious. He returned with a policeman who looked little elder than myself. He was wearing shades for sinister effect and stared at me icily. I put on my best 'stupid foreigner' look and pretended I could not speak Chinese.

"Who's this?" The policeman asked the driver.

"A foreigner. An official at the bus station in Yushu said he could board," he lied.

Clearly the policeman did not know what the rule was as regards me and only fleetingly glanced at my passport. He looked at my face hard and then appeared to decide that I would cause him more problems off the bus than on. He proceeded to search the bus for other passengers.

I reflected that allowing people in but not allowing anybody out was an extremely effective way of controlling access to the Yushu area.

"I was almost dying of fright just then," said my saviour after we had been allowed to pull away. "I wasn't sure what they would do. Obviously you're a foreigner but I could have received a big fine."

The road was very smooth. It was by far the best road I had experienced since Yunnan. I was told that it had been built after the quake to quicken access to the area. While I acknowledged the good it served in making relief efforts faster, I did not want to contemplate the long term prospects for Yushu now it was an easy day's drive from Xining. In several previous places I had seen the negative impact on minority culture caused by too close proximity to major Chinese cities. In one blow the earthquake had destroyed Yushu more completely than could be measured in statistics.

*

Maqin sat within striking distance of Amnye Machen, a holy Tibetan mountain, but its own Tibetan roots lay scattered. A wide boulevard ran through the middle of the town and contained the usual stalwarts: an Agricultural Bank of China and large Public Security Bureau. Most of the occupants I saw in the main square were Han men playing Mah-jong.

I found a dirty room in an ageing concrete hotel and set out to look around in the Tibetan district, which covered a small area on the edge of town. I passed Tibetan children walking home from school; their tracksuits and knapsacks very familiar. The prayer wheels in shrines on the hillside were being dutifully spun by a few aged women but the place had no soul. There was no concentration; no focal point: there was no monastery. Without monks, the Tibetan religion was rudderless. It was reduced to devoted laypeople walking around in circles.

Feeling depressed, I walked back into town and saw a crowd has gathered outside the police station. I moved closer, trying to avoid drawing attention to myself. A man was sitting in the road. He was a sorry sight. His face was covered in bruises and his lips were swollen. It was hard to see clearly but the fingers on his right hand appeared to be broken. He was bobbing his head slowly up and down and sobbing without tears. Nobody in the crowd moved to help him. They all just watched, knowing what had happened.

A police car pulled up because the crowd was blocking the entrance to the station. I moved away and spied from a doorway. There was nothing dramatic. The policemen spoke to a few people and shortly afterwards everyone started to trickle away. The battered man was made to move to one side and then the police car drove through the gates.

*

From Maqin I hitched a ride with a jeep-full of pilgrims. Tibetans walked around stupas, they walked around monasteries and they walked around mountains too. Amnye Machen was the holiest mountain in Amdo and a focal point for worship.

It was late April and some colour was starting to show on the hills. The pure white mass of the mountain stood out from the green land around. Even well into the twentieth century, before proper surveys were carried out, Amnye Machen had been considered a candidate for the highest mountain in the world because it rose so dominantly above the surrounding terrain. In fact it was only 6282m high; a figure that was only established when it was first successfully climbed in 1981.

I went to Amnye Machen with half a mind to walk a section of the kora but quickly realised that I lacked sufficient cash to hire the necessary equipment and guide. I had to content myself with visiting the hamlet that rested at the start of the pilgrim route. On arrival I climbed up a steep hillside in order to get a clear view of the distant peak. My breath rasped in my throat and I quickly became tired. Although I had been at altitude for a month, the thinness of the air was still noticeable. A Tibetan shepherd was reclining on the grass at the top of the hill. I walked over and sat beside him, breathing heavily. I explained that I was English and then asked whether he considered himself Tibetan or Chinese.

"Chinese of course. This is China," he replied, taking me by surprise. "Soon China's military will be the biggest in the world," he boasted. "Even now, England, Germany and France together cannot match it!" His Mandarin was heavily accented but probably better than my own.

"I don't know about that," I said. "Anyway, why does it matter? We don't want to fight."

"Yes you do! You like invading other countries. Look how you've invaded Iraq, Afghanistan and now Libya. It is we Chinese who don't want to fight. We love peace."

The NATO action in Libya was receiving plenty of coverage in the state media, particularly seeing as the conflict was at that point seemingly far from resolution. I found myself on the defensive: "Anyway, just because in China the Government says it likes peace . . . well . . . It's just . . . You have wars in your own country! I mean look at you Tibetans! I've just come through Western Sichuan and I've seen it for myself! Don't you think you're being crushed by the Chinese?'"

"The Kham Tibetans are different from us Amdo Tibetans," he replied. "In Kham they are always fighting and so it's right for the Government to prevent chaos. I like being part of China. We are becoming a great country. We are going to put a man on the moon. You English have never put a man on the moon, am I right?"

"I'm not sure."

"Well you haven't."

"But what does putting a man on the moon matter?"

"Our leaders at the moment are very good," he went on, ignoring my question. "Hu Jintao, Wen Jiabao . . . Mao was great: we all used to worship him . . . And Zhou Enlai."

His sheep had taken the opportunity of his distraction to scatter over a wide area and so he went to herd them back together.

I stumbled back down the hill to the village, which was little more than a cluster of low buildings scattered along a dirt track. A couple of the houses had spare beds for travellers and the simple restaurant where I ate conveniently had photos on the menu. I spotted a woman wearing a jumper that had '008 COOK NO CHEILY CFHGE' printed across the back. If distance from modern civilisation could be measured in the garbling of the English language then her jumper said a lot.

Down by the stream running through the village I saw four deer. They did not move for such a long time that I thought they were models. Then, when I approached closer, they all galloped away. As I was walking back to my room, a man in the red robes of a monk called me over. He had a muscular build and short hair. From the shortage of facial stubble, I guessed he was quite young. He introduced himself in English as Lama Wocai and welcomed me to the village. After a couple of sentences we switched to Mandarin, which he spoke fluently.

"Since you have come here I would like to teach you about the god Amnye Machen," he began in a calm and authoritative manner. "He is the lord of this area and rules over the people. He used to communicate with the locals very often but his revelations are much fewer these days. Some years ago, Amnye Machen saw how difficult life was becoming on the plateau. He decided to leave for India but another deity persuaded him to stay. She told him that if he went, the Tibetan people would forget their religion. And so he is still here, but his back is turned and he faces towards Dharamsala."

According to Tibetans mythology, their gods did not live on their mountains like the Greek gods on Olympus but rather they were the mountain. They saw the entire Tibetan Plateau as a living entity of insuperable majesty. Lama Wocai's anecdote about Amnye Machen struck me as very relevant to the current plight of the Tibetan people. They were divided, confused and indecisive, and it seemed their gods were too.

I asked Lama Wocai whether he was from the area.

"Oh no, my family is in Sichuan. But it is my purpose to be here. I am a lama; a living Buddha. I was recognised as the reincarnation of the previous lama when I was eight years old. Now I am twenty two," he explained. "My previous incarnation predicted that I would come here and so I came. At first it was very difficult for me because I could not understand the Amdo Tibetan language. It is so different from the language in the Kham region. But slowly I learnt. Now I teach the local people about the Buddhist scriptures and about being a good person. I teach them not to kill, not to steal, not to drink alcohol, not to smoke: that sort of thing. Many of the elder people understand—those aged forty and fifty—but it is more difficult with young people."

I was listening intently and did not interrupt. Lama Wocai remarked that I seemed a very wise man. I thought it was telling that he associated silence with depth of thought. It said a lot about Tibetan attitudes.

When I mentioned that I had come from Yushu, the lama's eyes took on the expression of sadness, which I had seen in the faces of so many people before. "What has happened there is terrible. But it is their own fault! The people in Yushu do not respect the Dalai Lama!" He proclaimed, referring to sectarian splits, which existed in Tibetan Buddhism just like other religions. "Now look what has happened to them: an earthquake and all their current problems! It is so important to respect the Dalai Lama. We must listen to the Dalai Lama."

I was shocked by his attitude. Attributing natural disasters to bad karma seemed strange to me and insulted my rational mind. Tibetan Buddhism had undisputable profundity but in a day to day sense I could not help but think its adherents might as well have been walking around with their eyes closed. I hid my disillusionment and asked, "Have you ever seen the Dalai Lama?"

"Yes," he said with a glow in his eye, "I went to Dharamsala in 2005. I stayed there for eight months and twice heard him preach. I have a large photo of him at home. Come to my home and I will show it to you."

I went with him to his house. It had two rooms: a living room for cooking and the room where he slept. An old television stood in the corner of the latter. "What did the Dalai Lama say when you heard him speak?" I enquired

"I do not know. The Dalai Lama speaks the language of Central Tibet. It is very different from the languages of Kham and Amdo. I could not understand a word but it was very special to listen to him."

A girl came in and served up tsampa. Then she sat down next to Wocai and started to tickle his feet. It was evident that she was more than a cook. Reading my expression, Wocai pointed out that he was a lama, not a monk. He had taken no monastic vows and was free to live as a normal man.

As we ate, Lama Wocai explained how he had introduced rules that helped the people of Amnye Machen preserve the Tibetan culture. Most interesting was one whereby the locals were not allowed to mix Mandarin and Tibetan in speech. In a conversation they could speak one language or the other but crossover was banned on pain of a fine. The idea was to prevent the Tibetan language becoming corrupted.

It was evident that Wocai's status as a Living Buddha gave him the respect of the local people and the mandate to exercise authority. He had provided to his small and isolated community the leadership that the Tibetan people as a whole—traditionally reliant on their Buddhist theocracy—so needed and so sorely lacked.

I knew, however, that the traditional hierarchy extant in the politically-irrelevant backdrop of Amnye Machen had not been allowed in the other areas I had travelled. I had seen how the monasteries had been restricted and how Tibetan resistance to Chinese rule had been reduced to uneducated, disoriented anger. I thought I understood what 'social harmony' meant as regards the Tibetans: divide and conquer.

*

I returned to Maqin the next day and discovered that no buses were leaving until the following morning. However, I found a policeman waiting outside the bus station who was driving to Xining that afternoon. He invited me to ride with him, we agreed on a price and immediately set off.

The policeman was a Tibetan but also a CPC member. He explained that his five year old daughter lived with his parents in a distant town. He and his wife, who was also in the police force, saw her only once every few months. Those pressures sounded familiar to me.

When I plucked up the courage to ask him whether he, a Tibetan but also a Party member, enjoyed living under Chinese rule, he simply replied,

"China is a country of fifty six ethnic groups." Beyond that, he did not elaborate.

He did, however, make an interesting remark when I asked him what his ambitions as a policeman were. "Of course I would like to be successful," he said, "but I do not want to reach the very top. I think that to reach the top you must have a good head but a bad heart. I do not want that."

At one point in the late afternoon I saw a large horse festival taking place on a slope to the left of the road. Colourfully dressed young men were riding bareback with their reins gathered in one hand like cowboys.

The policeman and I gradually relaxed into each other's company and he started asking me about England. Of particular interest to him was the cost of a bow and arrows. He explained that it was too expensive for him to buy the best quality bows in China because they were imported and had large taxes slapped on. This revelation made me warm to him slightly. He might be a Party Cadre but at least he liked archery!

He drove along at a tremendous pace, only slowing down when he saw yaks in the road ahead. It was a wise but unnecessary precaution. These yaks invariably had road-sense and scurried away at the car's approach. While it was a relief not to have to brake constantly, I nostalgically deemed that those yaks had lost something of that which made them Tibetan.

We crossed that icon of the Chinese world, the Yellow River, and began the long but gradual descent into Xining. My driver picked up yet more speed as the road widened and flattened out. On the final stretch of motorway he clocked over 140 Km/h. Cameras flashed as we passed but, as he explained, policemen were allowed to break the speed limit.

It was night by the time I was dropped off on a busy street in Xining, but not really dark. The lights of the big city shone all around me.

CHAPTER 13

When the Battle is Won

Xining exhibited all the characteristics of a flourishing Chinese city. Most of the money slung at Qinghai province by the Central Government seemed to have ended up in the provincial capital. Wealth, or at least relative wealth, was visible in the glitzy neon lights and in the western cars jamming the wide boulevards. The atmosphere of the city was pleasant but was not particularly inspiring to someone like me who had seen the same style of city several times elsewhere. However, I was tired from four weeks in the mountains so the charms of plumbing and clean sheets were infinitely magnified. The Chinese girls in their high heels and tight-fitting jeans also reminded me of what I had been missing during the roughness of the previous month. I paused for a few days to get my energy back.

Within the city, apart from the majority Han, there were a few Tibetans and a considerable Hui Muslim community. They formed a large proportion of the population in that region of China but were quite well integrated throughout the rest of the country too. By contrast to the Tibetans they made no claim to independence because they had historically always lived under Chinese authority anyway.

The Hui men tended to dress smartly with shining white skull caps perched on their scalps, while the women wore graceful silk veils. But any illusions I might have had about the Hui's refined ways were shattered when I walked into a backstreet in Xining's Hui district and found two brothels within twenty paces of each other. Fat Muslim girls with their breasts bulging out of their tops stood in the doorways. One rotund hooker, whose face was caked in make-up and lipstick, beckoned me to come inside. I smiled friendlily but did not feel particularly tempted.

A few sites of significance to the Tibetan people were within striking distance of Xining. On one day trip I went to Ping'an, the town in which the current Dalai Lama was born. Unfortunately, on the day I visited his home was closed to visitors. The Chinese authorities were being especially vigilant that month because it was the 60th anniversary of the Seventeen Point Agreement, the treaty by which the defeated Tibetans had ceded sovereignty of their land to the People's Republic of China in 1951.

On another excursion I went to the Kumbum Monastery. This was traditionally considered one of the six most important monasteries in Tibetan Buddhism. It was situated about twenty miles from the centre of the city on the burial site of Tsongkhapa, a late-fourteenth-century Buddhist leader who founded the Yellow Hat sect; the dominant branch of the Tibetan religion.

But when I visited I was disappointed. English notice boards stood outside each of the halls. Monks were scarce and tour leaders with microphones shattered any remnants of stillness. Despite the fine architecture and luxuriousness of the various temples, the atmosphere was destroyed by the hordes of visitors. Kumbum's long and illustrious history now lay in the past. These days it was less a monastery and more a tourist attraction.

The treatment of the heritage at Kumbum was dictated on the terms of the Chinese authorities. On all the information boards I read, great play was made of how the state's policies were 'protecting' sites of national importance. Certainly the roofs were gleaming and the statues were well polished, but I imagined the monastery could have done without those things. To my eyes, the 'protection' had, deliberately or not, ripped the soul out of the place.

*

Having rested and regained my zeal, I decided it was time to move on. Inside Xining's bus station there was anarchy. Tomb Sweeping Day, one of China's traditional festivals, meant everybody had the first weekend of May on holiday. Long lines of men and women jostled for position at the ticket counters.

Once I had bought my ticket and boarded the bus, however, the journey proceeded very quickly. Just like I had experienced outside Kunming in Yunnan province, the motorway leading out of Xining did not pass over the mountains but rather went through them. The tunnels made the journey much shorter and within a couple of hours I was in Tongren.

On first impressions the town was ugly. Concrete was the primary building material in the modern district. Many of the structures also had white tile facades, which made them look like the inside of public toilets. After a bit of exploration, however, I revised my opinion. I made my way to the large monastery standing among the more aesthetically-pleasing Tibetan houses. The pavement leading up to it was blocked by small stalls. Hui ladies were selling bread beside Tibetan ladies hawking off yak skins.

In the monastery I got the first good look of what I had come to see. In a small exhibition room was a collection of thangka; Tibetan religious art. These incredibly detailed canvases were an important feature of Tibetan culture and it was in Tongren that many of them were produced.

A friendly curator pointed out details for me to distinguish the various deities by: the seven eyes of White Tara, the thousand arms of Guanyin, the two disciples beside Sakyamuni . . . I looked, listened and tried to remember.

When the curator learnt that I was from England, he remarked in an off-handed manner that we had invaded Libya recently. I felt it was pointless to comment. What use was my word against the might of the state media?

Heading away from the monastery I found a few small studios where artists were working. Thangka artists painted with needle-thin brushes and with their faces just inches away from the canvasses. The concentration required was extraordinary. As was explained to me, the production of one of these pieces was in itself a religious experience; a chance for the artist to draw closer to the deity being depicted.

I met one Tibetan, calling himself by the Chinese name of Jiaxijiancuo, who was in the process of painting Guanyin on a black and gold background. He said that it would take him three months to complete the work. Now aged twenty three, he explained that he had been painting as an apprentice since the age of eight. He himself had just taken on his first apprentice, a sixteen year old boy.

In an extraordinary act of generosity, Jiaxijiancuo gave me a postcard-sized thangka as a gift. It had taken him five days to paint. I wanted to pay but he refused, saying that small thangka were almost unsellable anyway. Most orders now came not from monasteries but from private collectors, and it was big artworks that were most popular.

Wanting to show my gratitude, I invited him and his nineteen year old wife to dinner. She was pregnant with their child and said not a word. She did, however, write down the order at the restaurant. Jiaxijiancuo was illiterate because he had never gone to school.

*

Just outside Tongren was Wutun Si. Every hall in this monastery, which was split into an upper and lower section, had been reconstructed in the last thirty years. It had taken a severe battering during the Cultural Revolution; its ease of access from Xining and its association with religious culture having made it an obvious target. For it was there that some of Tibet's finest thangka were produced.

I went and watched, and watched, and watched. The thangka came to life before my eyes as I sat quietly on stools in the corners of various workshops. Most compelling was the patience of the painters. Every tiny brush stroke was measured and deliberate. One young man spent well over an hour on a section of one square centimetre. There was something profoundly spiritual in the strive for perfection. But the closer an artist got to perfection, the harder the road became. After many hours, I started being able to discern how some thangka were better than others. Colour control, detailing and the overall symmetry of the canvasses all varied from one to the next.

I had already resolved to acquire a second thangka by the time Lama Losang Pandan found me. He led me to his workshop and started talking. Apparently he had exhibited in Paris and had a back-log of commissions so long that it would take him years to complete. The key to his success was partly down to the quality of his pieces—they were, to my increasingly sharp eye, seriously good—but the rest was down to salesmanship. He showed me photos of him with innumerable customers; he took out his order book to prove how in demand he was; he explained how his age, forty, was the best age for producing thangka . . . The clincher was less his manner and more the fact that he had exactly what I was looking for. A golden Wenshu, Bodhisattva of Wisdom, flashed his eyes at me from the wall and I knew that it was the one.

After a lively round of bargaining I came away satisfied. Looking back I was not even sure whether Losang Pandan was a genuine lama. But he was a natural businessman and, as he made clear, the majority of his thangka were sold to newly-rich Han Chinese in Beijing, Shanghai and Guangzhou. No doubt those nouveau riche buyers thought they were getting a piece of 'real Tibet.' Most had no idea what that meant anyway.

*

Xiahe hung on the very edge of the Tibetan plateau just across the border from Qinghai in Gansu Province. Lying to the west of the small town was Labrang, another of the six seminal monasteries in Tibetan Buddhism. But, in stark contrast to the sterility of Kumbum outside Xining, Labrang was still a fully functioning religious establishment.

There were streams of pilgrims on the kora path. The weather-beaten faces; the thick clothes; the prayer beads thumbed in the left hand; the strange way in which the women leant forward, as if carrying a heavy load . . . all were familiar to me. Just as familiar was the activity they were engaged in: walking, walking, walking.

Whereas the devotion of the lay people was similar to what I had seen before, the activity of the monastic community was markedly different. I followed the crowds and ended up in the philosophy garden. Over two hundred monks were sitting in a large tent watching a debate. One novice stood in the middle and chanted, interrupting his own flow only to pose questions to a small circle of elder monks. It was a lively affair. Every now and then a section of the sitting monks would stand up and applaud wildly. I had absolutely no idea what was going on but it made for compelling viewing.

On the grass around the tent sat clusters of Tibetan men and women. Most were paying attention to the debate but a few were chatting quietly to their friends. The atmosphere was primarily social, not scholarly. It was good fun. This, I guessed, was how the religion was supposed to be.

I was shown around the rest of the monastery by a young monk who spoke excellent English. He had studied in Xining for three years so that he could be of service to the community as a guide to visitors. The temples he led me into were vibrant with spirituality. Whereas at Kumbum the statues had been fenced off behind barriers, here there was no obstruction between the worshippers and their deities.

I received a commentary on the philosophies and theologies contained within the Tibetan religion. It was fair to say that, without hard study, its depths were completely inaccessible. My capable guide did his best to satisfy my curiosity but came unstuck in the hall of the Seventh Buddha while trying to explain why the Tibetans believed there were one thousand Buddhas, and why the current Buddha was only the fourth. After I had asked yet another question, he turned to me with a patient smile on his face and said, "It is difficult for me to say in English. I do not want to say something wrong. We Tibetans believe that if you cannot speak the truth you should not speak at all."

We moved onto the subject of burial. The Tibetan tradition was 'sky burial,' whereby corpses were cut up in a special ceremony and left to the vultures. The purpose of this was both to effectively dispose of bodies, which could not be easily buried in the frozen winter ground, and also to release the soul of the departed from the flesh. However, my guide said that most monks were now cremated instead.

"Why is that?" I asked.

"Sky burial is the tradition but these days there are few vultures at the burial sites. I think it is because we Tibetans now use some western medicines. The vultures do not like the taste."

"Do the vultures refuse to eat the bodies?"

"Yes that sometimes happens," he said with a slight wince, "So now we mainly use cremation."

At the conclusion of the tour he led me into an exhibition room where intricate sculptures made entirely from yak butter were on display.

"Do you have problems with the Chinese government here at Labrang?" I asked. I had been avoiding the topic until that point out of respect for the holy atmosphere of the temples.

"No there are no problems."

"But I heard that, in 2008, some monks were killed."

"No monks were killed here."

"But there were protests?"

"Some monks were put in prison; that is all."

"But you said there were no problems?"

"I do not want problems. I just want peace."

He looked upset but I persisted. "Can you practise your religion freely here?"

"Yes the religion is free. Politics is not free but religion is free."

"But that could all change. Lots of the halls you are showing me have been rebuilt. They were damaged in the Cultural Revolution weren't they?"

"Yes, some were. But now it is much better. I am happy to be a monk."

I marvelled at how he could be so naïve. The Communists might no longer have been cracking down on religion for ideological reasons as they had in the earlier years of their rule, but they could still not tolerate anything that undermined their authority. I said as such, perhaps a little too harshly.

"I understand what you mean," he replied in a soft voice. "But I do not want to fight. Many monks have difficulties with this. We must protect the religion but we love peace and compassion . . ."

To the east of the monastery I saw a soldier bouncing a basketball in the courtyard of a military barracks. The barracks was small but I realised it did not need to be any bigger. It was easy to keep an eye on people whose thoughts were in the sky.

I retraced my steps to Xining. Tibetan architecture, Muslim architecture and Chinese architecture combined in the villages I passed. The cultural melting pot hinted at where my feet were now leading.

Tibet lay behind and a new journey lay in front. I was heading west into the heart of Asia. I was heading along the Silk Road.

CHAPTER 14

One Province: Two Worlds

I took an overnight train from Xining with a load of migrant workers. It was over a month since I had last caught a train and the relative comforts of hard sleeper were not wasted on me after all my extended bus journeys. The train was bound for Lhasa but I disembarked in the morning at Golmud, a city quite literally in the middle of nowhere. I was invited to breakfast by a construction worker from Hunan. He had not seen his wife and two year old daughter in months.

Then I boarded a rickety old bus, the driver strapped my rucksack to the roof and we set off west. The nondescript town of Huatugou lay on the Qinghai-Xinjiang border. Little more than a collection of cul-de-sacs, its existence was partly explained by the oil fields nearby. Pump-jacks bob up and down like prehistoric pterodactyls in the beige emptiness.

I did not linger and crossed into Xinjiang on a bus whose occupants were mostly Han Chinese. They were very curious about me, questioning why I was travelling alone, how much my watch was worth and whether I liked Chinese food . . . I replied as best I could and reflected that the Han people in remote areas were both less pretentious and friendlier than their city counterparts.

"Do you squat when you go to the toilet?" Asked one man dressed, like all Han migrant workers, in black trousers and black shoes.

"Yes, sometimes," I replied, thinking he was referring to when I was travelling.

"Outside?"

"If I have to."

The man looked puzzled. "I didn't realise that you had outdoor toilets in the West too. On TV it always seems that western toilets are inside . . ."

He thought for a while and then asked for clarification: "So you have an outdoor squat toilet at your home?"

I could not be bothered rectifying the misunderstanding. "Yes," I said.

*

I had started the day on the corner of the Tibetan Plateau at an altitude of over two thousand metres but by the time I reached Ruoqiang I was almost at sea level. The Tarim Basin, the huge depression in the heart of Xinjinag, brought its own climate. I climbed off the bus into the heat.

It was here, perched on the South Eastern corner of the Taklimakan Desert, that I first encountered the Uighurs. I was struck by the variety in their faces. Most had the dark features of Middle-Easterners but some had more olive-coloured skin with mousey brown hair.

The different culture meant I had to become accustomed to a new style of food. I ate kebabs and Nan breads in restaurants that were situated in basements to escape the heat and the flies. Apart from this, I found Ruoqiang dull, though I did chuckle at the names of the wide empty boulevards: 'Happiness Street', 'Peace Alley' and 'Liberation Road.'

I stayed a night in a large hotel that was owned by a Han Chinese couple. Xinjiang was prominent in the CPC's efforts to 'Develop the West' and this pair had been enticed by the incentives offered.

I caught another bus the next morning and continued relentlessly west. The road was flat and the landscape outside utterly barren: gravelly, grey and dusty. The only sign of civilisation off the road was the long line of electric pylons that stretched parallel to it. The bus passed few other vehicles.

This route had once been the southern branch of the iconic Silk Road. All the talk in China was of building a 'Modern Silk Road' into the heart of Asia, but I saw precious little evidence of development. The vast expanse of desert stretched to the horizon.

The bus went through a handful Uighur towns built on the sites of green oases. Young men played pool on tables by the roads and ate freshly baked Nan breads in shaded porches. The spire of an occasional mosque poked out from behind trees. There were rarely any women about.

Qiemo lay at the end of the day's drive. Its population was mostly Uighur but, just as on the previous night, the owner of the hotel where I stayed was a Han Chinese lady. She explained that she and her husband came to work there from March to October and then returned to their home province, Henan, for the winter. They too had been encouraged to set up business by the favourable economic incentives.

"Why have you come here?" The wife said, only half-jokingly. "It's the most boring place in China!"

Walking around, I thought the feel was similar to Ruoqiang. The street plan conformed to regular Han archetypes and once again I was subjected to vomit-inducing road names. Otherwise, the Uighur lifestyle dominated. There were a couple of mosques, a bazaar and lots of street food.

With difficulty, I found my way to the town's museum. It was difficult because none of the Uighurs seemed to understand my Mandarin. Whether they were unable or whether they chose not to, was a question I could not answer. Inside the museum was an exhibition on the archaeological sites in the desert to the north. Within striking distance of Qiemo were buried civilisations that formed part of Silk Road lore. Most notable was the ancient town of Loulan, which was abandoned because of the advancing desert sands in 330AD. Over the course of the twentieth century, excavations on the site yielded large numbers of preserved corpses, some of which dated back four thousand years. Two of these 'Tarim Mummies' were on display in the museum. Both had pointy noses and yellowing teeth. Their skin looked a little leathery but they still wore the remnants of clothing. Something else was clear from their appearance, though maybe it was just that I expected to see it: both looked indefinably European. The DNA signature of the Tarim Mummies was the source of considerable controversy but experts agreed that they were at least partly Caucasian. This issue did not merely concern academics and Silk Road fanatics; it was politically sensitive too. To counteract Chinese claims to Xinjiang, the Uighurs argued that they were the indigenous people of the region. The ancestry of the mummies was a high profile factor in the debate.

But I was not in Xinjiang to choose sides in the independence debate. It was a moot point anyway, because the Chinese were not going to let the region go. Instead I was there, just like at every other point of my trip, to see how well everybody was getting by.

Qiemo did not provide me with much insight. Apart from the museum there was very little of note in the town. Everyone's lives were just ticking on in the rather dusty environment.

*

I went from Qiemo to Hotan in one long day. The oasis towns I passed through were all Uighur. I saw the occasional donkey-drawn cart with goats cluttered in the back, and some earthen homesteads. On the long stretches between the towns, tarmac and dust were only enlivened by China Mobile telecom towers and petrol stations. So much for camels, merchants and Silk Road myth.

Even on the bus the atmosphere was dull. Uighur men with shaved heads and tidy beards patiently watched the movies shown on the bus' TV screen. These movies had frequent violent sections, which were allowed to run, but at the approach of anything resembling romance the Uighur driver skipped forward to the next scene. The women wore shawls and stared straight ahead. Neither men nor women seemed eager to start a conversation and they all kept themselves to themselves.

I reached Hotan late at night and booked into a very cheap hotel with two hardy French cyclers en route to Paris. The hotel room was about as far from the sophisticated charms of the city of love as it was possible to imagine. The sheets were yellowing, were covered in brown stains and stank of mature sweat. The air conditioning did not work and the toilet outside in the corridor smelt like a rat had died somewhere in the pipes.

The three of us went out to grab some food. It was Sunday evening and the mess from the daytime bazaar was visible everywhere. Litter and food lined the streets. We grabbed some greasy kebabs but none of us had much of an appetite. The prospect of returning to the room did not make for ease of digestion. When I did finally go to bed I slept fitfully in the smothering heat.

*

The areas I had come through had been sparsely populated and had been defined much more by the sand than the people, but Hotan was different. It lay to the south-west of the Taklimakan desert, in an oasis that was sufficiently lush to provide for a large city. Of more historical significance were jade deposits, which had made Hotan a significant trading post on the Silk Road. Nowadays the Han migration into Xinjiang was advancing steadily to the north of the Taklimakan but the regions to the south were still relatively untouched. Hotan's geographical location meant that its population remained almost completely Uighur.

In the morning after my arrival I ate a breakfast of noodles and cinnamon tea while sitting on a raised platform beside a main road. The streets were bustling but virtually none of the Uighurs in sight was a woman. It was men who drove the taxis, men who served at the restaurants, men who baked the Nan breads and men who stood in the shops. Whenever a small group of shawled Uighur women did pass by, I noted how their legs and arms were completely covered.

There was some confusion when I came to pay the bill for the meal. The owner tried to charge me twice as much as he had said originally, claiming I had misunderstood. I had a suspicion that he was using the excuse of his poor Mandarin to cheat me.

After we had agreed to halve the difference, I caught a bus to a traditional carpet factory beyond the dried bed of the Jade Dragon River. Inside the factory were lines of middle-aged women working away at looms. Using just knives, combs, and the dexterity of their fingers, they were producing beautifully colourful woollen carpets. Each lady had a section of roughly seventy centimetres by twenty centimetres that she was expected to complete in a day. Since some of the finished products were over ten metres long and five metres wide, even with teams of workers coordinating I it could take months just to complete one carpet.

Many of the women could not understand Mandarin. One managed to explain that she had been working there for twenty three years and indicated her neighbour who had apparently been making carpets for over forty years. The atmosphere and the techniques on display harked back to an older world.

I walked into another workshop. It was very cramped but perched on the benches were about a dozen young women wrapping up bundles of wool.

"Asallam Aleykum," I said, meeting the eyes of several dark-eyed girls who had turned to stare at me. Judging by the giggling response I guessed my accent sounded ridiculous.

"Do you speak Chinese?" I asked one girl who was staring at me cockily.

"A little yaar. Where you from yaar?"

"England."

"Angliar yaar?"

"Anglia? Yes that's probably right."

"You have girlfriend yaar?" Her husky voice had a sexy edge. The other girls were all looking at me curiously.

"Not at the moment."

"What job you do yaar?"

"Business," I said, sticking to the charade I had audaciously begun many months before. In fact I was so used to telling people I was a businessman that I had started to believe it myself.

"Rich yaar?" She asked cheekily.

"Not very."

I was half expecting music to start up and the girl to serenade me like some Uighur Carmen. It did not. I walked out into the boiling sunshine and returned to the city proper.

*

A huge bazaar occupied several blocks to the east of the centre. There I saw Uighurs of all ages swarming about but not a single Han Chinese person was in sight. Silk scarfs, carpets, knives, clothes, shoes, washing machines, fruit, kebabs, screws, notebooks; everything conceivable was being hawked and haggled over. Several sinks of murky coloured ice-water were scattered about. Although it looked dirty I drained a cup to slake my thirst, which had been brought on by the intense heat. An exhilarating anarchy pervaded most of the bazaar but in a shaded area I glimpsed a cluster of men kneeling on mats and praying towards the west; towards Mecca.

Sweating, I sat down for a mid-afternoon meal in a restaurant and ordered one of the pies that were fried in a stove outside. I ate the gristly, greasy and salty offering, and stood up to leave. The owner led me to a world map hanging on the wall and asked me where I was from.

"Anglia," I said, flaunting the word I had picked up earlier.

"Anglia," he repeated, pointing at a misshapen pink blob on the far left of the map. Then he covered up Xinjiang and pointed at China. "Han," he said. Finally, he covered up the rest of China and pointed at Xinjiang. "Uighur," he declared firmly.

After the frenetic buzz to the east, I was taken aback by the atmosphere in the middle of Hotan. The pavements were virtually deserted and the proportion of Han Chinese people was considerably higher. The recent immigrants seemed to have occupied the central portion of the city while leaving the outskirts to the natives. I walked into an air-conditioned shopping mall to escape the scorching sun. Han Chinese shop owners were watching over first-hand models of the same washing machines that were at that very moment being haggled over in the bazaar. Here, however, there were no customers buying anything. In the back of the mall I came across a Uighur couple whose job it was to clean the toilet. Apart from them there were no Uighurs to be seen. The bazaar and the mall were polar opposites of each other. It was as if two universes existed in the one city.

Back outside I met a Han Chinese man from Gansu province. "Your Chinese is much better than the local people's," he remarked when I had introduced myself. "Here, if you ask someone for directions in the street they can't even say."

"I think they can say," I suggested, provocatively, "but they just don't want to tell you. I don't think they like you Han Chinese very much."

"I know! It's like a foreign country here! We build their houses, their roads . . . We help them so much. But do they welcome us? No!" He said indignantly.

"Perhaps it's because they think you're destroying their culture?"

"What culture?"

"You don't think they have a culture?"

"Well, now you put it like that, well, erm, well obviously they do. But it's not as rich or old as China's."

Given the battering that China's 'rich and old' culture had taken under communist rule, I thought this was a bold statement, but I let it go.

*

In the evening I hopped onto the back of a motor cart outside my hotel. It trawled away, my legs dangling down from the side. Crossing a chaotic junction just outside the bazaar, I felt that my legs were in imminent danger of becoming trapped but I nonetheless revelled in the market atmosphere. The wind streamed through my hair and I finally felt like I was in the heart of Asia.

"You Blair, no?" Asked the driver of the motor cart when he learnt where I was from.

"Yes that's right," I replied. "Blair was our prime minister before."

"Blair good. America good. Bush, yes?"

"Yes they had Bush. Now it's Obama."

"Yes. Obama good. Bush good."

His casual comments resounded on two levels. Firstly, the Chinese authorities cited terrorism and threw large numbers of Uighurs into prison camps every year; a case of America's War on Terror spreading in unforeseen ways. Secondly, the subject of Western relations with

Muslims was very much the topic of the moment. Osama Bin Laden had been assassinated barely a week before.

When we reached Unity Square the driver tried to overcharge me. The amount in question was almost irrelevant and there was a chance that linguistic misunderstandings were really to blame. Nonetheless, I could not help but feel that everyone in Hotan was trying to rip me off.

Unity Square dominated the heart of the city. At one end was an enormous statue of Mao shaking hands with Kurban Tulum, a 'model Uighur' who welcomed the CPC's policies in Xinjiang. Towering prominently behind them was a new concrete high-rise cloaked in scaffolding. It was a potent image of what the Communist's policies had actually entailed.

I sat down in the square as the dusk started to settle. A large block of Han Chinese women were dancing to the music emanating from a CD player. Most were middle-aged and were lined up in neat rows, evenly spaced apart.

Right foot forward, left foot forward, kick, twirl, hop, skip . . . The steps looked the same as I had seen everywhere else in China; probably the same desexualised moves the elder women had learnt as children in their communist youth leagues. As I watched my mind turned to Shangri-la and to Kangding. There too, on the frontiers of the Han Chinese world, there had been these same women dancing, dancing, dancing. And there the Tibetans had come and danced with them. Those middle-aged ladies: the foot soldiers of 'social harmony'; the finest soldier the government had, I reflected with the force of revelation.

And now some Uighurs were drifting into the square: men, women, children; all. Each one had a beach ball and started smacking it high into the air.

The Han dancers continued, unperturbed by the disorder around them. Right foot forward, left foot forward, kick, twirl, hop, skip . . .

And more Uighurs were coming. And every one of them had beach ball and started smacking it into the air . . .

Right foot forward, left foot forward, kick, twirl, hop, skip . . .

And more Uighurs were coming, and more, and more, and every single one had a beach ball . . .

Right foot forward, left foot forward, kick, twirl, hop, skip . . .

And suddenly the square was a battle ground, the final frontier in a war whose fortunes reverberated in the corridors of Beijing. For it was all so obvious. The Uighurs, deliberately, defiantly and with solidarity of purpose, were saying that they would not dance along.

*

The next morning I was ill, presumably from the dirty water I had drunk at the bazaar. I dragged myself out of my bed and made my way to the bus station. Over the next couple of days of travelling I continued to make my way west through Uighur heartlands. As I left Hotan behind, the desert gave way to land that was greener and lusher. The Muslim culture was visible in the mosques I passed and also in the large cemeteries that lined the road. In Each grave had a headstone above it in the shape of hands clasped in prayer.

The day after leaving Hotan I stopped off in Yengisar. This small roadside town was the home of Uighur knife production and several shops were scattered along a stretch of the main highway. In the corner of one I saw a small group of men making blades with hammers, files and metal grinders. The rest of the shops, however, were just showrooms. I bought a tiny silver-laden folding blade and then continued perusing.

A dark-skinned Uighur with short hair called me into his shop. Ignoring my remark that I was just looking, he pulled out a ten inch blade with a handle made from deer antler. "It's very sharp, look." He demonstrated by shaving some hair off his forearm. He explained that his cousin had made the knife. "How much will you pay for it?" He asked.

"I have already bought a knife."

"Buy another one."

"I don't want another one. Anyway that knife is too big."

"It's only 1200RMB."

I jumped on the fresh excuse, "It's too expensive."

"1000RMB."

"Look, I really don't want it."

"800RMB. What price do you want?"

"I don't want any price."

"Say a price."

"100RMB," I quoted stupidly, expecting that such a ridiculously low offer would put him off the scent.

"600RMB."

"I can't even take it back home. I'd never get it through customs."

"You can ship it."

"I don't want to ship it."

"400RMB."

The situation was getting out of hand so I made to walk out of the shop. The owner ran around the counter and blocked the way to the door. "300RMB," He shouted.

"I don't want it."

"200RMB . . . Ok, Ok . . . 100RMB." His eyes blazed with humiliated anger. Before I could stop him he had seized my hand and shaken it.

"But I don't want it," I repeated.

He looked at me fiercely. Any playfulness that might have been in his manner before was now gone. I pushed past and headed for the door. He picked up a small knife from the counter and threw it at me. It bounced off my backpack and fell to the fall.

"Calm down," I said, angry too now.

I picked up the thrown knife and placed it back on the counter. I walked to the door again. He picked up the knife and once more threw it at my departing back. Once more it bounced off my backpack harmlessly. It was razor sharp. This time I did not put it back.

*

The Khunjerab Pass; the border with Pakistan. I took a few photos of the barbed wire and towering grey archway. A young soldier from Hebei watched on and made sure nobody walked too far. I felt a little sorry for him. He was a long way from home.

It was very cold, snow lay all around and the altitude was almost 5000m. And so, after a short time, I and five Han travellers climbed back into the car we had hired and headed back east. I was as far from Beijing as it was possible to be but, symbolically at least, I was heading back to the capital. We passed back down the Karakoram Highway, the iconic road over the western end of the Himalaya, only stopping off briefly in the border town of Tashkurgan, which has a Tajik population, and at the nomadic Krygz settlements around Karakul Lake.

At Karakul, a gang of motor-biking Krygz tradesmen located us and brought out exotically tinted rocks, which they had collected in the area. When we pulled away, all bar me were clutching amulets and necklaces. Then one of my fellow passengers, who had just coughed up large amounts of cash for a pebble, warned me to be careful when travelling alone.

"Many of the people in Xinjiang are thieves," he said.

I had heard the same refrain before. To Han Chinese, the ethnic groups in Xinjiang had reputations for being untrustworthy. My companions in the car had still come, however, on account of the natural beauty. And in truth all else paled in comparison. The massive bulk of Muztagh Ata stood to our right, its gradient so smooth that it appeared possible just to stroll up to the 7546m summit. Kongur's 7719m peak drifted in and out of view in the distance. The sun shone down from a perfectly clear sky and turned the snows a blinding white. The mountains shone like diamonds. They were the most magnificent peaks I had seen; their height and grandeur eclipsing anything I had come across in Sichuan and Qinghai. But amid the magnificence something felt odd. The road was smooth and the car was air-conditioned. It seemed a little too comfortable; too easy. It seemed a little hubristic.

A few hours later, in the suburbs of Kashgar, the driver pulled up outside the 'Kashgar Fok Products Store.' In the lobby, a solitary old Uighur lady worked away slowly on a smaller version of the same style of loom I had seen in Hotan. I walked past and found myself in a huge showroom. Han women in neat purple uniforms stood among piles of carpets while Han men in crisp-black suits sat behind displays of jade bracelets and pendants. By comparison to the authenticity of the workshop in Hotan, the atmosphere felt fake. When I defiantly suggested that some of the carpets were machine-made, however, a lady with dyed ginger hair—a Han fashion—rounded on me and vehemently told me that all products were genuine Uighur items. If so, I reflected, it was even worse that they were being sold by Han businessmen who would take most of the profits. But in the face of the bruising tirade I said nothing.

As I left, Wuzhe, a large and friendly holidaying-student, remarked in English: "Chinese woman is like tiger, yes?"

"Yes, but so is English woman," I replied with a sly smile, "The difference is that Chinese man is like mouse."

*

Kashgar was, quite literally, the end of the rail line. The train had first arrived in 1999 and was providing the means for more and more Han, enticed by the government's financial incentives, to come west. All the same there was no escaping the distance from eastern China. The Uighurs even used an unofficial time zone, two hours behind the nationwide standard Beijing time.

Around the centre, where People's Road and Liberation Road crossed at a busy intersection and where a huge statue of Mao watched over People's Park, the familiar high-rises and neon lighting of the newcomers were dominant. The area sprawled markedly wider than its equivalent in Hotan and was infringing heavily on the historic old Uighur district to the north. In the winding lanes of the sections that had thus far escaped demolition, however, the Uighur lifestyle continued in full force. One traveller I met, who had come from Afghanistan, said that the street life in Kashgar had much in common with that in Kabul. In the fierce heat people barged past each other while munching on water melons and Nan breads. In one side alley I saw a man slaughtering a chicken, proclaiming, "Allah O Akbar," as he ripped the bird's throat with a knife and let its scarlet life-source spill on the dusty ground.

I managed to navigate my way through the febrile but geographically disorienting streets to the Id Kah mosque. This, China's largest mosque, had a domed roof and twin minarets, and the outside walls were covered with shining yellow tiles. Previously at the heart of the old town, demolition and new construction had left this huge place of worship perched awkwardly just off Liberation Road. An English notice board at the entrance recounted the various reconstructions of the building, the most recent of which had taken place in 1999 with the aid of state funding. The final Chinglish paragraph caught my eye: "All of it shows fully that Chinese government always pays special attentions to the another and historical cultures of the ethnic groups, and that all ethnic groups warmly welcome Part's religious policy. It also shows that different ethnic groups have set up a close relationship of equality, unity and helps to each other, and freedom of beliefs is protected. All ethnic groups live friendly together here. They cooperate to build a beautiful homeland, support heartily the unity of different ethnic groups and the unity of our country, and oppose the ethnic separatism and illegal religious activity."

The CPC's explanation for the frequent outbursts of violence in Xinjiang—for example over two hundred people had been killed in ethnic riots in Kashgar in 2009—was that they were orchestrated by extreme Muslim terrorists who did not reflect the general feeling among the Uighur people. It claimed that the Uighurs were happy because they were getting wealthier, and it largely ignored any dissatisfaction with the changes to their cities and lifestyles. Given that Chinese traditional culture put great emphasis on the importance of architecture to the atmosphere of a place—most famously manifested in the principles of feng shui—it was surprising how insensitive they were to these concerns. The way of life and vibe in places like Kashgar were closely related to the physical buildings and streets that comprised them. Demolishing the old buildings and replacing them with modern and functional blocks was slowly plucking the soul from the Uighur people.

*

In the evening after returning from the Karakoram I met Mayira and Adziguli, two Uighur girls studying maths at Kashgar University. Mayira was wearing a black dress and black leggings. Adziguli had short hair and was in jeans, heels and a frilled top. Neither wore a shawl.

They could both speak excellent Mandarin because their entire education had been delivered in that language. They acknowledged the usefulness of the lingua franca to career opportunities but said that among themselves they only spoke Uighur. If the CPC's purpose in standardising Mandarin was to encourage national integration, then the Uighurs were playing the system.

As we chatted we walked down to the lake near the centre of town. A few pedalos were creeping across the water surface. We sat down on the pier and soaked up the evening sun. The lake did not look like a natural feature so I asked how long it had been there. Mayira told me that it had only existed in its present incarnation for a few years, before which it had been a bog. It went without saying that this sort of beautification marked the positive side of what state funding was able to achieve.

A little boy came over to us and pulled out a pack of chewing gum. "1RMB," he chirped.

Adziguli spoke with him and established that he was nine years old, before turning to me and adding, "But by the age of nine all Uighur men know how to do business anyway!"

I asked Mayira what she planned to do after graduating from University. "I want a career," she replied, "but I'll probably go back to my home town in Turpan. My family will want me to get married."

"Can you choose who you marry?"

"Of course," she said with a smile, "but my parents will have to approve."

"I want to marry for love," remarked Adziguli wistfully.

"But you will definitely marry a Uighur man?"

"Of course! My parents would not let me marry a non-Muslim anyway. Also I don't think the Chinese men are very attractive," Adziguli grinned, "I think most of them look like little boys."

A short while later she asked out of the blue whether I liked riddles.

"Yes, but I'm not very good at them!"

"Ok, listen to this one," she began: "A black cat and a white cat are sitting on the kitchen table. In front of them is a saucer of milk from which they are both drinking. Suddenly, the black cat pricks up his ears and bounds down from the table. He races to the cellar door, which is slightly ajar, and disappears into the darkness. For a few minutes all that is heard is a faint scrabbling. Then the black cat calls up to the white cat. The white cat instantly leaps down from the table and heads to the cellar. What does the black cat say?"

"So the black cat hears something and goes to the cellar?" I clarified, thinking hard.

"Yes," said Adziguli, wearing the patronising look that all people have when they know the answer to a riddle.

"And the white cat only goes down when the black cat has called out?"

"Yes."

"Well, I don't know . . . maybe: 'I've found a mouse.'"

"No, the black cat says 'miaow' because cats can't talk, stupid."

"Very good," I laughed, "But it's not really a riddle is it?"

"Whatever," said the girls together, laughing too.

After a pleasant couple of hours we parted. The two of them needed to get back to the University before the 10pm curfew.

*

The next day was Sunday and to the Uighurs that meant market day. The central bazaar was packed with people but its location in a new purpose-built hall took away some of the charm. Every now and then a bus disgorged a crowd of camera-wielding, colour-coded-sun-hat-wearing tourists at the entrance.

On the outskirts of the city I went to something much more genuine: a livestock market. Uighur farmers in skull caps were haggling over rows upon rows of bulls, sheep, goats and horses. Their ferocious exchanges invariably ended with the two participants slapping the hands together and shaking violently for several minutes. The sun blazed down and everyone was sweating, including the animals. The wobbly rear-ends of the sheep were shimmering with moisture while the severed heads of their less fortunate brothers lay in a pile over by the steaming canteens in one corner of the field.

I caused a little bit of confusion by asking several farmers how much a camel cost. Seeing as there were no camels anywhere to be seen, I received some strange looks. But I did not mind that I was making a fool of myself; I was feeding off the incredible atmosphere and loving every moment.

A young man started following me around. He seemingly had nothing better to do with his Sunday than walk behind me. I tried to engage him in conversation but he bordered on the monosyllabic so I soon gave up. He did, however, tell me that he had liked Osama Bin Laden for being a strong Muslim figurehead. Powerful symbols of resistance to outside forces had resonance in Xinjiang.

As I was leaving the market, a furious bull broke loose from his binding and ran rampage, knocking his attendant to the floor and charging in my direction. I scurried behind a car and watched a crowd of farmers attempt to bring the heaving titan back under control.

Later in the day, I and two other foreigners was invited by a local tour guide called Abdul to his family home, an hour's drive outside Kashgar. The house was made from earth and bricks. One section was for the family while the other section housed animals. They had eleven sheep, four cows and a few chickens. Behind the house, a few acres of land were used for cultivating wheat and apricots.

Abdul spoke decent English. I took the opportunity to raise the question on everybody's lips, "What do you think of the Americans killing Osama Bin Laden?"

He thought for a bit and then replied, "Some people here liked Bin Laden because he was strong and stood up for Muslims. Others, including me, thought that he was a troublemaker who made life harder for us all."

Despite being in a white shirt and black trousers, Abdul rolled up his sleeves and fed the cows. Clearly, whether he was a businessman in the city or not, he was expected to muck in when he returned to the home of his parents.

We ate dinner whilst sitting cross-legged on a platform, which during the night served as a communal sleeping area. The sleeping arrangements had presumably made the mechanics of marriage difficult when Abdul and his siblings had been living at home as children. I did not enquire about that topic.

The noodles we ate were cooked by Abdul's wife and mother. He, betraying that his day job was to dazzle tourists with phoney Silk Road myth, said, "The noodles are tasty, yes? Well, I'll tell you something true. You know Italian pasta? Marco Polo took the secret recipe for Uighur noodles with him when he returned to Venice in the thirteenth century. Whenever you sit down in an Italian restaurant it is the invention of the Uighurs that you are eating."

After we had arrived back in Kashgar, I paid 200RMB to the driver who had driven me back from the countryside. He, it now emerged, was Abdul's cousin. Abdul had 'invited' me to his home but he had been making money all along. The Uighurs were businessmen through and through but that was unsurprising; they had always been merchants, after all. And although its history was being steadily buried beneath concrete and tarmac, the Silk Road lived on in their calculating minds and unyielding ways.

*

I slept for most of the twenty four hour train journey to Urumqi. The heat made it hard to do anything else. Every now and then I noticed oil fields and wind farms outside. They hinted at an oft-cited reason for the Chinese government's determination to keep hold of Xinjiang. On the run in to Urumqi, the arid landscape gave way to a bit more greenery and the temperature fell. I got off the train under grey skies and made my way to a hostel.

A man on the train had told me that Urumqi was a 'little Hong Kong.' Clearly he had been referring to the economy and not the visual beauty because, in a nation of ugly modern cities, Urumqi was one of the very ugliest. Rows of low-rise concrete blocks lined every single street of the sprawling metropolis. A telling moment came when I caught a bus and continued on it for an hour, all the time thinking that I was almost back at my hostel because every road looked the same. Only when I reached the terminus did I realise that I had got on at the wrong side of the road. There were endless shopping malls, KFC branches, a Sheraton Hotel, a

Louis Vuitton shop . . . Urumqi was the capital of what was technically called the 'Xinjiang Uighur *Autonomous* Region' but the city's new design hardly resounded with Uighur aesthetics. There was barely a glimmer of the vibrant street life of the far west; it has been buried under concrete.

The city's main cultural feature was the Xinjiang Autonomous Region Museum and its star exhibit was the 'Loulan Beauty', the most famous of the Tarim Mummies excavated in the Taklimakan Desert. I rocked up to find that the Beauty was on loan to a museum in Shenzhen. Feeling disappointed, I perused the other exhibitions. The introduction to the first read: "The ancient Western Regions mainly refer to today's Xinjiang. Xinjiang has been an inalienable part of the territory of China." A separate exhibition was entitled 'Being with the Homeland Forever.'

The CPC were still relentlessly pushing their historical claims to Xinjiang but the question of whether they had a right to govern the region was fast losing relevance. The demographic changes In Xinjiang had made calls for Uighur independence nonsensical. So many people had been enticed west by the Government's incentives, or forced west during the harsh times of early CPC rule, that Xinjiang was now almost fifty per cent Han. Most were concentrated in the east of the region, around Urumqi but, as I had seen, they were gradually claiming a foothold in the far west. The Beijing government had proved unable to win the Uighurs' cooperation and integrate them into China willingly. Therefore, over many years, it had used the massive weight of the eastern Chinese population to swamp them.

*

On the next day, I visited Heaven Lake. It was situated in the mountains a couple of hours outside the city, so for convenience's sake I decided to take a tour bus there. I quickly regretted the decision. We stopped off at a shop selling herbal medicine and loitered there for half an hour so that the tour guide could pick up his commission. Then, when we arrived at the entrance to the park, the guide instructed everybody to pay up an extra 50RMB because the lake itself was a further thirty kilometres away and could only be reached via one of the fleet of buses that ran backwards and forth from the ticket office.

The lake itself was pretty but it was overrun by the tourist industry. I found 'genuine Kazakh yurts,' which could be entered for a cost, and a bowl of pasta cost me three times the amount it did anywhere else. Swarms of photographing tourists filled every available space by the lake shore. The last straw came when I spoke to another traveller, who had come to the lake independently. He said that he had not had to pay anything to board the buses inside the park. I went and accosted my tour guide. He told me to keep my voice down, smiled nervously and slipped me back my 50RMB.

*

Near the train station in Urumqi I met a Han Chinese man on his way home. He had just come back from a trip to Xi'an, a city that lay ahead of me. That he went back into heartland China for his holidays was unsurprising. He had only moved away from his home province of Henan in 1997 in order to find work in Xinjiang. He remarked that my toneless Mandarin sounded like a Uighur talking. He probably meant it as a playful jibe but I took it as a compliment. I asked what he thought of Xinjiang.

He paused for a moment. "It's ok," he said. "Xinjiang is now quite economically developed but it is not very stable. There are problems with terrorists and with the Taliban. Too much freedom is not a good idea here. It would be chaos."

"I thought the Taliban were mainly fighting against Western countries like America and England."

"The Taliban are also here in Xinjiang," he said.

"That makes things difficult," I commented. "The Taliban are not an easy group to defeat. At the moment my country has many soldiers in Afghanistan but I think victory is impossible."

"Yes I know you have soldiers in Afghanistan. You are also using military force in Libya now, am I right?" He said, taking the conversation down a different path. "You Westerners like to interfere in other countries."

"We are bombing Libya but I think we are doing it to help the Libyan people," I defended, "I think most of the people want our support."

"It is an invasion. Maybe you are helping the Libyan people now but you are doing it for your own good. Afterwards you will be friends with the government and will get oil. It is always wrong to interfere with other countries' affair. We Chinese love peace. If no country interfered with each other, the world would be peaceful."

I noted that Han people, often critical of the CPC when it came to their own lives, were generally supportive of its stance towards other ethnic groups and foreigner powers. More than anything else they were patriotic and that made them a powerful tool when it came to consolidating China's dominance over its least harmonious sections.

*

Turpan was officially the hottest place in China. The mercury there had been recorded touching 50 degrees Celsius. The town's atmosphere was defined by the heat. People—both Han and Uighur—moved slowly and sat quietly in the shades of green palms, which lined the oasis avenues. Earthen houses still sat among rows of green vines on the edges of the town. It was nearing the end of May when I arrived there and already the day time temperatures were stuck at over thirty degrees.

I found it an easy place to relax because everybody milling around in such a lethargic manner. One evening I and an American man bought a bottle of red wine made from the local grapes, sat in the middle of the town and watched the fountains that periodically sprang up in the main square.

After finishing the bottle, we went into a brick building, which had a simple sign on the door: 'Disco Club.' We ascended several flights of stairs and emerged into a large, dimly lit room. Absolutely everybody there was Uighur. Come to think of it I had not visited anywhere in Xinjiang where the Han and the Uighurs had crossed-over socially. They lived side by side but utterly separate.

Inside the club no one was drinking alcohol but a few people were smoking shisha. The men were in jeans and shirts and the girls, whilst not showing much skin, were shawl-less and wore high heels. A man started playing a song on an electric keyboard and several couples stood up to dance. Then, when the song was finished, they all went back to their tables and sat down again. The next time a song came on, everybody got up and started rotating around the dance floor. The rotation occurred in every way possible: a large moving circle formed so everybody was rotating relative to a common centre but then everybody was rotating their own bodies relative to each other and rotating their arms relative to their bodies and rotating their hands relative to their arms . . . I joined in the great dizzying mass of rotating humanity. No doubt religious reasons accounted for the absence of alcohol in the club but the Uighurs had found an ingenious way to make do without it. In fact, as I fast discovered, both drinking alcohol and dancing Uighur-style was almost too potent a combination.

The next morning I had to wake up depressingly early because I had arranged for a driver to take me to the sights around Turpan. My dedication meant that I beat the crowds to the village of Tuyoq. This beautiful collection of earthen houses in a desert canyon was almost empty as I walked around. I got the sense—one I had only experienced on a handful of occasions—that I had stepped into a lost world; a place without time. The blazing sun was already high in the morning sky, however, and I, given my hangover, could have done with it being a bit lower. Then, by the time I was feeling better, tour buses were starting to arrive and I was forced to scarper.

The other sights were all heaving with tour groups; a reminder that Urumqi lay just a few hours' journey to the north. Nonetheless a couple of the sights were remarkable, particularly the remains of the ancient desert city, Jiaohe. Unfortunately the crumbling ruins provided no shade whatsoever from the sun and I quickly became uncomfortably hot. I went over to cower in the shadow of a large parasol, which had been erected by a lady in traditional Uighur silken clothing. The lady's job was to pose for pictures with tourists for 10RMB a shot. When I remarked that the price seemed exorbitant, she laughed heartily and said that she agreed, adding, "But the tourists will pay that much so I'll charge that much!"

"It can't be much fun for you to be outside in the heat every day," I noted. "It's boiling."

Again she laughed. Her large dark fixed on me and she said, "Today is quite cool. It's only about 35 degrees. In July and August it reaches fifty."

Amongst the fossilised earthen building I found the shell of what had once been a Buddhist temple. The niches that had held statues were still visible. Long before Islam first appeared on the scene, Buddhism had dominated Xinjiang. In fact Buddhism had first reached China via the ancient caravan routes around the Taklimakan. The tantalising niches at Jiaohe were a fascinating glimpse of that legacy, but I was on my way to see much more incredible sights.

At the end of the day I boarded a train and left Xinjiang. I was heading east but I was moving against the tide. The Han were pouring west, escaping the over-populated crush of eastern China and spilling out into Xinjiang. Between the two existed an intermediary zone. During the middle of the night the train ghosted into a province synonymous with the Chinese Silk Road: Gansu.

CHAPTER 15

Down the Silk Road

The Hexi Corridor was a long stretch of arid plain in the north-west of Gansu province, hemmed in by mountains to north and south. The strange shape of the terrain had historically made it the main thoroughfare through which goods came into and went out of China. Whether merchants or camels, religions or inventions, poets or armies; all things in the bottleneck had always been moving onwards. I decided to align myself with the Hexi Corridor's transitional nature and flew down its length in three brisk days.

By the wayside lay icons of Silk Road lore, places whose very existences were owed to the crossing of peoples and cultures. Coming back from Xinjiang, my first stop was at Dunhuang and the legendary Mogao Caves. Carved over almost a thousand years, beginning from the fourth century AD, these grottoes were widely considered one of the world's finest collections of Buddhist art.

I arrived with my excitement on hold. Although the Mogao Caves were one of the sights I had been most looking forward to visit in the whole of China, I was wary of the rampant tourism that I imagined would accompany them. My pessimism proved unjustified. Dunhuang was situated hundreds of miles from anything resembling a city and it appeared that its isolation had preserved it from all but the most determined seekers. There was an organised system whereby caves could only be entered with a guide, but the emphasis of this was to protect the artwork rather than exploit visitors.

Hundreds of caves were chiselled into the long hillside, only about a dozen of which are open to the public. Within these dozen, however, the art I saw was entrancing. Towering Buddhas disappeared into the gloomy darkness tens of metres above my head and murals betraying the cultural influences of places far distant stretched around the walls before me. The Pegasus of Ancient Greece flew alongside Chinese deities and testified to a globalisation that had lived and died in an age long forgotten. The colours of the paint had sometimes faded or the lines thickened with oxidisation, but these factors only served to witness the passage of time; to witness, as the Buddhists who carved the caves had known, that nothing was permanent.

While the guide was waiting for some slower members of my group, I slipped ahead and found Cave Sixteen unlocked. A cavernous space greeted me and a golden phoenix coiled on the roof above. Carved into a side wall was the innocuous Cave Seventeen. A simple mural was faintly visible on the back wall and a small statue of a monk sat in the gloom. I thought nothing of it until my guide caught up and then I realised that Cave Seventeen was none other than the Library Cave. In a place of mysteries, the Library Caves' story was the most mysterious. In 1900 the Taoist guardian of the grottoes, Wang Yuanlu, discovered that a mural on the side wall of Cave Sixteen had cracked. Seeing as the caves were hewn into the solid rock, cracking should have been impossible. Wang realised that something must lie behind. He smashed through and discovered Cave Seventeen. But he did not find it empty like it was today. There were manuscripts! Scrolls and scrolls and scrolls were crammed into every available space. There were over fifty thousand in total. They recorded anything and everything from details of the Mogao Grottoes' construction, to ancient medical prescriptions, to Buddhist Sutras . . . They were written in scripts as varied as classical Chinese, ancient Uighur and Sanskrit . . . It was a find of unimaginable importance.

News of the discovery spread and most of the collection was weaned away over the next decade by determined western archaeologists, whose 'theft' continued to gripe with Chinese national sentiment. Many of the manuscripts found their way into foreign museums and private collections. Now, over one hundred years later, a whole realm of academia existed, entitled simply 'Dunhuang Studies.' Experts gathered on a yearly basis to discuss the finds and to speculate on some of the many remaining questions.

Why, for example were the manuscripts hidden in the first place? What impending disaster led the unknown guardian to seal away so precious a collection a thousand years ago? And why was the cave forgotten? I came away from Dunhuang hoping that the answers would never be found. It was life-enriching to have a few mysteries left.

*

Jiayuguan was known to as 'the mouth of China.' As the final outpost on the Great Wall, its fortress had seen everything from exiled officials to invasion forces pass through its legendary Jade Gate. Symbolically at least, it had always delineated China-proper from the start of the great wilderness 'out there'.

I found a desert-coloured fortress in a desert-coloured landscape. Mountains apparently lay in the distance to north and south but they were invisible because of the dusty haze. I climbed up onto the mighty bastions and gazed west. I tried to imagine the fear of the unknown that the Chinese of the past must have felt on heading out through the gate. A line of pylons stretched away from me and startled me out of my daydreams. It was not unknown any more. For better or for worse, the frontier had disappeared far to the west. It would not return any time soon.

I gave up my imaginings and climbed down from the wall. A girl with a camera asked to take a photo of me. I smiled in acceptance and posed with her. Unlike me she had not come with useless fantasies, I reflected. She understood better than I that Jiayuguan was just a relic; a museum piece; a place to smile on camera with. Its world was long gone.

Not far from the fortress stood a restored section of the Great Wall. It stretched up a steep hillside just like the Great Wall always did in promotional photos. Far smaller than the mighty obstacles that lay in the vicinity of Beijing, I guessed that I would have been able to climb over it myself.

The Great Wall had never proved much use as a defensive barrier but that observation was to misunderstand its significance. The section I stood on near Jiayuguan had been constructed from the compacted sand and rocks of the nearby desert, just as every section of the five-thousand-mile colossus had been made with the local resources. That had been done for pragmatic reasons, yes, but it also represented how China had never been uniform. Every section of the vast land had always been diverse in terms of geography and resources, but also in terms of the people. Turning the Chinese landmass into a monoculture was to go against all the trends of history.

*

While Jiayuguan was 'the mouth of China', the land to the east of it was known as 'the throat'. It seemed to me an unfortunate metaphor that anyone heading west rose up the throat and spewed out of the mouth. I had barely paused at Dunhuang and Jiayuguan and so had largely ignored the small and nondescript settlements that existed there, but I did pause at the considerably larger town of Zhangye.

I arrived in the early evening and set off in search of a hotel. A Qing dynasty archway dominated the main intersection and in the streets around it a lively atmosphere prevailed. To everyone I asked for directions, I said that I wanted to stay in the cheapest place in town. Somehow that did not sink in because each and every one of them kept pointing me towards the town's finest establishment. They obviously inferred from my foreign-ness that I was rich.

By luck I stumbled across a cramped hotel just off a main road. The friendly girl at reception smiled at me and gave me a room. The standard cheap accommodation in off-the-beaten-track areas of China was the 'putongjian'-'ordinary room.' Invariably there was a communal toilet at the end of the corridor and a floor attendant. This hotel was no different except that the floor attendant's office was, simply put, a cage. The thick metal bars seemed appropriate for imprisoning a tiger, or more relevantly, for keeping out a tiger. What sort of place was this? I put down my bags, stepped back out of my room and almost bumped into a thin girl with an older man on her arm. Another girl in high heels and thick red lipstick strutted past, her miniskirt barely stretching below her waist. I walked down the corridor and passed a room where the door was ajar. A girl was selecting some of the items from the various paraphernalia strewn across the bed. I glimpsed a few pieces of lingerie and unmistakable small square packages.

Chuckling, I went out and bought a beer. I found a statue of Marco Polo standing on a roundabout and raised my bottle in salute. So much for the legacy of the Silk Road.

*

The next day I visited the Horse Hoof Temple, a Tibetan-Buddhist retreat in the Qilian Mountains to the south of Zhangye. There were just a handful of monks in attendance but I was still dazzled. The temples had been cut literally into a sandstone cliff face and were linked by claustrophobic staircases within the rock. I slithered my way up through dark passages and found myself in shadowy grottoes watched over by serene Buddhist deities.

The natural setting was also beautiful. A grassy valley floor gave way to forested slopes, which themselves gave way to craggy and snow-capped mountains. The whole area smacked of peace and solitude.

Back in Zhangye, I whiled away an evening sitting on a bench in a small park. After the underlying tensions I had felt in ethnic minority areas over the previous few months, it was nice to be in a place that seemed at ease with itself. Zhangye was majority Han Chinese, had historically always been part of China and lay in an area where there was nothing much of political or economic importance going on. The Government had no reason to interfere there and the absence of pretence was tangible.

As I sat and watched the world go by, a couple of teenage girls in tracksuit school uniforms came over. One was tall with frizzy hair and glasses while the other was slight and had long straight locks.

"Where are you from?" The tall one asked in English, before bursting into fits of embarrassed giggles.

"I'm from England," I replied encouragingly. "Do you learn English at school?"

We began a simple conversation. Neither girl can have had many opportunities to speak with a foreigner so I tried to be friendly. Their efforts to practise their English were stymied, however, by a crowd of onlookers who gathered around to see what was going on. When it emerged that I could speak Chinese, questions started coming my way in a ceaseless flow.

"What currency do you use in England?"

"How many RMB to the pound?"

"Ten! Wow, English people must be very rich."

"What are salaries like in England?"

"Your walking boots look well-made. Did you buy them in England?"

"How much did they cost?"

I did my best to satiate their financial curiosity.

After a while an elder man cut in, "Do you mind if I look at your hand?"

I acquiesced, not quite sure what he wanted. The man took my hand and started feeling it thoroughly. He traced the lines on my palm and peered closely at my fingertips. After about a minute of intent concentration, he announced his conclusion to the onlookers: "It's the same."

"Of course it's the same," I remarked. "We are all people."

"We are all people," repeat a few meditatively, turning over the words in their mouths.

A sharp-minded little boy in the front row lisped, "But if we're all the same, why do we speak different languages?"

*

I took an overnight train all the way to Lanzhou, Gansu's provincial capital but did absolutely nothing other than transferring from the train station to the bus station and continuing my journey. The road out of Lanzhou was fast and smooth. I was certainly spotting a pattern as regards where most state funding was being invested in the western parts of China. Kunming in Yunnan, Xining in Qinghai, Urumqi in Xinjiang and now Lanzhou in Gansu: all the provincial capitals I had seen were disproportionately well-developed compared to the land around them.

I disembarked at Tianshui, a town of little significance other than that it was situated on a major train line. In the centre, lines of small restaurants selling cheap noodles and dumplings contributed to a loud evening atmosphere. I stayed one night in a grimy hotel manned by five attractive girls and the next morning made my way into the surrounding countryside.

The bus rose gradually into a wooded and hilly area, where bees hummed beneath the baking sun. My destination was Maiji Shan, a Buddhist cave complex with a history stretching back one and a half millennia. The artwork I saw there was impressive but after Dunhuang I found it hard to be wowed. The standout feature of Maiji Shan, however, was the grottoes' precarious location on a vertical rock face. Some of the carvings were at dizzying heights up to one hundred metres above the ground. A large network of staircases has been nailed into the cliff to allow people to get close to the carvings. Unfortunately there were too many people there at the same time as me and large numbers were getting vertigo on the narrow steps. The circulation of human traffic ground to a congested standstill and the squashed atmosphere made it hard to enter into the reflective mind-set I wanted. I could still feel awe, however, at how the sculptors had managed to go so high into the air and not only avoid nausea but also chisel religious masterpieces into the mundane rock.

It was a fitting conclusion to my Silk Road travels. That evening I boarded a train with a crowd of migrant workers and when I got off I was in Xi'an.

CHAPTER 16

Cities of the Future

It was late in the evening by the time I checked into a hostel and took a shower. I had not had a chance to wash since leaving Turpan, so the combined dirt, grease and smell of the entire length of Gansu fell from my skin. It was extremely refreshing.

Next morning I went to a hairdresser. Off came the locks that I had left untrimmed for months. Off too came three months' worth of beard. I had let it grow wild as I tramped through China's untouched borderlands but now I was back in back in one of China's civilised ancient capitals, and so it had to go. I walked out of the hairdresser looking at least five years younger and set out to take in the city.

As I was walking down a quiet street not far from the city centre, a woman beckoned to me from a doorway. "Massage?" she called out.

I paused and decided that a massage was not a bad idea. Carrying a rucksack every day had hardened up my shoulders and I thought it would be nice to have the tightness eased out. I went inside and sat down on a sofa. A second lady came over. She was a lady in the sense of being over forty years old but otherwise there was very little lady about her. She was wearing a corset and was caked in make-up.

"What sort of a massage do you want?" She asked.

"Just a massage," I replied, feeling self-conscious of my freshly shaved look. Situations like these were easier to handle with a manly beard.

"Body massage or foot massage?"

I told her that I wanted a body massage and that I would pay twenty RMB. Looking at me with a motherly expression she said that it cost thirty RMB.

"Twenty Five."

"Thirty RMB," She repeated, "but I'll strike your aeroplane at the end if you want."

"Strike my aeroplane?"

She mimed her meaning. "That's alright," I said hastily. "I don't need you to strike my aeroplane. I'll just have the massage."

"Are you sure?"

"I'm sure."

"It's the same price," she said, giving me a dirty look. For some reason, in that moment I remembered that the Chinese word for a prostitute, 'jinu,' translated as 'hen.' Something about this old crone did indeed call to mind the adjective 'clucking.'

Before I could conclude our negotiations, however, there was a more pressing problem. "Do you have a toilet?" I asked.

"You need the toilet?" she repeated, looking sceptical.

When I confirmed that I did she disappeared for a few seconds and returned with a bucket. "You can use this," she said.

"So you don't have a toilet?"

"No but all the clients use this."

"No I'm not pissing in that. I'll go to a public toilet."

"There isn't a public toilet near here."

"There are public toilets everywhere."

"Will you come back?"

"Yes of course."

"Ok, there's one just round the corner."

"Cool. I'll go to that one."

"You promise you'll come back."

"Of course. It won't take long."

I walked out and scarpered. China's untouched borderlands had proved far from untouched, I reflected. Unsurprising, therefore, that its civilised ancient capital had proved itself far from civilised.

Considerably more disappointing was that China's civilised ancient capital proved itself far from ancient. As I quickly discovered, very little of Xi'an's incomparable heritage had been left untouched by the passage of time or by the tide of modern construction. Even the small amounts that had survived looked awkward, none more so than the fourteenth century Ming Dynasty Bell Tower, which sat unceremoniously in the middle of the congested central roundabout. Xi'an had been the capital of China for more than a thousand years, most notably during the political and cultural flowering of the Tang Dynasty of 618-907AD, but now it was just another in the long line of China's industrial and commercial centres.

Many of the people strutting along the pavements and driving fast down the wide roads struck me as very pretentious. The thing I noticed most was how everything they did was western. They were wearing western clothes, listening to western songs, drinking western drinks and driving western cars. I wondered whether perhaps China's civilised ancient capital was not even China's anymore. But no, that was pushing it a bit far.

In fact, despite the limited amount of things pertaining to Xi'an's glorious past, I thought it was quite a pleasant city. Optimism hung in the air and quality of life took a front row seat. Even the western influences betrayed the new wealth and aspiration of the population. Xi'an put on its best show in the evenings when the lights flickered into life on the city walls and the commercial rat race of the day gave way to the up-beat casualness of the night. Restaurants served until late to people sitting at outside tables; buskers sat on the roadsides and serenaded the passing crowds; girls put on their sexiest outfits and accompanied their boyfriends to bars, and drag queens tottered down the pavements in platform heels.

After a couple of days in Xi'an I headed into the outskirts of the city to its most prestigious attraction. Given that I had an acute dislike of all things related to the rip-off Chinese tourist industry, I went to the Terracotta Warriors with low expectations. I was surprised. The tour groups might have outnumbered the warriors a hundred to one but the warriors had a mean look in their eyes, which said they would win if it came to a fight.

In fact, if asked to choose whether the robotically-photographing visitors or the subterranean army looked more human, I would have gone for the two-thousand—two-hundred-year-old pottery pieces every time. With a little bit of imagination I could picture the battalion break into a march. None of the warriors would break rank, none would glance sideways: all would stride steadily and relentlessly forward.

In their day the soldiers of the Qin faction were the most formidable in China. Their leader used their might to conquer all opposition and become China's First Emperor in 221BC. Ultimately he had his troops modelled in terracotta to accompany him into the afterlife. Probably he feared the avenging spirits of the underworld because during his lifetime the First Emperor got himself a brutal reputation for tyranny.

The Chinese people had a long-term view of history and the Qin Emperor was back in vogue. A spate of publications and recent films had tried to resurrect his legacy, praising his far-sighted efforts to unify China under a powerful central government and largely ignoring his methods. It was pertinent to note, however, that the modern Government was cherry-picking a contradictory selection of precedents to suit their purposes. That the moral influence of Confucius could today be trumpeted alongside the unification-at-all-costs and authoritarian mentality of the Qin Emperor was an irreconcilable paradox, not least because the Qin Emperor actually persecuted the Confucian scholars of his time.

*

I caught a train out of Xi'an in early June. While I was eating a pot noodle and looking out of the window into the darkness, the middle-aged woman reclining on the bottom bunk opposite me asked where I was going. When I said that I was going to Chengdu she said that she was doing likewise. This was not particularly surprising: the train was going to Chengdu.

Nonetheless small talk of that sort was good for breaking the ice and we proceeded to chat for some time.

"Are you travelling alone?" I asked.

"No I'm with some friends. I just have a holiday for a few days."

"Are you married?"

"Yes and I have one son," she replied. "He's twenty six but he has not found himself a wife so he just sits around at home. I tell him he should go and get a girlfriend but he does not worry about it like I do. I'm nervous that he can't look after himself. He can't cook, he can't clean: I do everything for him."

Her anxiety was etched all over her face so I offered reassurance. In the back of my mind I suspected that her son's behaviour was a problem of the woman's own making. The spoilt upbringing of China's One Child Policy generation was a well-documented problem. The mocking term for a boy who had received excessive pampering from his parents was 'a little emperor.'

"Do you take holidays often?" I asked.

"This is the first time I have gone away this year," she replied. "Last year I did not go away at all. My husband is no good around the house either, you see. Both he and my son hate it when I go away but sometimes I just need time to myself." She looked both feisty and pensive at the same time. "I have cooked lots of food so all they need to do is heat it up."

"It sounds like they'll be ok," I said soothingly.

*

When I woke the next morning the train was on the run in to Chengdu but the landscape was still agricultural. Male and female farmers were wading knee deep in sodden paddy fields and planting fresh shoots in the underwater sludge. A few glanced up at the train as it flew by, revealing the sun-tanned faces beneath their wide-brimmed hats. Barely thirty minutes later I disembarked at the station in Chengdu and was greeted by a completely different way of life: a new metro line, racing taxis, wide streets and an all-embracing haze.

Chengdu, the capital of Sichuan province, was modernising fast and I saw the new wealth visible in the shape of flashy sports cars racing down the roads. It was strange for me to think that Kangding, one of the first Tibetan towns I had visited, could be just one long bus journey to the away. While Kangding's weather had exhibited the freshness of the mountains, Chengdu's was the epitome of river basin mugginess. The humidity induced a lethargic attitude in the locals, which they either defeated by eating very spicy food or else cultivated by relaxing further. Rather like in Xi'an, in Chengdu quality of life seemed an important consideration. The city's parks were full of people moving slowly and playing games.

The lifestyle appealed to me and I spent one afternoon loitering in the tea garden of Chengdu's largest temple while playing cards with some other travellers. All around us groups of local people were sitting on the wobbly chairs and tables, which had been squashed into every nook and cranny. Some of the locals were playing cards too, others were chatting and others were eating melon seeds. Everybody was sipping tea from China pottery and having their cups periodically re-filled by attendants with huge kettles.

On my left sat a girl called Jiena who was in Chengdu for a job interview. She was twenty two years old and was just about to graduate from university before diving into working life.

"I'd love to be able to travel like you guys," she said enviously, addressing both me and a couple of other foreigners at the table, "but my father wants me to get a job."

"Where are you from?" I asked.

"Mianyang. It's a small city about an hour from Chengdu."

"How small?"

"About one million people."

"Chinese small," I said, smiling, before remarking how good her English was.

"I don't think it's any good," she said, looking embarrassed. "I mainly learnt it from watching American movies so I'm sure I make all sorts of mistakes. My Korean is probably better than my English."

"It sounds like you'll wasted in an office," I remarked, knowing that her job interview had been for a secretarial post.

She looked at me with a hint of regret. "Yes, I want to go away to Shanghai or Beijing. Do something different, you know? But I can't. My family's very traditional."

Her words reminded me that Sichuan was still very deprived. It lacked the same relentless pace but, to my eye, Chengdu might almost have been one of the booming cities on the east coast. Its surrounds, however, were evidently not seeing the benefits of the increase in wealth. When Jiena described her family as 'traditional,' what she of course meant was that they were poor.

A man came over armed with cotton buds, a tuning fork and some lethal-looking rods. He offered to clean my ears. Jiena explained the process: "What happens is that he rings the tuning fork next to your ear to loosen the wax. Then he scrapes the wax out with the rod and cleans it with the cotton wool."

"Is it painful?"

"Most of the time it's nice," she said casually, "but the man who did me yesterday touched my ear drum. That hurt."

The prospect of having a spike inserted into the side of my head made me shudder so I decided to pass on the ear cleaning. Walking away from the tea house a short while later, I saw an old man spinning a diablo in the shade of some bamboos. He was seriously good. Knotting, flicking, twisting, curling, and flinging; the diablo seemed like an extra limb. In fact he was so good that it looked a little boring. Where was the fun if he never dropped the thing?

*

Other than sipping tea with the locals, there was one main thing for a traveller to do in Chengdu. The Giant Panda Breeding Research Base lay on the edge of the city. The paths inside the base wove gently through green bamboo thickets. The only place where there was no bamboo was inside the enclosures themselves. Presumably this measure was to prevent the pandas eating it.

Eating was all the overweight bears seemed to do. I arrived shortly after feeding time and found every single panda munching away contentedly from a pile of bamboo shoots situated conveniently close by. Sleeping also seemed popular. I watched one panda that had even combined the two past-times. He lay on his back with his eyes closed while chewing his way through a delicious piece of bamboo bark.

All the black and white furry beasts seemed to want was to be left in peace. They were not having their wish granted. Crowds of tourists, a disproportionate number of them foreigners like me, were gazing on in rapture. The high point came when one bear stood up and started to itch his rear against a tree. Cameras clicked wildly and one excited lady cried out, "He's just like me!" Quite what she meant I could only speculate.

*

Given what I had seen of the earthquake aftermath in Yushu, I decided to visit the sight of an even more catastrophic tremor. The Sichuan Earthquake of 2008 killed over sixty thousand people and destroyed virtually all buildings near the epicentre in Wenchuan County. The collapse of a number of schools had caused great controversy, with questions raised and then stifled about whether poor construction standards caused the death of the children inside. By the time I visited it was three years since the disaster and there had been sufficient time to rebuild.

The unique circumstances had given the Government the chance to recreate the Wenchuan in its own image. Everywhere I had travelled previously, the influence of current policy had mixed with the stew of what had already been there. But Wenchuan provided me with a one-off opportunity to see how the Government designed a town when it could start from scratch.

I set off for the region early one Sunday morning. Even at the bus station in Chengdu the first signs of the quake's impact were visible. A large poster read: "Humanitarian Aid for a Harmonious Society."

Chengdu was humid and warm that day but as my bus left the city behind and started to climb into the mountains to the north-west, the air became increasingly cold. The road was new and passed through a couple of tunnels. Billboards beside the road spewed out the rhetoric of the moment, including one from State Grid, the national electricity provider, that proclaimed: "Delivering Clean Energy to a Harmonious World."

As we drew closer to Wenchuan collapsed sections of the old road were visible and the mountainsides were scarred by landslides. The villages we passed, however, were newly built and undeniably pretty. The local ethnic minority in Wenchuan were the Qiang—a people related to the Tibetans—and traces of their traditional architecture were visible in the reconstructed buildings.

From the station at the town of Wenchuan I caught a local bus into the town centre and found myself sitting next to a local Qiang man. I enquired where he had been when the earthquake had struck.

"I was very lucky because I was in Chengdu on the day it happened. All the buildings there shook but none collapsed. My wife was in Jinchuan, a village near here. She was stuck there for ten days because none of the aid workers could reach them for that long."

"Then what happened?"

"My wife and I lived in a tent for a year. Then our son was born so we went to Chengdu and lived there for another year. Last year we were told our new home was ready so we came back."

I asked what he thought of his new house and received a very positive response. "I really like it," he said. "It's a lot better than what I had before the quake. I didn't even have to pay much because the government covered most of the costs."

"Is it in the same place as your previous home?" I asked, bearing in mind what I had seen in Yushu of people being relocated.

"Of course not! Nothing is in the same place anymore! I grew up in Wenchuan but now I can get lost in the streets," he said with a laugh.

I asked whether any of his family had died in the tremor, to which he replied, "Luckily none of my friends or family was killed. Here in Wenchuan town there were not so many deaths. Much larger numbers of people were killed in Yingxiu and a few other small towns around here."

He was on his way into town to do some shopping ahead of his young son's second birthday. The little boy's birth must have been a symbol of hope in the darkness.

A solitary crane hovered over Wenchuan's skyline but when I looked around most buildings seemed to have already been completed. I bought a snack at the shop of a lady from Hubei—a neighbouring province—who had come to Wenchuan in the aftermath of the quake to set up her business. When she had first come, the town had still lain in ruins and so she had lived in a blue tent like everyone else.

The Min River, bloated by the summer melt, powered past the town. The sky was grey and a gusty wind occasionally picked up. It was a reminder that Wenchuan lay in a properly mountainous area.

On the new promenade beside the rushing river, a man was fishing with a bamboo rod. I asked him the same question that I was asking everybody: "Where were you when the quake struck?"

"I was here in Wenchuan," he said slowly. "I was outside when it happened so I was not hurt."

"Did you have to live in a tent?"

"Yes, I lived in a tent. Most of the buildings here were destroyed. Almost everyone lost their home. The area we are standing on now used to be covered with tents."

He explained that he had helped out in the aftermath of the quake by carrying water to remote mountain villages, which had been inaccessible except on foot. I did not ask him too many questions because he seemed keen to drift back into contemplation. I felt that he deserved some peace.

A bustling street market occupied the main road in the centre. The majority of people belonged to the area's ethnic groups. Qiang women in sky blue dresses called out to me to buy their cherries. Behind where the ladies were selling fruit was a large building, which housed a new museum. Inside were some excellent exhibitions on the Qiang culture and also some detailing the earthquake and its aftermath. The word 'harmonious' cropped up a too much for my liking but I was interested to see the efforts being made to move on. In particular the emphasis was on transforming Wenchuan and its surrounds into a hub of regional tourism.

Outside once more I met a group of four men from Hubei who had come to Wenchuan the year before to build houses. They said the town was unrecognisable from when they had first come. I could well believe it. Were it not for the fact that everything was new, I would have struggled to guess there had been an earthquake at all. There were phone shops and jewellery stores, banks and dentists. There were also several sections that had been pleasantly beautified. As well as the promenade down by the river, there were small parks and wide pedestrian streets. Wenchuan seemed a nice place to live.

Later in the afternoon I was approached by three boys as I walked down the pavement. They were aged seventeen and attended the Number 1 High School, which had recently been built on the road leading out of Wenchuan. One of the three boys was very articulate and wanted to practice his English.

"What are you doing in Wenchuan?" He asked me.

"I have just come to have a look because there was the earthquake here," I replied. "Are you from here?"

"No, we are from different villages in the interior," he said, referring to the mountainous terrain west of Wenchuan.

After a while we switched to Mandarin. Both he and his two friends were ethnic Tibetan but they did not speak their mother tongue.

"Was your home destroyed when the quake struck?" I asked.

"No it was protected by the mountains. I was not at home anyway because I was living in my middle school at the time." He gestured to his companions and said, "None of us live at our family homes because they are too far away. We sleep in dormitories at our school."

"But weren't your schools destroyed in the quake?"

"Some schools were," said another of the three. "My middle school was damaged so the government sent all of us to Jiangsu province on the east coast to continue our education until they could repair the buildings. The teachers came too. We stayed there for over a year."

When we reached the new high school I saw a sprawling complex of white and brown buildings. A large football field was visible behind the fence but the security guard did not allow me to enter. I took a photo with the boys and a couple of other students who had gathered around.

"By the way, what do you want to do when you finish high school?" I asked as I left.

"I want to go to University," said the first boy. "Probably I'll go to Sichuan University in Chengdu but my ambition is to go to Tsinghua."

I wished him luck. I knew that Tsinghua, located in Beijing, was arguably the best university in the entire land. A Tibetan boy in a resurrected town dreaming of gracing China's most prestigious educational institution . . . A poignant story indeed.

CHAPTER 17

On the Mighty Yangtze

The Chengdu to Chongqing train link was part of the high speed rail network. In Chengdu it was raining as I left at ten o'clock but when I got off the train around midday, I felt like I had walked into an oven.

I undid all the buttons on my shirt and boarded a public bus. A young child was sitting completely naked on her mother's lap. Everyone was coated in a thin film of sweat and was moving as little as possible. A lady climbed on to sell newspapers. Several people bought one and started fanning themselves. The bus crossed a bridge into central Chongqing where I saw bleached high-rises reaching skywards with laundry hanging from the balconies. Few people were out on the streets.

Like Nanjing, Chongqing was one of China's 'three furnaces'. I had visited Nanjing in February and it had been cold. Now it was June and I understood what 'furnace' meant. When I emerged from my hostel in the late afternoon, Chongqing's streets were marginally fuller, especially down by the waterfront of the peninsular, where the Jialing River flowed into the Yangtze. I had travelled near the source of this colossal waterway in the mountains around Yushu; I had trekked past the roaring rapids of one of its early tributaries at Tiger Leaping Gorge, and I had chugged out of its enormous delta near Shanghai. Here in the middle of its course, China's mightiest river looked dirty, green and sultry.

In 1997 Chongqing separated from Sichuan province and was given special status as a municipality which answered only to the central government. The idea was to turn both the city and its agricultural surrounds into a bastion of economic growth for China's interior. To escape the apathy-inducing stickiness of the outdoors, I dived into the air-conditioned Chongqing Planning Exhibition Gallery. I had gone to an equivalent exhibition in Beijing, where the focus had been on making the capital more liveable but, judging by what I read, in Chongqing liveability was a distinct second priority. The first priority was to build quickly enough to support the weight of people flooding in from the countryside. The urbanisation projects had to deal with what was by some reckonings the world's largest municipal population. The ambitious target of making the existing city the central hub of a multi-district super-metropolis was described in the exhibition as analogous to 'the many stars encircling the moon.'

With that image in mind, I set out to take a look. Down by the riverfront the Yangtze eased by lazily. The rusting hulks of unused cruise ships were tied to the jetties and naked children swam around them, seemingly inured to the smell of rotting fish and sewage that permeated the air.

Chongqing was a hilly place and the centre stood high above river. I could find no roads leading inland from where I was walking so I decided to climb up some steps between residential tower blocks. I ascended a few flights and then found the path in front of me blocked by garbage and slime. I clambered over it, filthy liquid seeping into my sandals, and soldiered on. Brown droplets dripped from a flaking balcony above me, struck my head and ran down my face. The steps in front petered out and I was faced by a solid wall. I was forced to descend again through the garbage and broken glass. By the time I reached the bottom my shins were covered in black ooze and my feet were squelching in my sandals.

I went back down to the Yangtze and tried to wash off the grime. I was only partially successful. It was a case of washing the filth of one sewer in another. In the circumstances I decided to return for a shower before heading out for dinner.

Chongqing's favourite food was hot pot, whereby thinly-sliced assortments of meat and vegetable were cooked in a bubbling and extremely spicy broth. I passed hot pot restaurants everywhere but when it came to dinner time I chose a particularly cheap-looking canteen. If it was the local favourite, I reasoned, the best would be found in the grubbier establishments.

I was barely able to understand the owner's thick dialect. She could not tell me how much it was per skewer of fatty meat so we agreed, or at least I thought we agreed, on 30RMB all included. I ordered a beer, selected the items I wanted to eat and sat down on one of the wobbly plastic stools. Although I ate alone, I noticed that the couple next to me only paid half as much for twice the amount of food. Having eaten, I stood up to go and handed the boss thirty RMB. When I started to walk out, she barred my way.

"40RMB," She said

"You said 30RMB."

"Plus a beer," She remarked. "40RMB."

"You said all included."

"No I didn't."

"Look at the people who just left," I said indignantly. "They paid 17 RMB for two meals."

"40RMB," she said aggressively.

"Don't be an idiot!" I was becoming more heated, though I was not sure whether she could understand what I was saying. "You know I've eaten about 10RMB worth of food and you agreed 30RMB anyway."

"40RMB!" She snarled.

"How is the beer 10RMB anyway?" I pointed out, angrily. "These bottles cost 3RMB everywhere else."

I tried to slip past her but she sidestepped and cut off my escape. She stood only about five feet tall but was built like a tank. She took my arm in a vice-like grip.

"Don't try to cheat me!" I shouted, sounding not quite as commanding as I would have liked.

She let go of me but continued blocking the exit. The other diners were watching on as if my predicament were mild entertainment. I retreated into a corner of the restaurant and waited. Sure enough, she took her eye off me for a couple of seconds and I made a break for it. She lunged at me but I was no longer in the mood to be gentlemanly and shoved her arm away. As I ran off I uttered a resounding, "Fuck off!"

It came out more squeaky than resounding.

*

I spent the next day accompanying Zhu, a girl who was in Chongqing to get a tattoo. We caught a string of buses to a suburb that lay an hour outside the centre. There was no let-up in the built-up environment, with cranes and scaffolding constant sights. More than construction, however, the area was defined by destruction. Old buildings stood waiting for the wrecking ball, their fates sealed by the character slapped onto their facades in red paint: 'chai—'for demolition.'

The tattoo parlour was located in a disused factory building. An art college lay opposite and studios had taken over much of the industrial site. Many of the brick buildings were covered in colourful graffiti. Students with sketch pads sauntered around, middle-aged women in pyjamas gossiped in doorways and children with naked bottoms ran around. It was grimy, funky and cool.

By contrast to the vibrancy outside, the tattoo parlour itself had plain white walls and a simple couch. Zhu had 'cogito ergo sum' inked into her side by the kindly female tattooist while I tried not to appear indecently interested in the flesh on show. Afterwards we explored the area and then caught a bus back into the centre.

The bus was absolutely packed. Chongqing was not a place for people who cherished their personal space. I found myself standing near the doorway at the front, pressed up close to a small man with greasy black hair. At one point I became aware that he had slipped his hand into my pocket.

"What are you doing?"

He withdrew his fingers from where they had been wrapping around my wallet. I pushed him away and took him by the throat.

"You dare try to steal my stuff," I muttered quietly. I was gratified to see he looked scared.

I continued gripping his throat for a few seconds and then realised that there was nothing else to be done. There was no way either of us could move because the bus was too full. I drew away my hand and instructed him to get off at the next stop. We stood facing each other for a few minutes, trying not to catch each other's eyes. Only when the bus drew to a halt did he climb down. Compared to the incident the previous day, I had emerged with flying colours. Men were easier to deal with than women, I reflected.

*

I stayed in Chongqing for a few days and got a thorough feel for the city. It had its glamorous features, including several expensive restaurants and bars. Even these, however, only looked the part in the evenings when the darkness descended and masked the imperfections of the day. The outrageously-fast rate of growth was leaving a lot of skeletons in its wake. Within short walking distances of neon-lit shopping complexes—in one of which I found the sort of duty free shop more often seen in airports—were areas of real poverty. In these backstreets I saw children going to the toilet on the floor; street markets selling mangy poultry and dirty vegetables, and even a 'cinema' that was just an old TV playing videos to people on wooden stools. Large amounts of litter gave off pungent smells and several beggars, some of them crippled, moved helplessly about.

In Chongqing all the excitements, difficulties and paradoxes of China's development were taken and then exaggerated. Some of the results were surprising. One thing I spotted was an interactive machine built into a wall rather like an ATM, but on which it was possible to learn who the local policemen and senior officials were. This innovation probably owed itself to a well-documented crackdown on crime led by the then mayor of the city, Bo Xilai. For a country in which I had barely found transparency anywhere it was a remarkable step. It was with regret that I left Chongqing behind. Crazy it might have been but stereotypical it most certainly was not.

The next section of my trip quickly erased any sense of nostalgia. From Chongqing I set off for the Three Gorges, the Yangtze's most renowned section. I bought a third class ticket on an old cruise ship, which entitled me to a cramped bunk in a six-person cabin on the bottom deck near the engine room. Cruises through the Three Gorges brought in large amounts of tourist dollars and I did not want to spend the time with a crowd of nouveau riche. By opting for the cheapest option I judged that I might meet some interesting people. It proved a good decision.

One man in my cabin was a retiree from Dunhuang who had cycled over four thousand miles within China since finishing his working life. Most memorable, however, was an old man from a village in Sichuan with whom I shared a cigarette in the gloom of the first evening. His native tongue was the Sichuanese dialect of Chinese, which was almost impossible for me to understand. He did speak some Mandarin but only in a thickly accented and elaborate manner. Together with the frequent pauses he made for effect, this made him sound a bit like the Chinese characters in Hollywood movies. Despite the difficulties, we managed to hold a reasonable conversation. More to the point I listened while he talked. His monologue began when I asked him what he did.

"I am over seventy years old now so I do not work, but I used to be a farmer. I grew my own food . . .Do you have farmers in England?"

"Yes but not many now," I said.

"There are not so many in China now either . . . Everybody used to be a farmer . . . China is better since Deng Xiaoping's reforms . . . It was bad before . . . Chairman Mao's economic policies were bad . . ." I kept my ears peeled as he went on, "Before we had no money, no food . . . Under Chairman Mao we had no freedom and could not speak openly . . . We had to close our eyes . . . It is much better now . . . China is all about politics and under Chairman Mao there were bad decisions."

I knew Sichuan had suffered particularly harshly from Mao's agricultural policies. The old man had lived through hard times and was now happy to be living without the constant pressure of starvation. All the same, every time he referred to Mao he automatically used the respectful title of 'Chairman.'

Over the next two nights, the ship chugged smoothly down the Yangtze River. A few barges were carrying coal downstream but the majority of traffic was caused by cruise ships such as my own. Occasionally my boat pulled up at a town and the tour guides on board started shouting out instructions. I had no interest in visiting the faux attractions that everybody was herded towards and took these opportunities to walk around by myself. The towns were generally quiet and relatively empty. The local lifestyles had clearly been reoriented around the cruise industry. Even the people selling smoked fish waited down by the jetties for the tourists, rather than having shops in the towns.

Apart from the stops I spent the time relaxing on the deck of the ship and watching the scenery roll by. The finest moments came at the points where the river narrowed and passed into the enclosing grandeur of the Gorges. Late on the second night, when the bustle on deck had quietened and the ferry was slipping silently through the darkness of the Wu Gorge, I felt like I was drifting through an enormous cathedral. The moon shone down on the black cliffs and reflected in the passive waters. The timelessness of the Yangtze left a deep impression on me and I felt very small.

On the final morning the sky was grey. I and all the other passengers disembarked and climbed onto tour buses, which delivered us to the Three Gorges Dam. This was one of the most controversial structures in China but there was no denying that it was astonishing to look at. It stretched for one and a half miles across the Yangtze River and had the appearance of a fortress wall. I was no engineer so could not understand the importance of every tower and symmetrical dint in the massive blockade, but I nonetheless had the rare feeling of beholding man's supremacy over nature. The Dam was a demonstration of human vision and a testament to China's ambition. It had harnessed the Yangtze River for energy production and was apparently going to regulate its tendency to flood. The waters of the world's third longest river looked rather pathetic to me as they lapped tamely against the concrete colossus.

It was hubris, or so the critics claimed. And looking at the Dam's sheer perfectness I myself felt a hint of misgiving. Building something so manifestly powerful was inviting nature to reassert its authority. And every year the vengeful Yangtze, to the eye so timid, was carrying millions of tons of silt into the reservoir behind the dam. The river was timeless; that I knew. Man's vigilance would now have to prove timeless too.

*

Downstream I entered Hubei. This province was defined by water and contained not only the Yangtze but also a large number of lakes. Floods had always been a feature of its existence, and their prevention was part of the reason for the construction of the Three Gorges Dam.

I saw this wateriness first hand. It started to rain while I was at the Dam and it was still raining when I reached Yichang, the nearest town. It was still raining at Wuhan, the provincial capital, when I arrived there that evening. It was still raining the next morning but I decided to go out and explore anyway. I bought a plastic poncho and a cheap umbrella, and braved the conditions.

Wuhan was the third of China's 'three furnaces' but in the circumstances it was hard to imagine. I visited the Yellow Crane Pavilion, an ancient pagoda and the city's primary landmark, and from the top floor gazed out over a city that looked ugly and grey because the light was ugly and grey. Clusters of skyscrapers were visible in the distance and betrayed that

Wuhan was one of China's inland boomers. But even China's economic growth was largely eclipsed by the weather on that day.

Traffic jams formed on the main roads and the car drivers honked at each other angrily. On the pavements, everybody I saw was rushing except for one man walking his dog in nothing but his boxer shorts. Seeing as he was wearing nothing worth keeping dry, he seemed very relaxed about things.

I made my way down to where the wide Yangtze River flowed fast through the middle of the city. It was so wide at that stage of its course that the districts on opposite sides of the river, *Wu*chang and *Han*kou, had for centuries been separate cities. Now a huge railway bridge spanned the gap.

As I was standing by the river, three men wearing speedos and carrying orange floats walked down to the edge of the water. They dived in and started swimming towards the far bank, which was roughly a kilometre away. I watched the three orange dots inch their way across the gap, willing them to make it. Large container barges complicated the crossing but the real difficulty was the current. To swim the Yangtze was to cross swords with a titan. By the time the men were half way across, they were almost a kilometre downstream. Then they were lost to my sight.

The next morning I caught a train out of Wuhan. It was still raining. A few days after that, parts of the city flooded.

CHAPTER 18

The End of all my Exploring

My time in China was drawing to a close and so I returned to Beijing. As I was coming out of the toilet on the train there, a man approached me. He had a tanned and handsome face. I guessed he was less than forty years old. His shirt was undone, he was wearing shorts and the effects of alcohol were visible in his red cheeks. We smoked a cigarette together and started chatting. His name was Wang but he could not pronounce my name. He explained that he was on his way home to Hebei, the province encircling Beijing.

"What were you doing in Wuhan?" I asked.

"Some work and some fun, Neekuh. I and my colleagues attended a conference there."

"I see. What job do you all do?"

"You have so many questions, Neekuh," he said with a patronising smile. "We are policemen."

We went and sat down on the folding chairs in the aisle of the hard sleeper carriage. Wang leaned close, the familiar stench of baijiu exuding from him, and looked me straight in the eye. "Neekuh, how long have you been in China?"

"Over ten months."

"And what part of England are you from, Neekuh?"

"Manchester."

"Manchester. That was the centre of the Industrial Revolution wasn't it Neekuh?" He asked, knowing the answer.

"That part of England, yes."

"Well Neekuh, England is a very developed country and has a very stable society. Tell me Neekuh, because you are from a developed and stable society, Neekuh, tell me what you think of China."

"That's a big question," I said warily.

"Be honest, Neekuh. We are friends. Tell me honestly, Neekuh, what you think of China."

"There are many pressures here. Many difficulties."

"Very good Neekuh. You are a clever man Neekuh," he said smugly. "What difficulties?"

I decided to play it safe: "For example, there are big inequalities with wealth."

"That is correct, Neekuh, there are big inequalities with wealth. To become a harmonious society we must lift poor people out of poverty. What else, Neekuh. Be honest."

"People have few rights here. There is no democracy and lots of corruption."

"Very good, Neekuh. There is too much corruption. As China develops it must also become a more open society."

A man stumbled down the aisle. He had muscular shoulders and a round face. He sat down on a bottom bunk and gazed at us with bleary eyes.

"Li this is Neekuh. Neekuh is a friend from England. Neekuh, this is Li."

Li hiccuped in greeting.

"I was speaking with Neekuh about politics, Li," said Wang smoothly. "You should listen closely. Neekuh is a very clever man."

Li looked admiringly up at Wang then turned to me and said proudly, "Wang is one of the leaders of our town."

"Hush hush, Li," said Wang, looking pleased, "Listen to Neekuh."

"So Neekuh," he said, turning to me again, "you are being very honest. What else do you think Neekuh? Your country is very developed and our society is still immature. Tell me, what other problems are there here?"

"You are destroying the cultures of your ethnic minorities."

"No, Neekuh," said Wang, "that is incorrect. You see Neekuh, we Chinese have a great respect for all our minorities."

"I am not so sure."

"No, Neekuh. You are a very clever young man but this you do not understand. I will teach you Neekuh. You see, China is a country of fifty six minorities. We are all brothers. United we are strong and divided we are weak. We are one family, Neekuh."

I knew I had reached the bottom line and did not argue. Another man wobbled towards us. He was fat and had a friendly face. He nodded his head towards Wang and sat down.

"Neekuh, let me introduce this man," Wang said with a passive face. "Neekuh let me ask you, in England do you have men who lie and cheat, kidnap and steal? Yes? Well, this man is *not* that sort of a guy. In fact he's a policeman."

I laughed and the new arrival turned red. Shortly afterwards Wang stated that he felt tired. He turned to Li and said, "Go and fetch two of the boxes of the tea that I bought."

A few seconds later Li returned with two red tins. Wang offered the first to me and then, taking the second tin, offered it back to Li. Li looked embarrassed and thanked Wang many times. I smiled at how skilfully Wang twisted the younger man around his finger. No doubt this skill was what allowed him to succeed as an official in China.

Although Wang then left to sleep off his drunkenness, I continued chatting to one of his companions, a large teddy bear of a policeman. We continued in the same vein of conversation, talking about how China could improve as a society. Despite being a member, the man criticised the CPC, referring to it as 'trash'. His words reminded me that the CPC was not a machine but rather a collection of eighty million individuals. I realised that although the political system was opaque, within that system there were still a range of opinions.

Paradoxically given his criticisms, however, he then stated that the only way things could change for the better in China was for the CPC to become stronger: "If we were stronger, more powerful, then the conditions in this country would quickly improve," he asserted with a thoughtful but confident demeanour. "For example, if Taiwan Island was returned to us peacefully and our waters in the South China Sea were acknowledged, the government would relax controls. How can the leaders allow criticism within China when our outside enemies are so close? If our borders were secure then more freedom would exist within China."

I questioned whether the government would really use any of the hypothetical additional power to liberate its people, rather than just consolidating its on position.

"No I don't think so," he said, sounding less sure of himself than he had before. He had clearly bought into the same idea as most of the Han population: that the Government, which had showed scant evidence of trustworthiness, would prove trustworthy when it came to gradually reducing its own power.

After turning over his thoughts in his mind he declared that, even though the leaders might not live up to their rhetoric about gradual opening up, the only alternative was attempted revolution. I was surprised to hear a party official talking like that at all and came out with encouraging remarks.

He looked at me sadly and said: "But there is no way to win like that."

"Because of Tian'anmen Square?" I prompted.

"Yes, Tian'anmen Square proved it was impossible. I am forty five years old. You are a young man and you do not have life experience like me. I know there is no way."

"Maybe Tian'anmen Square showed how divided the government was, not how strong?" I offered hopefully.

"No. Tian'anmen Square proved that there is no way. Even if the government was divided then, it is not the same now . . ." He trailed off.

*

I returned to Beijing to coincide with the July 1st anniversary of the founding of the Chinese Communist Party. It was ninety years since the original thirteen members had first gathered in Shanghai. I arrived expecting some sort of hoo-hah to have taken over the capital. Far from it: a commemorative film had been made and there were various things on television, but Beijing itself was largely indifferent. Many of the local people looked at me strangely when I asked whether there were any special events. Several did not even know it was the ninetieth anniversary at all.

With thought I realised I had been stupid to expect a big fuss. The CPC was of course not going out of its way to remind people how thorough its current monopoly on power was. The recent Arab Spring had received a lot of coverage in China and its leaders were treading carefully. I reflected that of the ordinary Chinese I had met around the country, most had not had a Western sense of human equality and, while I had heard plenty of criticisms of the CPC, I had never heard anyone suggest that they could do the job better. Many had laboured under the impression that those in high office, even if corrupt, were invariably exceptionally intelligent. As such the CPC was still benefitting from most Chinese people's historically-entrenched sense that government was something for an elite few, though I thought it ironic that communism had served to strengthen rather than dissolve this instinct. The internet and globalisation were threatening to shake it all up, however. If the common people in Arab countries could rise up and take power, what could stop the Chinese people doing likewise?

Because there was relatively little going on by way of public events, I did just as I had done in January in Beijing and walked around. To the south of Tian'anmen, I discovered that the bars, hotels and fresh paving had advanced further into several hutongs. Time had not stood still.

Feeling hungry one day I entered a restaurant and ordered a dish, the photo of which looked a bit like liver. The waitress said the name and looked questioningly at me, before looking for confirmation to her boss. I assumed that they took me for a weak-stomached tourist and combatively bluffed, "I know what it is. I want to eat it."

No further questions were asked. In the interlude before my food arrived, the boss took a live fish from a tank and placed it on a set of scales. The fish flapped, fell off and hit the floor with a thud. In revenge, the boss picked it up and then flung it to the ground again. Presumably its fate was to be cooked alive.

When my dish came the taste was strong and I vaguely recognised it. The small lumps of elastic meat in it had the consistency of intestines but had strange lumps of soft fat inside. Some were ovular in shape, but open at one side as if lopped off. It took me surprisingly long to work out that I was eating balls. The rich taste was familiar from my Baotou barbecue days. These balls were very small though. Perhaps they belonged to chickens? Either that or impotent sheep? If chicken, then why did they taste like the lamb balls I had eaten in Baotou? Did testicles taste the same whatever the species? By the time I realised what I was eating, the dish was mostly finished. I did not finish it. Suddenly the long misshapen pieces drew to mind the rear ends of the sheep in Kashgar's livestock market, their ripped testes dripping blood.

Nearby the restaurant I went to a small tea house, which I had first visited in the winter. The friendly owner, who spoke good English, was surprised to find me still in China and poured me a drink while we chatted. She listened politely to my account of my trip but the stories seemed to sadden her. She never had time to travel. Seeing her melancholy, I changed topic and remarked that her hutong had changed enormously.

She looked at me sadly and said, "Yes, everything is changing."

I asked whether she preferred it now or before.

"Before of course," she replied. "In the past the hutongs were communities and they were everywhere. They were part of old Beijing. I have lived in hutongs all my life. Now they are building these new high-rises full of apartments. I would not like to live in one of them."

"Are you being forced to move out of here?"

"No, I do not have to move," she said. "But after seventy years all property returns to the government anyway and then they can do with it what they want. My daughter, she is eleven years old. By the time she is my age, maybe all of old Beijing will be gone."

The changes to Beijing's hutongs were designed to attract more tourists, but the owner said that it had been a very bad year for her business.

"What do you think the reason is?" I asked.

"Probably the world financial crisis," she answered. "There have not been so many foreign tourists recently. On some days earlier in the year I had no customers at all in the shop. Even now in the summer the number of people is small compared to two years ago."

She went out of the room to cook dinner in the kitchen at the back. Her husband came in to keep me company. By contrast to his wife, my travelling tales seemed to energise him. When I mentioned that I had been to Xinjiang, his eyes lit up and he said that he had previously worked in Urumqi.

"What did you do?" I asked.

"I bought cheap water melons in Urumqi, took them on the train down to Guangzhou and sold them for a high price."

"Really! How long did the journey take?"

"About a week. I usually stopped off in Chengdu and sold some of the melons before carrying on to Guangzhou."

"Did you just take them the melons into the passenger carriages?" I enquired, chuckling at the thought.

"Oh yes. I used to take a big crate onto the train and then I spent most of the journey watering the melons from the tap in the toilet. Do you know why I did that?" He asked, tantalisingly.

"Tell me."

"I did it so that the melons would not shrivel and split. The first time I did the trip, I arrived in Guangzhou to find half of my melons were tiny and half of them had rotted!" He laughed happily at the memory.

"So you enjoyed the job?" I asked, smiling too.

"Oh yes! It was hard work but I could travel around and see places. It was a good life."

"Why did you stop?"

"It was many years ago now. There were new leaders and they changed the rules so I couldn't take my melons on the train anymore. And so I came back to Beijing. Since then I've been working mornings on the rail tracks, and every afternoon I come back home and help in the shop."

He threw an affectionate glance over his shoulder to where his wife was half visible chopping vegetables behind a curtain. I discerned a small hint of nostalgia lingering on his face. Perhaps his inner Ulysses still dreamt of adventure.

*

It was summertime and large numbers of people were moving within China. For the first time since Spring Festival I was unable to get anything other than a standing ticket on a train and resigned myself to a sleepless night on the way to Baotou. I ended up sitting on my backpack in the cold section between two carriages; my knees hugged up tight to my chest. A group of migrant workers were hemmed in around me, all holding similar postures. We were next to the toilet and the stench was pungent.

"Where are you from?" Asked the man crouched next to me.

"England," I replied, not feeling much like chatting.

"What are salaries like in England?"

"On average about £15,000 per year."

"How much is that in RMB?"

"150,000RMB."

"Over 10,000RMB per month?" He calculated, unbelieving. It was about seven times what he earned. "Do you have migrant workers in England?"

"Not many."

"What about if I wanted to go to England as a migrant worker? Is it possible?"

"Not really."

"But if I really wanted too?"

"Not it's not possible. You wouldn't be given a visa."

"How about if I said I was a traveller?"

"It's very difficult for Chinese people to get English tourist visas."

"Why?"

"Because there are lots of people like you who would actually try to work."

He looked thoughtful for a moment. "But you could take me?"

"No, I couldn't."

My efforts to dodge conversation failed miserably. The men scrunched up all around me had taken an interest in me and started asking other questions.

"Is life better in England?" Asked one.

"People are wealthier," I said, "but one big difference is how governments work."

"Yes," said the man, "we have trouble here with corruption. I have heard that in the West you have problems with drugs. Is that true?"

"It's not a huge problem in Britain but yes, some people do take drugs."

"Drugs are very bad. We have no drugs here. It is illegal and the punishments are very strict."

The night passed slowly. Most annoying was the lady with the food cart who came through regularly until after 2am. Because I was in the path of the trolley, I had to stand up and press myself into the wall every time she came through. An old lady with a sick bag passed on her way to the toilet and spilled some of the vomit on my leg. Nonetheless, I managed to get some rest.

*

One poem by T.S.Eliot rang very true for me as I reached the culmination of my travels in China: "And the end of all our exploring/ Will be to return to where we started / And know the place for the first time."

I returned to Baotou to see some friends prior to the final leg of my trip. Having seen much of the rest of China I was able to place the city better into context. I understood well that, in the grand scheme of things, it was insignificant and ignored. I also recognised that this made it one of the most unpretentious places in the country.

Only after arriving did I realise how tired I was. I finally had nothing to do and nowhere to go, and the strain of five months on the road poured out of me. On the second evening I ate an enormous and cheesy Italian calzone, went out for some drinks and topped it all off with an early-morning barbecue bonanza. My gut, used to simpler fare, rebelled; my body, fatally relaxed, gave way, and my mind, distracted and in no position to martial its defences, was routed. I got ill and remained so for a few days.

When I went to the pharmacy I was given two types of medicine. One was western and one was Chinese. I doubted that they complimented each other but the nurse behind the counter seemed to think that twice the cultural influences made for twice the effectiveness. I understood that my illness was primarily psychological anyway and so bought both.

Some of the high-rises behind the University, which had been under construction when I left in the winter, had since been completed, but otherwise everything in the city was the same. A few more foreign teachers had come during my absence but the core people were identical. One Englishman, who had come to Baotou at roughly the same time as me, had become a very regular frequenter of whorehouses. The irony was that he had studied Philosophy and Ethics at Manchester University and had given me a lecture on the immorality of prostitution shortly after he had first arrived.

My Filipino friend, Ryan, had continued getting himself into trouble. The latest incident had nothing to do with gangs. He had slept with the wife of a rich businessman, who was now threatening to exact his revenge and have Ryan killed. Soon after I departed China, Ryan was thrown out of the country, albeit for entirely different reasons: the Government was stamping down on Filipino's because of a dispute with the Philippines over the South China Sea and the Baotou authorities felt compelled to do their bit. Ryan's timely exit saved the humiliated businessman from having to make good his threat.

Other than that the main news was that riots had taken place in Inner Mongolia in the spring. Given that the Mongolian people had a homeland of their own, there was relatively little open conflict between them and the Han, despite the manner in which they were being squeezed out culturally. However there was still the potential for unrest: I was told that the riots in question had erupted over the detention of some Mongolian men by Chinese police. The disorder had not spread to Baotou but as a precaution all university students across the city had seen their dormitory curfews changed to ten o'clock during the tense period.

*

After recovering from my sickness I went to Pingyao, an ancient walled city in Shanxi province. I got off my train in the morning at a small station and was driven into the centre on the back of a motor cart. It passed through a gate of the angular city wall and drove through quiet streets. A maze of grey brick buildings spread out before me. But this was a different sort of Chinese grey. This was a grey from times before.

The shutters on many windows were still closed, despite the fact that it was no longer early. Very few people were outside; those that were all seemed old. Grey hair matched the grey bricks. Every breath of air drew in the unfamiliar smell of longevity. Like in Shanghai many months before, I could scarcely believe I was still in the same country. Then it had been the impossible future, now it was the impossible past.

This sense of disbelief died down as the day wore on and the aged streets filled with people, but I never entirely lost the feeling. Founded in its current form in the 14th Century, Pingyao had been a thriving city throughout the Ming and Qing dynasties and had become an important commercial centre during the latter: China's first ever draft bank, the Rishengchang, had been established there in 1823. Most remarkably, Pingyao had survived the massed demolition that marked the CPC's early years. That made it almost unique.

I hired a bike and tried to avoid the congestion of the main streets. I was partially successful, discovering dusty back alleys and forgotten courtyard houses hidden in the maze. Each alley quickly led back to a noisier street, however, or ran out at the impassable city wall because Pingyao was only little.

But even if it was small, in the context of China it was astonishing enough that it existed at all. Shanxi province, which I had first visited during the

National Holiday while I was still a teacher in Baotou, was one of the provinces from which the earliest semblances of Chinese civilisation had sprung forth. Now, however, it was caught in no man's land; neither the booming east coast nor the focus of political attention in the far west. Rather like Inner Mongolia it was industrial, unglamorous and not a feature of people's thoughts. Perhaps the survival of Pingyao's heritage owed something to the fact that it was ignored.

In the evening, I went outside the walls and looked back. The towering bastions, over six hundred years old, were silhouetted black in the dusk and the elegant pagoda atop the north gate stood erect and proud. But it was the sinking orb behind that caught my eye. That universal symbol of ancient China; that sight I had rarely seen: a red sun set over the twilight city.

*

From Pingyao I went down to Henan, another of the provinces that gave birth to Chinese civilisation. It was one of the most populous areas in the country but was still relatively poor. A disproportionate number of the people I had met trying their luck in the far west hailed from Henan.

First I visited Luoyang, a city whose glorious history as the capital of various dynasties had climaxed at the same time as the European Dark Ages. Its star had faded after that time and it had gradually drifted into insignificance. Now it was a polluted and overpopulated scar on the landscape.

Just outside the city, however, was a reminder of the ages gone by. I had visited Yungang near the beginning of my time in China; I had passed by Mogao during the heart of my trip, and so it seemed apt to me that I visited Longmen, the third of China's most famous Buddhist cave groups, as my travels drew to a close. When I got there off the bus, I discovered a less poetic progression. I had been able to enter the grottoes at Yungang independently; I had gone into the gloomy hollows at Mogao but only with a guide, and now at Longmen I was forced to stand outside the caves and peer in from behind barriers.

Notwithstanding this, the caves were impressive. Even the mutilation of many statues, some by the ravages of time but most by the wilful destruction of man, lent to the scene. To me it said that the past had not always been smooth; that the glories of one age could so easily be purged in the next; that China—in contrast to the prevailing narrative of '5000 years continuous civilisation'—had always been a place of upheaval. But I was trying too hard to spot patterns. After all, much of the destruction at Luoyang had been caused by foreign museum collectors and not by the Chinese themselves. I wanted to feel that I knew China after almost eleven months' exploration but the contradictions still left me disoriented. I worried whether my conclusions were not purely subjective, whether I was not just as ignorant as when I set out.

*

Kaifeng, my final stop, had a good amount of its heritage intact. Mighty walls and restored palaces greeted my arrival. I did not have much time and allowed myself to follow the tourist trail around the various historical sites. Although I could have done without the accompanying promotional blurb, which tried to tell me that the Chinese had invented virtually everything worth inventing, I was delighted to find a disproportional amount of extant history. Some of the stories associated with the old architecture were very interesting. It seemed that every preserved archway had an anecdote lying behind it: the itinerant monk, the flatulent prince, the incorruptible juror . . .

Much more than Kaifeng's historical narrative, however, I enjoyed its unpretentiousness. Three wheel motor carts chugged down the streets;

old men in boxer shorts cycled up on rickety bicycles and dived into the green lake at the centre of the city; people ate barbecued chicken feet off wooden skewers and then casually tossed the litter on the floor, and women in pyjamas breastfed bare-bottomed babies while squatting outside grubby canteens. Kaifeng was continuing as it always had, in spite of the changes in the nation around it.

On my second evening I was sitting on a narrow bench park outside the city walls and eating quail eggs when a group of old ladies lined up on the far side of the square. A song started up. Right foot forward, left foot forward, kick, twirl, hop, skip . . .

There they were, just like I had seen them everywhere. I watched quietly, memories washing over me.

Right foot forward, left foot forward, kick, twirl, hop, skip . . .

Children on roller skates weaved around the dancers, recalling the chaos in the square in Hotan. But Kaifeng was no distant province; Kaifeng was one of China's heartlands; a place about which nobody gave a damn. And still they were dancing.

Right foot forward, left foot forward, kick, twirl, hop, skip . . .

The faces of the women were blank. But I knew why they danced so.

Right foot forward, left foot forward, kick, twirl, hop, skip . . .

And why should they not enjoy themselves?

As I watched I realised that, after a year's exploration throughout the land, I had at last found China.

*

Back in Beijing for the last time I walked down to Tian'anmen Square, that symbol of frustrated hopes, and thought about my year. My mind ranged from the western borders to the Pacific coast; from the Himalayan heights to the desert flats; from the wealth in the cities to the poverty in the countryside; from the optimism of Wenchuan to the despair in Yushu. In some places I had found a 'harmonious society' and in others I had certainly not. Of one thing I was fairly sure: that the future for China's ethnic minorities was bleak, at least as far as their traditional cultures went. As for the Han, I guessed their future was generally positive.

To my right lay the Great Hall of the People, the Soviet-style titan from which the country was ruled. So much, I realised, depended on the unclear intentions of the men walking its corridors of power. But so much, too, depended on incalculable outside factors. If my travels had taught me anything, it was just how big China was; how populated; how diverse.

Given this melee of factors, I knew that, even after a year of travelling, I still could not confidently predict where the country would go in the future. But if asked, "What will happen in China?" I reflected that I could at least understand the question.

That night I boarded my final train, the Trans-Siberian Express, and left a year behind. Behind me the dance went on.

About the Author

Nico Hobhouse is currently a student reading Classics at Oxford University. He has broad interests, including religion, politics, history and literature. He is as an especially keen linguist and became fluent in Mandarin over the course of the year described in this book.

Whenever he has time Nico travels, usually alone. Apart from his journey through China and Tibet, he has crossed America by land from the Pacific to Atlantic coasts, has taken the Trans-Siberian Railway through Russia and has spent a month in Mongolia.

Dancing on the Frontier is his first book.

Lightning Source UK Ltd.
Milton Keynes UK
UKOW042059160113

204983UK00001B/207/P